BREAKDOWN AND REBIRTH, 1914 TO THE PRESENT

A Documentary History
of Modern Europe
Volume IV

Edited by

Thomas G. Barnes
Gerald D. Feldman
University of California, Berkeley

Originally Published by
Little, Brown and Company

UNIVERSITY
PRESS OF
AMERICA

LANHAM • NEW YORK • LONDON

University Press of America,™ Inc.

4720 Boston Way
Lanham, MD 20706

3 Henrietta Street
London WC2E 8LU England

Library of Congress Cataloging in Publication Data
Main entry under title:

Breakdown and rebirth, 1914 to the present.

(A Documentary history of modern Europe ; v. 4)
Reprint. Originally published: Boston : Little, Brown,
1972. (A documentary history of modern Europe / Thomas
G. Barnes, Gerald D. Feldman ; v. 4) With new introd.
1. Europe–History–20th century–Sources. I.
Barnes, Thomas Garden. II. Feldman, Gerald D. III.
Series: Barnes, Thomas Garden. Documentary history of
modern Europe ; v. 4.
D411.B73   1982   940.5   82–45164
ISBN 0–8191–2366–8 (pbk.)   AACR2

All University Press of America books are produced on acid-free
paper which exceeds the minimum standards set by the National
Historical Publications and Records Commission.

PREFACE

"For I do not see the whole of anything; neither do those who promise to show it to us." Michel de Montaigne's frank disclaimer of his own capacity and scathing rejection of the vaunted capacities of others to see all was written almost exactly four centuries ago, in an age of fanaticisms and all-embracing visions. It is relevant for our own age of fanaticisms and all-embracing visions. Fanaticism aside, it is a particularly apt motto for authors and editors of books for introductory courses in history. Where not downright messianic, or even prophetical, such books tend to be pontifical — if not by the authors' intentions, then at least in the student's reading of them. Some notions guided us in this compilation, and it is good to make those notions and their manifestations clear at the outset, not only that we might not be thought messianic, prophetical, or pontifical, but also that those who choose and those who use this book will know what we think it does and does not do. At the outset, we make no claim that it will enable the student to "see the whole" of modern European history, or even as much of it as is treated here.

We believe that even the most general study of history requires awareness of historians' dependence upon the sources for history. It is as well that the novice understands from the start that all historiography is based on a broad but still selected body of sources. The very selectiveness of this collection reflects the nature of the historian's job in writing history. We believe that the student cannot begin to understand either history or the historian's task without himself exercising his intellect on the sources of history. This compilation, highly selective though it is, demands that the student use his critical faculties in weighing what he reads as historical evidence; indeed, it demands that he determine from the variety of sources presented what constitutes historical evidence and how evidence can be analyzed and understood in different ways. For example, a student with the psychological interests of Erik H. Erikson, another with the politico-social bent of Roland H. Bainton, and another given to the avowedly theological focus of James Atkinson would all approach Martin Luther differently, but they would all have to meet and begin with Luther's own writings.

For that reason, if for no other, this series includes a major segment of Luther, which, though it comprises only a fraction of his considerable output, provides a common ground for all who would understand Luther and Lutheranism and a common origin for each interpretation of the man and his movement. So have we in every volume of this series aimed at providing a large enough selection from major historical figures (both thinkers and doers), commentaries by lesser men, descriptions of events, laws and government directives, manifestoes and platforms, some correspondence and belles lettres, to suggest the variety of sources for Europe's past, to allow each student to bring into play his own critical acumen, and to provide illustration of men, events, and ideas which might otherwise prove elusive.

This series is intended to be a *documentary history* of Europe. By this we mean that a student using — not merely reading — these volumes can come to some understanding of modern Europe's past by the documents alone aided by the explanation of the headnotes to the selections and the longer introductory essay to each chapter, which provides context and continuity both to the documents in that chapter and with the chapters preceding and succeeding. The series is not meant to serve as a substitute for a text, but it is intended to be as self-sufficient as is necessary to fit with any textbook or narrative history, sometimes in agreement with and sometimes in contrast to the interpretations that will be found elsewhere in what a student can be expected to read in an introductory course in modern European history at any college level. We have sought to make the selections long enough to give real substance for reflection and analysis. Perforce, this has limited the number of selections and therefore has caused us to exclude some men, events, and ideas that others would think of prime importance. We have felt no call to mirror the broad consensus as to which documents are and are not important. Although our colleagues will find a number of selections that all agree are "major," they will also find many that are rarely if ever found in books of readings and a few that have not previously appeared in English. We have sought significance, freshness, insightfulness, and incisiveness in our selections, and these concerns rather than idiosyncrasy, a penchant for novelty, or a commitment to a specific historical interpretation have determined that much of the material in this series will be new and different.

ACKNOWLEDGMENTS

The permission of authors and publishers in whom copyright is vested has been acknowledged where the selection appears. We would, however, tender special thanks to those holders of copyright who allowed us to use material either gratis or for a nominal fee, a practice that is no longer universal. A number of our colleagues assisted us with sage advice and tips for finding materials, and we are in yet greater debt to Lawrence Levine, Martin Malia, Robert Middlekauff, William Slottman, and Engel Sluiter than that already incurred by many years' close service together at Berkeley. Two students, Murray Bilby and Jeffrey Diefendorf, served us as bibliographical assistants and rendered aid beyond what we paid them. Malgorzata I. Winkler of the University of California, Berkeley, Library translated the Union of Lublin from Polish, a difficult task well done. The College Department of Little, Brown and Co. was always helpful, and we perhaps tumble into invidiousness in singling out the history editor, Charles Christensen, and the three copyeditors who wrestled with the series and its authors, Jane Aaron, Lynne Marcus Gould, and Patricia Herbst. To all, our most sincere thanks.

T. G. B.
G. D. F.

CONTENTS

BREAKDOWN
AND REBIRTH
1914 to the Present

THE FIRST WORLD WAR
Chapter 1

The origins of the First World War are still the subject of historical debate, but the perspective provided by more than a half century of scholarship and recent German research have provided the foundation for a measure of consensus on the general, though not on the specific, aspects of the war's origins. Although it is clear that none of the great powers had a monopoly on imperialism or militarism, Germany emerges as the power most disruptive of Europe's international relations. The responsibility for this can be attributed only in part to the incompetence and bluster of Emperor William II and the chancellors and foreign secretaries who served him. Fundamentally, it was an expression of Germany's position in world affairs and place in the development of the European state system.

The German historian Ludwig Dehio has argued that Germany was the last of the European hegemonial powers. Like Spain of Charles V and Phillip II and France of Louis XIV and Napoleon Bonaparte, the Germany of William II and Adolf Hitler attained a position of material strength that virtually compelled it to become the most dynamic power on the Continent. As with its predecessors, its expansive tendencies called forth a hostile coalition, and it sought to defend itself with ever increasing ruthlessness until its only security seemed to lie in assuming hegemony over the entire Continent. Like Spain and France, Germany was finally beaten by maritime powers, but where the power of Britain had been sufficient to restore the balance before, now the power of the United States was necessary. Germany, then, was the last of the hegemonial powers because its downfall marked the transformation from a diplomatic system centering on Europe to one dominated by great world powers of continental magnitude — the United States, Russia, and China.

Dehio's thesis is too deterministic to be entirely acceptable. Germany may have been fated to be the most dynamic power in Europe in this period, but the peculiarities of its imperialism and its failure reflected problems in domestic politics rather than some necessity inherent in its international position. Nevertheless, the Dehio thesis is highly suggestive. Germany's belated appearance as a unified state, its search for world-power status after most of the colonial world had already been divided up, its ambitions in Africa, the Balkans, and the Middle East, and its naval building programs did frighten England, France, and Russia and caused them to abandon their rivalries and unite in the Triple Entente. The more Germany's leaders felt encircled and denied of their rights, the more desperate they became. Many of Germany's most distinguished statesmen and scholars thought that it was "now or never" and that if Germany did not become a world power, it would soon fall behind not only England but also the United States and Russia. In 1914, therefore, Germany's leaders were more willing to break out of their encirclement and risk war than their enemies.

Germany clearly was not alone in feeling that a reckoning had to come sooner or later, however. These feelings developed quite naturally in the context of an increasingly expensive arms race, but they also reflected a psychological atmosphere in which each succeeding crisis raised international tension and made men almost yearn for war as a release. In part this psychological tension explains the enthusiasm with which soldiers of all nations marched off to war in 1914. All the combatants claimed that they were fighting a defensive war and denied ulterior motives, even though the realities were otherwise. World War I was a war in which the various powers sought to achieve imperialist ambitions unattainable by purely diplomatic means. Germany, first under the leadership of Chancellor Theobold von Bethmann-Hollweg and then under the stubborn military leadership of Paul von Hindenburg and Erich Ludendorff, sought hegemony on the Continent through control of Belgium, the industrial regions of France, and central Europe, and sought world-power status in the form of a central African empire and domination in the Ottoman Empire. France fought for Alsace-Lorraine, control of the Rhineland, and the permanent weakening of Germany, and Russia sought control of the Straits and Constantinople and improved borders with Germany and Austria-Hungary. England strove to eliminate Germany as a sea power and destroy Germany's colonial position, while Italy wished to take the Tyrol and secure a slice of the Ottoman Empire. Indeed, Germany's enemies demonstrated particular interest in carving up the Ottoman Empire. Thus, no European power was free of imperialist war aims. One may argue that Germany's aims were the most dangerous because they were primarily continental, but this perspective is no testimony in favor of the moral qualities of Germany's opponents. Unfortunately, Germany could not afford to stubbornly maintain its aims as demanded by its military leaders because time was on the side of its enemies.

Although the question of war aims became a source of domestic tension within all the warring states, particularly after the Russian Revolution and America's entry into the war, the first months of the war were marked by remarkable domestic harmony within the warring states. To the relief of some worried conservatives, the socialists marched off to war behind their national banners and the Second International suffered an ignominious collapse. Nationalism had proven more powerful than class consciousness and might have remained so if the war had been as short as the generals and political leaders anticipated. Unhappily, the generals were more or less consistently wrong throughout the war, and the war proved to be a disaster from which Europe never fully recovered. The slaughter in the trenches destroyed or spiritually and physically maimed the best of a generation, while the mobilization of the homefront made combatants of the civilian population and had a distorting effect upon economic and social life. The optimism and calculability, the sense of predictability, of prewar Europe were gone forever. Europe's societies were more divided than ever by the end of the conflict. The Western allies, under the virtually dictatorial direction of Lloyd George, Clemenceau, and Wilson, managed to hold out, but the empires of Germany, Austria-Hungary, and Russia collapsed under superior material force and internal conflict.

England and the "Encirclement" of Germany

Perhaps the greatest miscalculation of German prewar diplomacy was that England could never reconcile her imperial rivalries with France and Russia. The differences between England and those two powers were real enough, but Germany failed to respond to periodic English overtures and establish some formal friendly connection. Germany insisted on too high a price — namely, English membership in the Triple Alliance of Austria, Germany, and Italy — for German support of England in colonial disputes with the alliance of France and Russia. England, because of a diplomatic tradition that militated against binding commitments, parliamentary checks on foreign policy, and an unwillingness to throw the balance of power on the Continent entirely to Germany's favor, refused to adhere formally to the Triple Alliance. Germany responded to England's refusal by trying to bully England into accepting Germany's colonial demands. Germany opposed English ambitions in South Africa and elsewhere and, most important, in 1898 began constructing a high seas fleet directed against England. England was willing to let Germany have the strongest land army in the world but could not accept a challenge in the realm most vital to British interests — the sea. Having forced France to retreat in colonial matters at Fashoda, England began pursuing a policy of reconciliation with France that culminated in the creation of the Entente Cordiale of April 8, 1904. In the public clauses of the treaty, the two powers agreed to recognize one another's respective spheres of interest in Egypt and Morocco, but in the all-important secret clauses England was given a free hand in Egypt and France a free hand in Morocco. The Germans were shocked by the Anglo-French entente and sought to break it by challenging French claims in Morocco in 1905 and 1911. The last crisis proved particularly severe, and England was prepared to support France by force if necessary. The English also reconciled their differences with Russia in 1907, thus completing Germany's "encirclement." Nevertheless, they wished peace with Germany and in 1912 tried without success to reach an agreement on naval questions. An agreement seemed particularly vital because improved weapons technology, particularly the development of the Dreadnought, a fast battleship, was intensifying the naval race. First Lord of the Admiralty Winston Churchill concluded that England had to meet the German challenge by increasing the British program. At the same time, England's foreign secretary, Sir Edward Grey, strengthened his country's commitment to France without informing Parliament by an exchange of letters with the French ambassador, Paul Cambon. England moved most of its fleet into home waters, while the French concentrated on the Mediterranean. After making this arrangement, England could hardly leave the French coast undefended in the event of German attack.

The Anglo-French Entente of April 8, 1904

ARTICLE 1. His Britannic Majesty's Government declare that they have no intention of altering the political status of Egypt.

The Government of the French Republic, for their part, declare that they will not obstruct the action of Great Britain in that country by asking that a limit of time be fixed for the British occupation or in any other manner. . . .

ARTICLE 2. The Government of the French Republic declare that they have no intention of altering the political status of Morocco.

From Great Britain, *Parliamentary Papers,* vol. 103 (1911), Cmd. 5969. Reprinted by permission of Her Majesty's Stationery Office.

His Britannic Majesty's Government, for their part, recognise that it appertains to France, more particularly as a Power whose dominions are conterminous for a great distance with those of Morocco, to preserve order in that country, and to provide assistance for the purpose of all administrative, economic, financial, and military reforms which it may require.

They declare that they will not obstruct the action taken by France for this purpose, provided that such action shall leave intact the rights which Great Britain, in virtue of treaties, conventions, and usage, enjoys in Morocco, including the right of coasting trade between the ports of Morocco, enjoyed by British vessels since 1901.

ARTICLE 3. His Britannic Majesty's Government, for their part, will respect the rights which France, in virtue of treaties, conventions, and usage, enjoys in Egypt, including the right of coasting trade between Egyptian ports accorded to French vessels.

ARTICLE 4. The two Governments, being equally attached to the principle of commercial liberty both in Egypt and Morocco, declare that they will not, in those countries, countenance any inequality either in the imposition of customs duties or other taxes, or of railway transport charges.

The trade of both nations with Morocco and with Egypt shall enjoy the same treatment in transit through the French and British possessions in Africa. An agreement between the two Governments shall settle the conditions of such transit and shall determine the points of entry.

This mutual engagement shall be binding for a period of thirty years. Unless this stipulation is expressly denounced at least one year in advance, the period shall be extended for five years at a time.

Nevertheless, the Government of the French Republic reserve to themselves in Morocco, and His Britannic Majesty's Government reserve to themselves in Egypt, the right to see that the concessions for roads, railways, ports, etc., are only granted on such conditions as will maintain intact the authority of the State over these great undertakings of public interest. . . .

ARTICLE 9. The two Governments agree to afford to one another their diplomatic support, in order to obtain the execution of the clauses of the present Declaration regarding Egypt and Morocco. . . .

SECRET ARTICLES

ARTICLE 1. In the event of either Government finding themselves constrained, by the force of circumstances, to modify their policy in respect to Egypt or Morocco, the engagements which they have undertaken towards each other by articles 4, 6, and 7 of the Declaration of to-day's date would remain intact.

ARTICLE 2. His Britannic Majesty's Government have no present intention of proposing to the Powers any changes in the system of the Capitulations, or in the judicial organisation of Egypt.

In the event of their considering it desirable to introduce in Egypt reforms tending to assimilate the Egyptian legislative system to that in force in other civilised Countries, the Government of the French Republic will not refuse to entertain any such proposals, on the understanding that His Britannic Majesty's Government will agree to entertain the suggestions that the Government of the French Republic may have to make to them with a view of introducing similar reforms in Morocco. . . .

Churchill's Speech on the German Naval Bill of 1912, Before the House of Commons, July 22, 1912

I think it will be for the convenience of the Committee if first of all this afternoon I proceed to examine in detail the scope and character of the new German Navy Law. The main feature of that law is not the increase in the new construction of capital ships, though that is an important feature. The main feature is the increase in the striking force of ships of all classes which will be available, immediately available, at all seasons of the year. A Third Squadron of eight battleships will be created and maintained in full commission as part of the active battle fleet. Whereas, according to the unamended law, the active battle fleet consisted of seventeen battleships, four battle or large armoured cruisers, and twelve small cruisers, in the near future that active fleet will consist of twenty-five battleships, eight battle or large armoured cruisers, and eighteen small cruisers; and whereas at present, owing to the system of recruitment which prevails in Germany, the German fleet is less fully mobile during the winter than during the summer months, it will, through the operation of this law, not only be increased in strength, but rendered much more readily available. Ninety-nine destroyers, torpedo-boat destroyers — or torpedo-boats, as they are called in Germany — instead of sixty-six, will be maintained in full commission out of the total of 144. Three-quarters of a million pounds had already been taken in the general estimate for the year for the building of submarines. The new law adds a quarter of a million to this, and that is a provision which, so far as we can judge from a study of the finances, would appear to be repeated in subsequent years. Seventy-two new submarines will be built within the currency of the law, and of those it is apparently proposed to maintain fifty-four with full permanent crews.

Taking a general view, the effect of the law will be that nearly four-fifths of the entire German navy will be maintained in full permanent

From *Parliamentary Debates, Commons,* vol. 41 (1912), pp. 838–42. Reprinted by permission of Her Majesty's Stationery Office.

commission — that is to say, instantly and constantly ready for war. Such a proportion is remarkable, and, so far as I am aware, finds no example in the previous practice of modern naval Powers. So great a change and development in the German fleet involves, of course, important additions to their personnel. In 1898 the officers and men of the German navy amounted to 25,000. To-day that figure has reached 66,000. Under the previous Navy Laws, and various amendments which have preceded this one, the Germans have been working up to a total in 1920, according to our calculations, of 86,500 officers and men, and they have been approaching that total by increments of, approximately, an addition of 3,500 a year. The new law adds a total of 15,000 officers and men, and makes the total in 1920 of 101,500. The new average annual addition is calculated to be 1,680 of all ranks, but for the next three years by special provision 500 extra are to be added. From 1912 to 1914, 500 are to be added, and in the last three years of the currency of the law 500 less will be taken. This makes a total rate of increase in the German Navy personnel about 5,700 men a year. The new construction under the law prescribes for the building of three additional battleships — one to be begun next year, one in 1916, and two small cruisers of which the date has not yet been fixed. The date of the third battleship has not been fixed. It has been presumed to be later than the six years which we have in view. The cost of these increases in men and in material during the next six years is estimated as £10,500,000 above the previous estimates spread over that period. I should like to point out to the Committee that this is a cumulative increase which follows upon other increases of a very important character. The law of 1898 was practically doubled by the law of 1900, and if the expenditure contemplated by the law of 1900 had been followed the German estimates of to-day would be about £11,000,000. But owing to the amendments of 1906 and 1908, and now of 1912, that expenditure is very nearly £23,000,000. The actual figures of the expenditure have been given by my right hon. Friend the Chancellor of the Exchequer on a recent occasion in Committee of Supply. But the fact that personnel plays such a large part in this new amendment and that personnel is more cheaply obtained in Germany than in this country makes the money go further there than it would do over here.

The ultimate scale of the new German fleet, as contemplated by the latest Navy Law, will be forty-one battleships, twenty battle or large armoured cruisers, and forty small cruisers, besides a proper proportion — an ample proportion — of flotillas of torpedo-boat destroyers and submarines. [An Hon. Member: "By what year?"] By 1920. That is not on paper a great advance on the figures prescribed by the previous law, which gave thirty-eight battleships, twenty battle or large armoured cruisers, and thirty-eight small cruisers. That is not a great advance on the total scale. In fact, however, there is a remarkable expansion of strength and efficiency, and particularly of strength and efficiency as they contribute to striking power. The number of battleships and large armoured cruisers alone which will be kept constantly ready and in full commission will be raised by the law from twenty-one, the present figure, to thirty-three — that is to say, an addition of twelve, or an increase of about 57 per cent. The new fleet will in the beginning include about twenty battleships and large cruisers of the older type, but gradually as new vessels are built, the fighting power of the fleet will rise until in the end it will consist completely of modern vessels. This new scale of the German fleet — organised in five battle squadrons, each attended by a battle or armoured cruiser squadron, complete with small cruisers and auxiliaries of all kinds, and accompanied by numerous flotillas of destroyers and submarines, more than three-fourths, nearly four-fifths, maintained in full permanent commission — the aspect and scale of this fleet is, I say, extremely formidable. Such a fleet will be about as numerous to look at as the fleet which was gathered at Spithead for the recent Parliamentary visit, but, of course, when completed it will be far superior in actual strength. This full development will only be realised step by step. But already in 1914 two squadrons will, so far as we can ascertain, be entirely composed of "Dreadnoughts," or what are called "Dreadnoughts," and the third will be made up of good ships like the "Deutschlands" and the "Braunschweigs," together with five "Dreadnought" battle-cruisers. It remains to be noted that this new law is the fifth in fourteen years of the large successive increases made in German naval strength, that it encountered no effective opposition in its passage through the Reichstag, and that, though it has been severely criticised in Germany since its passage, the criticisms have been directed towards its inadequacy.

Before I come to the measures which will be necessary on our part, perhaps the Committee will permit me to make a general observation. There are two points with regard to navies and naval war which differentiate them from armies and land war. The first is the awful suddenness with which naval warfare can reach its decisive phase. We see on the continent of Europe immense military establishments possessed by nations dwelling on opposite sides of political frontier lines; yet they dwell and have dwelt for a whole generation in peace and tranquillity. But between those armies and any decisive collision there intervenes an inevitable period of delay that acts as a great buffer, a cushion of security. I mean the vast process of mobilisation, the very first signs of which must be noticed, and which, once it begins, lays idle the industry of both countries and dominates the whole course of national life. So it is that through all these years nations are able to dwell side by side with their tremendous military establishments without being a prey to undue anxiety as to immediate attack. But none of these considerations apply to fleets. The Fleet which was assembled for the manoeuvres the other day was fully capable of going into action as soon as the ammunition could be brought up and put by the side of the guns. And that is true of all the great highly efficient navies of the world.

I am bound to say, looking far ahead, and farther than the purposes of this Vote, at the aspect which Europe and the world will present when the power of States, which has been hitherto estimated in terms of armies, will be estimated very largely in naval strength, and when we have a number of Great Powers all possessed of very powerful navies, the state of Europe and of the world would seem to contain many more germs of danger than the period through which we have been passing in our lifetime.

The second general point to which I would direct the attention of the Committee is the extreme slowness with which naval preparations can be made. Small ships take eighteen to twenty months to build; large ships take from two to three years, sometimes four years. Docks take more than four years to build. Seamen take from two to three years to train; artificers take much longer; officers take between six and seven years. The efficiency which comes from the harmonious combination of these elements is a plant of very slow growth indeed. Cool, steady, methodical preparation, prolonged over a succession of years, can alone raise the margin of naval power. It is no use flinging millions of money about on the impulse of the moment, by a gesture of impatience, or in a mood of panic. Such a course only reveals your weakness and impotence. Those who clamour for sensational expenditure, who think that the kind of danger with which we are faced needs to be warded off or can be warded off in that way, are either ignorant themselves of naval conditions or take advantage of the ignorance of others. The strain we have to bear will be long and slow, and no relief will be obtained by impulsive or erratic action. We ought to learn more from our German neighbours, whose policy marches unswervingly towards its goal across the lifetime of a whole generation. The two general principles which I would deduce from these observations, and which will guide my remarks this afternoon, are, first, that we have an ample margin of strength instantly ready; and, secondly, that there must be a steady and systematic development of our naval forces untiringly pursued over a number of years. . . .

Exchange of Letters Between Sir Edward Grey and Paul Cambon, November 22–23, 1912

My dear Ambassador,

From time to time in recent years the French and British naval and military experts have consulted together. It has always been understood

From Great Britain, Foreign Office, *Collected Diplomatic Documents Relating to the Outbreak of the European War* (1915), pp. 260–61. Reprinted by permission of Her Majesty's Stationery Office.

that such consultation does not restrict the freedom of either Government to decide at any future time whether or not to assist the other by armed force. We have agreed that consultation between experts is not, and ought not to be regarded as, an engagement that commits either Government to action in a contingency that has not arisen and may never arise. The disposition, for instance, of the French and British fleets respectively at the present moment is not based upon an engagement to co-operate in war.

You have, however, pointed out that, if either Government had grave reason to expect an unprovoked attack by a third Power, it might become essential to know whether it could in that event depend upon the armed assistance of the other.

I agree that, if either Government had grave reason to expect an unprovoked attack by a third Power, or something that threatened the general peace, it should immediately discuss with the other whether both Governments should act together to prevent aggression and to preserve peace, and if so, what measures they would be prepared to take in common. If these measures involved action, the plans of the General Staffs would at once be taken into consideration, and the Governments would then decide what effect should be given to them.

Yours, etc.,
E. Grey

Dear Sir Edward,

You reminded me in your letter of yesterday, 22nd November, that during the last few years the military and naval authorities of France and Great Britain had consulted with each other from time to time; that it had always been understood that these consultations should not restrict the liberty of either Government to decide in the future whether they should lend each other the support of their armed forces; that, on either side, these consultations between experts were not and should not be considered as engagements binding our Governments to take action in certain eventualities; that, however, I had remarked to you that, if one or other of the two Governments had grave reasons to fear an unprovoked attack on the part of a third Power, it would become essential to know whether it could count on the armed support of the other.

Your letter answers that point, and I am authorised to state that, in the event of one of our two Governments having grave reasons to fear either an act of aggression from a third Power, or some event threatening the general peace, that Government would immediately examine with the other the question whether both Governments should act together in order to prevent the act of aggression or preserve peace. If so, the two Governments would deliberate as to the measures which they would be prepared to take in common; if those measures involved action, the two Governments would take into immediate consideration the plans of their general staffs and would then decide as to the effect to be given to those plans.

Yours, etc.,

Paul Cambon

Germany's Strategy

As twentieth-century man has discovered in a fateful way, armaments races and military planning for war develop a logic and dynamic of their own that limit the maneuverability of statesmen trying to maintain peace or at least choose the most favorable options in case of war. This happens particularly when military authorities are highly regarded and have too much independent power. Imperial Germany had the misfortune to have highly regarded and independent military authorities, and the plan put into effect by the German general staff in August, 1914, demonstrates how disastrous militarism can be. The plan was devised in 1905 by Count Alfred von Schlieffen, chief of the great general staff from 1891 to 1905. It underwent many revisions of detail, but its basic purpose was to solve the problem of fighting a two-front war and to give Germany the quick and total victory Schlieffen was convinced Germany needed. The goal was to defeat Germany's continental enemies one at a time. Since Russia was so large and would mobilize slowly, Schlieffen decided that a defensive action could be fought in the east while a great blow was struck in the west. However, a speedy victory over France was difficult because of the French fortress system. To solve this problem, Schlieffen called for the violation of Belgian neutrality and a gigantic enveloping action by Germany's right wing, which would encircle and destroy the French armies. The task was to be accomplished in six weeks, and then the German armies were to be shifted to the east.

The military timetable established by Schlieffen and his successor, General von Moltke, caused Germany severe political difficulty in 1914. Although the war began as a conflict between Austria-Hungary and Serbia and expanded to include Russia and Germany, the Schlieffen-Moltke timetable required Germany to begin operations by sending an ultimatum to Belgium and finding an excuse for war with France. England probably would have entered the conflict on the side of France anyway, but the invasion of Belgium rallied English public opinion behind the government's decision. Worst of all, the Schlieffen Plan didn't work. Moltke has often been accused of watering down the plan, but the chief problem, as historians investigating the question with fresh evidence have discovered, was that the plan was a gamble from the start, leaving little room for change and requiring that nothing go awry. The French armies were able to stop the German right wing at the Battle of the Marne in September, 1914. Schlieffen died in 1912 and did not live to see the failure of his plan. His final draft of the plan, written in 1912, is a good illustration of this military technician's mind at work.

The Schlieffen Plan

The Triple Alliance developed out of an alliance between Germany and Austria-Hungary. Both Powers felt threatened by Russia: Austria due to serious political differences which could easily have led to a war, Germany because of personal irritations which might nevertheless soon have given way to traditional friendship again, had they not been aggravated by the signing of a treaty with Russia's enemy. The alliance was conceived defensively, but in case of war was to be carried into effect offensively.

At that time the Russian army was distributed throughout the vast expanse of the empire, and the Russian railway system was altogether inadequate. Therefore in the first stages of a war it would only have been possible to assemble a part of the army in Poland right of the Vistula. Against this part the allies intended to advance from north and south in order to crush the enemy in the middle of the country.

While the two allies were still enjoying this pleasant prospect, rumours got about that Russia was pulling her corps stationed in the East westwards and preparing to assemble an army on the Niemen, on the German's left flank, and on the eastern frontier of Galicia, the Austrians' right flank. Austria intended to clear her flank first and postpone the offensive into Poland until this was done. Unless Germany were prepared to invade Poland alone, she had no choice but to follow her ally's example. Thus two quite separate prospective theatres of war were created: one in Eastern Galicia, the other in East Prussia, each with its adjoining Russian provinces.

Austria, with only the smaller part of the Russian army against her, had a relatively easy task. She would always have forces to spare for the pursuit of her aims in the Balkan peninsula. Germany faced not only the greater part of the Russian army but also, as became soon apparent, the French army.

This disproportion might have been rectified by Italy, which had joined the Alliance. Indeed, in the hope of regaining Nice and Savoy,

From Gerhard Ritter, *The Schlieffen Plan: Critique of a Myth*, trans. Andrew and Eva Wilson (New York: Praeger, 1958), pp. 169–76. Reprinted by permission of Oswald Wolff Publishers Ltd.

the latter was intending to cross the Alps and to invade central and southern France, thereby relieving Germany of a great part of the French army. The plan had to be abandoned when France fortified all the Alpine passes. But in order to take part in the expected Franco-German war, Italy was to bring some corps over the Austrian and south German railways to the Upper Rhine, where she would unite with Germany in a common campaign. This plan also was eventually abandoned, because it was thought dangerous to send a large part of the army abroad when the French could cross the Alps and invade the Po valley.

So Italy left the Triple Alliance, at least as a working member. Austria kept far away in a separate theatre. Germany meanwhile faced the greater part of the Russian, and the whole of the French army, without any support.

If both her enemies were to advance from east and west, Germany would certainly find herself in a serious situation. But neither dared take the decisive step. Each feared the other would let her down or come too late, and that she alone would be saddled with the whole German army. Secure behind fortresses, rivers, mountains and swamps, both were lying in wait for their unprotected weaker adversary who was entirely on his own.

So it was not the Triple Alliance, but solely the Germany army which held Russia and France in check, preventing the former from giving Austria, and the latter Italy, a taste of her superiority. Peace was kept in Europe. It mattered little that Italy, prevented by the French Alpine fortifications from attacking France, tried to vent her expansionist desires on Austria. When the Austrians, too, fortified their Alpine passes, the Italians were forced to give up their lust for conquest here as well.

The power and prestige of the German army proved their worth in 1905 and 1909. Neither France nor Russia was willing to take up arms once Germany left no doubt about her determination to fight back. This favourable state of affairs underwent a change in 1911. German resolution was paralysed by England's threat to come to the assistance of France with 100,000 men. In 1911 England would have yielded before Germany's manifest intention of using the army if necessary, as France had done in 1905 and Russia in 1909. But on this occasion it was Germany who yielded, and so the spell was broken which had so far made her army seem invincible. Nor could the lost prestige be restored by the army reform of 1912, which brought little more than changes in organisation — none in power. This time it was not Germany's promise to stand by her Austrian allies which secured peace, but only England's wish, for economic reasons, to avoid a world war.

It is to be hoped that England's will may not for ever be decisive, and that Germany will one day regain the position of power necessary to her economic prosperity. Without a war this will scarcely be possible. How it will come about remains to be seen. How it is to be conducted must be left to Germany. She has done her duty as a member of the Triple Alliance by making an enemy of Russia, from whom she was not divided by any conflicting interests — and of whom she could have won nothing worth while — and by drawing upon herself the greater part of the Russian army. As a result she stands between two powerful enemies. . . .

The *whole* of Germany must throw itself on *one* enemy — the strongest, most powerful, most dangerous enemy: and that can only be the Anglo-French!

Austria need not worry: the Russian army intended against Germany will not invade Galicia before the die is cast in the West. And Austria's fate will be decided not on the Bug but on the Seine!

Against Germany, the French intend to hold a position extending from the frontier at Belfort along the Upper Moselle as far as Toul, from there following the course of the Meuse to Verdun and leaning on neutral Belgian territory as far as the neighbourhood of Montmédy. In front of this position they will further occupy the passes across the Vosges, the fortified city of Nancy, Manonvillers, the heights right of the Meuse between Toul and Verdun, and also Longwy. Should the Germans succeed in breaking through the left wing of this position, they will still find the enemy behind the Meuse betwen Verdun and Mézières. Below the latter the river is not easily accessible. The first important crossing, farther north, is blocked by the fortress of Givet. The Germans cannot therefore count on crossing the Meuse without serious fighting so long as it runs through French territory. Beyond Givet the river enters Belgium. This country is regarded as neutral, but in fact it is not. More than thirty years ago it made Liège and Namur into strong fortresses to prevent Germany from invading its territory, but towards France it has left its frontiers open. The French will therefore be free to send as many reinforcements as they wish into the position which the Belgians apparently intend to occupy between these two fortresses. The English may also be present. In 1911 they threatened to land with 180,000 men in Antwerp. On its landward side the latter is heavily fortified. It is unlikely that the Dutch will bring their Scheldt batteries into action against the English, upon whose goodwill they depend for their colonies. Therefore via Antwerp, or if need be Dunkirk, the English can join up with the Belgians and French in the position Liège-Namur. From there the three, or two, of them will be able not only to prevent the Germans crossing the Meuse between Givet and Liège, but also most effectively to flank a German attack on the French position Belfort-Mézières.

Unless, therefore, the Germans are prepared to suffer a serious defeat, they are obliged to attack the offensive flank which the Belgians have added to the French position. This can be done if at an early stage a German army crosses the Meuse below Liège, wheels left and invades Belgium and France left of the Meuse and Sambre, while a second army supports the attack between Givet and Namur on the right of those rivers, a third advances on the sector Mézières-Verdun, and a fourth advances on the front Verdun-Belfort.

An attack on so large a scale requires a large army. The German corps, with a column-of-march length of twenty-nine kilometres excluding train, have become very cumbrous. If only their infantry strength were not in unfavourable proportion to the artillery, they could be divided and each half be treated as a new corps. But as the Reserve divisions are allotted too little artillery in proportion to infantry, a more favourable arrangement of the army might be achieved by a combination of army corps and Reserve divisions. . . .

. . . It will be advisable to confront the Belgian Government with the choice of a bombardment of its fortified towns, particularly Liège, as well as a considerable levy — or of handing over all fortresses, railways and troops. But to turn the threatened bombardment into reality if necessary, the heavy artillery must be suitably equipped. The latter will also prove necessary in the further course of the campaign. To begin with, the great industrial town of Lille offers an excellent target for bombardment.

For the investing of fortresses which have not capitulated, for the occupation of conquered territory, and for securing lines of communication, the army will be followed as soon as possible by the Landwehr, the Ersatz troops, and, since these alone will not be sufficient, the mobilised Landsturm.

Level with the first army, a second army of eight divisions will advance south of the Meuse, using one division to invest Liège and Namur on the south. It will cross the Meuse betwen Namur and Mézières, the right wing following the right bank of the Sambre, leaving a division before Maubeuge and taking the direction of St. Quentin, while the left wing takes the direction of Rethel.

The third army will advance with five corps through southern Belgium and Luxembourg against the Meuse betwen Mézières and Verdun.

The fourth army, with six corps, will attack the front Verdun-Belfort, resting its left wing against the area of Porrentruy in neutral Switzerland. So far as Belfort and Epinal are concerned, this attack cannot do more than seal them on the east side. Against the forts of the Upper Moselle, the gap betwen Epinal and Toul, and the hill position between the latter fortress and Verdun, siege tactics will have to be used. The fortifications round Nancy can be reduced by the bombardment — threatened or actual — of the town. If this succeeds, the Germans will come into possession of the high plateau opposite Toul, which is washed by the Meurthe and the Moselle. A break-through in the strongly held position Belfort-Verdun, however, can only be hoped for when the third army has crossed the Meuse, and this in turn can only succeed when the second and first armies have crossed the French frontier.

A successful march through Belgium on both sides of the Meuse is therefore the prerequisite of a victory. It will succeed beyond doubt, if it is only the Belgian army which tries to obstruct it. But it will be very difficult if the English army, and perhaps even part of the French, is present. The area between Namur and Antwerp is so confined that it can easily be blocked by the English and Belgian corps, supported if necessary by a few French corps. In this case, the advance of the second army on the right of the Sambre must create a breathing space. If they, too, find the Meuse blocked between Namur and Mézières, help can come only from an attack on the whole front, with a break-through at some point after large-scale heavy artillery preparation.

But in general we must put our trust in an overwhelming right wing, which will progressively bring the whole line forward. When the latter reaches the approximate level Abbeville, St. Quentin, Rethel-Verdun, the French will slowly evacuate the position Verdun-Toul, Toul-Epinal, etc. Their general retreat will first be towards the position Rheims–La Fère, then towards Paris. The first, second and third German armies, joined by the released corps with strong cavalry on their wings, will follow in a wide arc with the intention of completely encircling the greatest possible part of the enemy army.

For the occupation of the conquered territory and the covering of the lines of communication, the Landwehr and Ersatz troops will not be sufficient. The Landsturm must be mobilised.

War Aims

As might be expected, the various combatants during World War I all claimed that they were the victims of aggression. They frequently justified their imperialist war aims on the grounds that they needed security against future aggression. Although the chief supporters of extreme war aims were military men and conservatives, the far-reaching demands of even moderate statesmen were quite remarkable. It was always assumed, for example, that the German chancellor, Theobold von Bethmann-Hollweg, was a moderate. The recent discovery of his war aims memorandum of September 9, 1914, however, has dealt a fatal blow to his reputation. Bethmann-Hollweg deviated from his program for European hegemony and world power after the defeat on the Marne, but Germany's basic goals remained fairly constant throughout the war. The draconian terms imposed on Russia at Brest-Litovsk in March, 1918, proved that the Germans meant business.

Allied arrangements for European and non-European territorial rearrangements were no less cynical. They were, however, well kept

*secrets until the Bolsheviks published the secret treaties after the
October Revolution. Of all Germany's opponents, the Italians were
probably the most honest in expressing their intentions. They frankly
entered the war on the side they believed would win and would give
them the most gain. Their terms were stated in the Treaty of London
signed with the Allies on April 26, 1915. The Italian contribution to
the war effort was rather undistinguished, and Italy's territorial ambitions caused severe conflicts at the Paris peace conference.*

Bethmann-Hollweg's Provisional Notes on the Direction of Policy on the Conclusion of Peace, September 9, 1914

[The] general aim of the war [is] security for the German Reich in
west and east for all imaginable time. For this purpose France must be
so weakened as to make her revival as a great power impossible for all
time. Russia must be thrust back as far as possible from Germany's
eastern frontier and her domination over the non-Russian vassal peoples
broken.

1. *France.* The military to decide whether we should demand cession
of Belfort and western slopes of the Vosges, razing of fortresses and cession of coastal strip from Dunkirk to Boulogne.

The ore-field of Briey, which is necessary for the supply of ore for our
industry, to be ceded in any case.

Further, a war indemnity, to be paid in instalments; it must be high
enough to prevent France from spending any considerable sums on armaments in the next 15–20 years.

Furthermore: a commercial treaty which makes France economically
dependent on Germany, secures the French market for our exports and
makes it possible to exclude British commerce from France. This treaty
must secure for us financial and industrial freedom of movement in
France in such fashion that German enterprises can no longer receive
different treatment from French.

2. *Belgium.* Liège and Verviers to be attached to Prussia, a frontier
strip of the province of Luxemburg to Luxemburg.

Question whether Antwerp, with a corridor to Liège, should also be
annexed remains open.

At any rate Belgium, even if allowed to continue to exist as a state,

From Fritz Fischer, *Germany's Aims in the First World War* (New York: Norton, 1967),
pp. 103–05. Copyright © 1961 by Droste Verlag und Druckerei GmbH, Dusseldorf;
translation copyright © 1967 by W. W. Norton & Company, Inc., and Chatto and Windus, Ltd. Reprinted by permission of W. W. Norton & Company, Inc., and Chatto and
Windus Ltd.

must be reduced to a vassal state, must allow us to occupy any militarily important ports, must place her coast at our disposal in military respects, must become economically a German province. Given such a solution, which offers the advantages of annexation without its inescapable domestic political disadvantages, French Flanders with Dunkirk, Calais and Boulogne, where most of the population is Flemish, can without danger be attached to this unaltered Belgium. The competent quarters will have to judge the military value of this position against England.

3. *Luxemburg.* Will become a German federal state and will receive a strip of the present Belgian province of Luxemburg and perhaps the corner of Longwy.

4. We must create a *central European economic association* through common customs treaties, to include France, Belgium, Holland, Denmark, Austria-Hungary, Poland [sic], and perhaps Italy, Sweden and Norway. This association will not have any common constitutional supreme authority and all its members will be formally equal, but in practice will be under German leadership and must stabilise Germany's economic dominance over Mitteleuropa.

5. *The question of colonial acquisitions,* where the first aim is the creation of a continuous Central African colonial empire, will be considered later, as will that of the aims to be realised *vis-à-vis* Russia.

6. A short provisional formula suitable for a possible preliminary peace to be found for a basis for the economic agreements to be concluded with France and Belgium.

7. *Holland.* It will have to be considered by what means and methods Holland can be brought into closer relationship with the German Empire.

In view of the Dutch character, this closer relationship must leave them free of any feeling of compulsion, must alter nothing in the Dutch way of life, and must also subject them to no new military obligations. Holland, then, must be left independent in externals, but be made internally dependent on us. Possibly one might consider an offensive and defensive alliance, to cover the colonies; in any case a close customs association, perhaps the cession of Antwerp to Holland in return for the right to keep a German garrison in the fortress of Antwerp and at the mouth of the Scheldt.

The Treaty of London, April 26, 1915

ARTICLE 1. A military convention shall be immediately concluded between the General Staffs of France, Great Britain, Italy and Russia. This convention shall settle the minimum number of military forces to

From Great Britain, *Parliamentary Papers,* vol. 51 (1920), Cmd. 671. Reprinted by permission of Her Majesty's Stationery Office.

be employed by Russia against Austria-Hungary in order to prevent that Power from concentrating all its strength against Italy, in the event of Russia deciding to direct her principal effort against Germany.

This military convention shall settle question of armistices, which necessarily comes within the scope of the Commanders-in-chief of the Armies.

ARTICLE 2. On her part, Italy undertakes to use her entire resources for the purpose of waging war jointly with France, Great Britain and Russia against all their enemies.

ARTICLE 3. The French and British fleets shall render active and permanent assistance to Italy until such time as the Austro-Hungarian fleet shall have been destroyed or until peace shall have been concluded.

A naval convention shall be immediately concluded to this effect between France, Great Britain and Italy.

ARTICLE 4. Under the Treaty of Peace, Italy shall obtain the Trentino, Cisalpine Tyrol with its geographical and natural frontier (the Brenner frontier), as well as Trieste, the counties of Gorizia and Gradisca, all Istria as far as the Quarnero and including Volosca and the Istrian islands of Cherso and Lussin, as well as the small islands of Plavnik, Unie, Canidole, Palazzuoli, San Pietro di Nembi, Asinello, Gruica, and the neighbouring islets. . . .

ARTICLE 5. Italy shall also be given the province of Dalmatia within its present administrative boundaries. . . .

ARTICLE 6. Italy shall receive full sovereignty over Valona, the island of Saseno and surrounding territory of sufficient extent to assure defence of these points (from the Voïussa to the north and east, approximately to the northern boundary of the district of Chimara on the south).

ARTICLE 7. Should Italy obtain the Trentino and Istria in accordance with the provisions of Article 4, together with Dalmatia and the Adriatic islands within the limits specified in Article 5, and the Bay of Valona (Article 6), and if the central portion of Albania is reserved for the establishment of a small autonomous neutralised State, Italy shall not oppose the division of Northern and Southern Albania between Montenegro, Serbia and Greece, should France, Great Britain and Russia so desire. The coast from the southern boundary of the Italian territory of Valona (see Article 6) up to Cape Stylos shall be neutralised.

Italy shall be charged with the representation of the State of Albania in its relations with foreign Powers.

Italy agrees, moreover, to leave sufficient territory in any event to the east of Albania to ensure the existence of a frontier line between Greece and Serbia to the west of Lake Ochrida.

ARTICLE 8. Italy shall receive entire sovereignty over the Dodecanese Islands which she is at present occupying.

ARTICLE 9. Generally speaking, France, Great Britain and Russia recognise that Italy is interested in the maintenance of the balance of power in the Mediterranean and that, in the event of the total or partial partition of Turkey in Asia, she ought to obtain a just share of the Mediterranean region adjacent to the province of Adalia, where Italy has, already acquired rights and interests which formed the subject of an Italo-British convention. The zone which shall eventually be allotted to Italy shall be delimited, at the proper time, due account being taken of the existing interests of France and Great Britain.

The interests of Italy shall also be taken into consideration in the event of the territorial integrity of the Turkish Empire being maintained and of alterations being made in the zones of interest of the Powers.

If France, Great Britain and Russia occupy any territories in Turkey in Asia during the course of the war, the Mediterranean region bordering on the Province of Adalia within the limits indicated above shall be reserved to Italy, who shall be entitled to occupy it.

ARTICLE 10. All rights and privileges in Libya at present belonging to the Sultan by virtue of the Treaty of Lausanne are transferred to Italy.

ARTICLE 11. Italy shall receive a share of any eventual war indemnity corresponding to her efforts and her sacrifices.

ARTICLE 12. Italy declares that she associates herself in the declaration made by France, Great Britain and Russia to the effect that Arabia and the Moslem Holy Places in Arabia shall be left under the authority of an independent Moslem Power.

ARTICLE 13. In the event of France and Great Britain increasing their colonial territories in Africa at the expense of Germany, those two Powers agree in principle that Italy may claim some equitable compensation, particularly as regards the settlement in her favour of the questions relative to the frontiers of the Italian colonies of Eritrea, Somaliland and Libya and the neighbouring colonies belonging to France and Great Britain.

ARTICLE 14. Great Britain undertakes to facilitate the immediate conclusion, under equitable conditions, of a loan of at least £50,000,000, to be issued on the London market.

ARTICLE 15. France, Great Britain and Russia shall support such opposition as Italy may make to any proposal in the direction of introducing a representative of the Holy See in any peace negotiations or negotiations for the settlement of questions raised by the present war.

ARTICLE 16. The present arrangement shall be held secret. The adherence of Italy to the Declaration of the 5th September, 1914, shall alone be made public, immediately upon declaration of war by or against Italy.

.   .   .   .   .

After having taken act of the foregoing memorandum the representatives of France, Great Britain and Russia, duly authorised to that effect, have concluded the following agreement with the representative of Italy, also duly authorised by his Government:

France, Great Britain and Russia give their full assent to the memorandum presented by the Italian Government.

With reference to Articles 1, 2, and 3 of the memorandum which provide for military and naval coöperation between the four Powers, Italy declares that she will take the field at the earliest possible date and within a period not exceeding one month from the signature of these presents.

In faith whereof the undersigned have signed the present agreements and have affixed thereto their seals.

Done at London, in quadruplicate, the 26th day of April, 1915.

> (L. S.) E. Grey
> (L. S.) Imperiali
> (L. S.) Benckendorff
> (L. S.) Paul Cambon

DECLARATION BY WHICH FRANCE, GREAT BRITAIN, ITALY, AND RUSSIA UNDERTAKE NOT TO CONCLUDE A SEPARATE PEACE DURING THE COURSE OF THE PRESENT EUROPEAN WAR

The Italian Government, having decided to participate in the present war with the French, British and Russian Governments, and to accede to the Declaration made at London, the 5th September, 1914, by the three above-named Governments,

The undersigned, being duly authorised by their respective Governments, make the following declaration:

The French, British, Italian and Russian Governments mutually undertake not to conclude a separate peace during the course of the present war.

The four Governments agree that, whenever there may be occasion to discuss the terms of peace, none of the Allied Powers shall lay down any conditions of peace without previous agreement with each of the other Allies. . . .

DECLARATION

The Declaration of the 26th April, 1915, whereby France, Great Britain, Italy and Russia undertake not to conclude a separate peace during the present European war, shall remain secret.

After the declaration of war by or against Italy, the four Powers shall sign a new declaration in identical terms, which shall thereupon be made public. . . .

Trenches and the Home Front

Historians have yet to explore seriously the social and psychological consequences of the First World War. Fortunately, major twentieth-century writers have provided historians with valuable clues about what to look for when they finally get around to this task. Life in the trenches and patrol duty, which provided a way of life and death for millions of men, are vividly described by the English writer Robert Graves in his autobiography, Goodbye to All That. *Life on the home front also provided a theme of great complexity and significance. On the one hand, war brought privations and required participation on some level by almost everyone. On the other, the length of the war and its hardships often served to deepen class barriers and promote privateering and high living by those with wealth and influence. A gulf developed between the men at the front and the people back home. French novelist Marcel Proust, in the last portion of his autobiographical* Remembrance of Things Past, *describes how decadent French aristocrats and pretentious members of the upper middle class tried to cope with the war.*

Graves' *Goodbye to All That*

My first night, Captain Thomas asked whether I would like to go out on patrol. It was the regimental custom to test new officers in this way, and none dared excuse himself. During my whole service with the Welsh I had never once been out in No Man's Land, even to inspect the barbed-wire; the wire being considered the responsibility of the battalion intelligence officer and the Royal Engineers. When Hewitt, the Welsh machine-gun officer, used to go out on patrol sometimes, we regarded this as a mad escapade. But both battalions of the Royal Welch Fusiliers had made it a point of honour to dominate No Man's Land from dusk to dawn. There was never a night at Laventie when a message did not come down the line from sentry to sentry: 'Pass the word; officer's patrol going out.' My orders for this patrol were to see whether a certain German sap-head was occupied by night or not.

Sergeant Townsend and I went out from Red Lamp Corner at about ten o'clock; both carrying revolvers. We had pulled socks, with the toes cut off, over our bare knees, to prevent them showing up in the dark and

From Robert Graves, *Goodbye to All That* (© 1957 by Robert Graves), new ed. (London: Cassell, 1957), pp. 114–19. Reprinted by permission of Robert Graves and Collins-Knowlton-Wing, Inc.

to make crawling easier. We went ten yards at a time, slowly, not on all fours, but wriggling flat along the ground. After each movement we lay and watched for about ten minutes. We crawled through our own wire entanglements and along a dry ditch; ripping our clothes on more barbed-wire, glaring into the darkness until it began turning round and round. Once I snatched my fingers in horror from where I had planted them on the slimy body of an old corpse. We nudged each other with rapidly beating hearts at the slightest noise or suspicion: crawling, watching, crawling, shamming dead under the blinding light of enemy flares, and again crawling, watching, crawling. A Second Battalion officer, who revisited these Laventie trenches after the war ended told me the other day of the ridiculously small area of No Man's Land compared with its seeming immensity on the long, painful journeys that he had made over it. 'It was like the real size of a hollow in one's tooth compared with how it feels to the tongue.'

We found the gap in the German wire and at last came within five yards of the sap-head. We waited quite twenty minutes, listening for any signs of its occupation. Then I nudged Sergeant Townsend and, revolver in hand, we wriggled quickly forward and slid into it. It was about three feet deep and unoccupied. On the floor were a few empty cartridges, and a wicker basket containing something large and smooth and round, twice the size of a football. Very, very carefully I groped and felt all around it in the dark. I was afraid that it might be some sort of infernal machine. Eventually I dared lift it out and carry it back, suspecting that it might be one of the German gas-cylinders we had heard so much about.

We got home after making a journey of perhaps two hundred yards in rather more than two hours. The sentries passed along the word that we were in again. Our prize proved to be a large glass container quarter-filled with some pale yellow liquid. This was sent down to battalion headquarters, and from there to the divisional intelligence officer. Everybody seemed greatly interested in it. The theory was that the vessel contained a chemical for re-damping gas-masks, though it may well have been dregs of country wine mixed with rain water. I never heard the official report. The colonel, however, told Captain Thomas in the hearing of the Surrey-man: 'Your new wart seems to have more guts than the others.'

After this I went on patrol fairly often, finding that the only thing respected in young officers was personal courage. Besides, I had cannily worked it out like this. My best way of lasting through to the end of the war would be to get wounded. The best time to get wounded would be at night and in the open, with rifle fire more or less unaimed and my whole body exposed. Best, also, to get wounded when there was no rush on the dressing-station services, and while the back areas were not being heavily shelled. Best to get wounded, therefore, on a night patrol in a quiet sector. One could usually manage to crawl into a shell hole until help arrived.

Still, patrolling had its peculiar risks. If a German patrol found a wounded man, they were as likely as not to cut his throat. The bowie-knife was a favourite German patrol weapon because of its silence. (We inclined more to the 'cosh,' a loaded stick.) The most important information that a patrol could bring back was to what regiment and division the troops opposite belonged. So if it were impossible to get a wounded enemy back without danger to oneself, he had to be stripped of his badges. To do that quickly and silently, it might be necessary first to cut his throat or beat in his skull.

Sir Pyers Mostyn, a Royal Welch lieutenant who often went out patrolling at Laventie, had a feud with a German patrol on the left of the battalion frontage. Our patrols usually consisted of an officer and one, or at the most, two men; German patrols of six or seven men under an N.C.O. German officers did not, as one of our sergeant-majors put it, believe in 'keeping a dog and barking themselves'; so they left as much as they decently could to their N.C.O.s. One night Mostyn caught sight of his opponents; he had raised himself on his knees to throw a percussion bomb, when they fired and wounded him in the arm, which immediately went numb. He caught the bomb before it hit the ground, threw it at them with his left hand, and in the confusion that followed got back to the trench.

Like everyone else, I had a carefully worked out formula for taking risks. In principle, we would all take any risk, even the certainty of death, to save life or to maintain an important position. To take life we would run, say, a one-in-five risk, particularly if there was some wider object than merely reducing the enemy's manpower; for instance, picking off a well-known sniper, or getting fire ascendancy in trenches where the lines came dangerously close. I only once refrained from shooting a German I saw, and that was at Cuinchy, some three weeks after this. While sniping from a knoll in the support line, where we had a concealed loophole I saw a German, perhaps seven hundred yards away, through my telescopic sights. He was taking a bath in the German third line. I disliked the idea of shooting a naked man, so I handed the rifle to the sergeant with me. 'Here, take this. You're a better shot than I am.' He got him; but I had not stayed to watch.

About saving the lives of enemy wounded there was disagreement; the convention varied with the division. Some divisions, like the Canadians and a division of Lowland territorials, who claimed that they had atrocities to avenge, would not only avoid taking risks to rescue enemy wounded, but go out of their way to finish them off. The Royal Welch were gentlemanly: perhaps a one-in-twenty risk to get a wounded German to safety would be considered justifiable. An important factor in calculating risks was our own physical condition. When exhausted and wanting to get quickly from one point in the trenches to another without collapse, we would sometimes take a short cut over the top, if the enemy were not nearer than four or five hundred yards. In a hurry, we would take a one-in-two-hundred risk; when dead tired, a one-in-fifty risk. In battalions where morale was low, one-in-fifty risks were often taken in laziness or despair. The Munsters of the First Division were said by the Welsh to 'waste men wicked,' by not keeping properly under cover while in the reserve lines. The Royal Welch never allowed wastage of this sort. At no time in the war did any of us believe that hostilities could possibly continue more than another nine months or a year, so it seemed almost worth while taking care; there might even be a chance of lasting until the end absolutely unhurt.

The Second Royal Welch, unlike the Second Welsh, believed themselves better trench fighters than the Germans. With the Second Welsh it was not cowardice but modesty. With the Second Royal Welch it was not vainglory but courage: as soon as they arrived in a new sector they insisted on getting fire ascendancy. Having found out, from the troops whom they relieved, all possible information as to enemy snipers, machine-guns, and patrols, they set themselves to deal with them one by one. Machine-guns first. As soon as a machine-gun started traversing down a trench by night, the whole platoon farthest removed from its fire would open five rounds rapid at it. The machine-gun would usually stop suddenly, but start again after a minute or two. Again five rounds rapid. Then it gave up.

The Welsh seldom answered a machine-gun. If they did, it was not with organized local fire, beginning and ending in unison, but in ragged confused protest all along the line. The Royal Welch almost never fired at night, except with organized fire at a machine-gun, or a persistent enemy sentry, or a patrol close enough to be distinguished as a German one. With all other battalions I met in France there was continuous random popping off; the sentries wanted to show their spite against the war. Flares were rarely used in the Royal Welch, except as signals to our patrols that they should be starting back.

When the enemy machine-guns had been discouraged, our patrols would go out with bombs to claim possession of No Man's Land. At dawn next morning came the struggle for sniping ascendancy. The Germans had special regimental snipers, trained in camouflaging themselves. I saw one killed once at Cuinchy, who had been firing all day from a shell-hole between the lines. He wore a sort of cape made of imitation grass, his face was painted green and brown, and his rifle was also green-fringed. A number of empty cartridges lay beside him, and his cap bore the special oak-leaf badge. Few of our battalions attempted to get control of the sniping situation. The Germans had the advantage of having many times more telescopic sights than we did, and bullet-proof steel loop-holes. Also a system by which snipers were kept for months in the same sector until they knew all the loop-holes and shallow places in our trenches, and the tracks that our ration parties used above-ground by night, and where our traverses occurred, and so on, better than most of us did ourselves. British snipers changed their trenches, with their battalions, every week or two, and never had time to study the German trench-geography. But at least we counted on getting rid of the unprofessional sniper. Later we secured an elephant-gun that could send a bullet through enemy loop-holes; and if we failed to locate the loop-hole of a persistent sniper, we tried to dislodge him with a volley of rifle-grenades, or even by ringing up the artillery.

It puzzled us that when a sniper had been spotted and killed, another sniper would often begin operations next day from the same position. The Germans probably underrated us, and regarded their loss as an accident. The willingness of other battalions to allow the Germans sniping ascendancy helped us; enemy snipers, even the professionals, often exposed themselves unnecessarily. There was one advantage of which no progress or retreat of the enemy could rob us, namely that we always more or less faced east. Dawn broke behind the German lines, and they did not realize that for several minutes every morning we could see them, while still invisible ourselves. German night wiring-parties often stayed out too long, and we could get a man or two as they went back; sunsets went against us, of course; but sunset was a less critical time. At night, our sentries had orders to stand with their heads and shoulders above the parapet, and their rifles in position. This surprised me at first, but it implied greater vigilance and self-confidence in the sentry, and also put the top of his head above the level of the parapet. Enemy machine-guns were trained on this level, and it would be safer to get hit in the chest or shoulders than in the forehead. The risk of unaimed fire at night being negligible, this was really the safest plan. It happened in battalions which did not insist on the head-and-shoulder rule, but let their sentries just steal an occasional peep over the top, that an enemy patrol would sneak up unseen to the British wire, throw a few bombs, and get safely back. With the Royal Welch, the barbed-wire entanglement became the responsibility of the company it protected. One of our first acts on taking over trenches was to inspect and repair it. We did a lot of work on our wire.

Proust's *The Past Recaptured*

At dusk, before the hour when the afternoon teas ended, while the sky was still light, one saw little brown spots in the distance which might

From Marcel Proust, *Remembrance of Things Past* (© 1932; renewed 1960 by Random House), vol. 2, trans. C. K. Scott Moncrieff and Frederick A. Blossom (New York: Random House, 1932), pp. 901, 924–26. Reprinted by permission of Random House, Inc., Chatto and Windus Ltd., and George Scott Moncrieff.

have been mistaken, against the blue evening sky, for gnats or birds. In the same way, when one sees a mountain very far away, one might think it a cloud. But one is impressed, knowing that this cloud is immense, solid, unyielding. Just so was I deeply moved because the brown spot in the summer sky was neither a gnat nor a bird, but an airplane piloted by men who were watching over Paris. The recollection of the airplanes I had seen near Versailles the last time I went out with Albertine had no part in this emotion because the memory of that occasion had become a matter of indifference to me.

At the dinner hour the restaurants were crowded and if, passing by, I saw a poor soldier on leave, who had escaped for six days from the constant danger of death and was about to go back to the trenches again, fix his gaze for an instant on the brightly lighted windows, I suffered as I used to at the hotel at Balbec when the fishermen watched us dining, but now I suffered more because I knew that the misery of the soldier is greater than that of the poor man, being a merging of all miseries and still more touching because more resigned, more noble, and because, with a philosophical shake of the head, without hatred, about to return to the front, he said, as he saw the slackers jostle one another as they reserved their table, "You would never think there was a war going on here." Then at half-past nine, before anyone had had time to finish dinner, all the lights were suddenly put out on account of the police regulations, and the new jostling of the slackers, snatching their overcoats from the doormen of the restaurant where I had dined with Saint-Loup one evening when he was on leave, took place at nine thirty-five in a mysterious half-light like that of a room where a magic lantern is being shewn or of a playhouse used for projecting the films of one of those very cinemas to which these men and women diners were going to rush. But after that hour, for those who, like me on the evening I am speaking of, had stayed at home for dinner and were going out to call on friends, Paris was, at least, in certain quarters, darker than the Combray of my childhood; when we went to see one another, it was like calling on country neighbours. . . .

As for the change which had taken place in M. de Charlus's form of enjoyment, it was intermittent. Keeping up an extensive correspondence with soldiers at the front, he did not suffer from any lack of fairly mature men on leave. In short, speaking generally, Mme. Verdurin continued to hold her receptions and M. de Charlus continued to indulge his tastes as if nothing had changed. And yet for two years that immense human being called 'France' (the colossal beauty of which, even from the purely material point of view, one does not feel unless one perceives the cohesion of the millions of individuals who, like multiform cells, crowd it full to its outermost perimeter, like so many minute interior polygons, and unless one views it on the same scale as a single cell or a microscopic organism would view a human being, namely, as huge as Mont Blanc) had been face-to-face in a gigantic collective quarrel with that other immense agglomeration of individuals 'Germany.' In the days when I believed what people said, hearing first Germany, then Bulgaria and then Greece protest their peaceful intentions, I would have been tempted to have faith in their declarations. But since living with Françoise and Albertine had gotten me into the habit of suspecting them of harbouring thoughts and schemes which they did not tell me about, I did not let any statement from William II, Ferdinand of Bulgaria or Constantine of Greece, however fair it seemed, mislead my intuitive understanding of what each of them was contriving. It is true that my quarrels with Françoise and Albertine had been merely private quarrels, which involved only the life of one little spiritual cell, namely, a human being. But, just as there are animal bodies and human bodies, that is to say, combinations of cells each of which, as compared with a single cell, is as big as a mountain, in the same way there are huge organised agglomerations of individuals, which are called 'nations'; their existence simply repeats on an amplified scale the existence of the component cells, and whoever is unable to comprehend the mystery, the reactions and the laws of the latter, will utter only empty words when he comes to speak of struggles between nations. But if he has mastered the psychology of the individual, then these colossal masses of conglomerate individuals, lined up opposite one another, will take on in his eyes a beauty more imposing than the struggle that springs merely from the conflict of two natures, and he will view them on the scale on which tiny organisms, so microscopic that ten thousand would not measure one cubic millimeter, would view the body of a man of great size. Just so for some time that great body, 'France,' filled to its perimeter with millions of multiform little polygons, and that other body, 'Germany,' filled with still more polygons, had been having a quarrel such as, to a certain extent, individuals have.

But the blows they exchanged were governed by the rules of that mass prize fighting the principles of which Saint-Loup had explained to me, and since, even considered from the point of view of the individual, they were gigantic aggregations, their quarrel assumed immense, magnificent forms, like the upheaving of an ocean of millions of waves which is endeavouring to break down an age-old line of cliffs; or like gigantic glaciers which seek with their slowly destructive oscillations to cut a path through the encircling ring of mountains. Notwithstanding all this, life went on almost unchanged for many persons who have figured in this narrative and particularly for M. de Charlus and the Verdurins, just as if the Germans had not been so near them, because a standing menace — although in this case, to be sure, the peril had now been removed — leaves us completely indifferent if we do not picture to ourselves what it really is. People usually go about their pleasures without ever reflecting that, if the etiolating and moderating influences should happen to cease, the proliferation of the microscopic organisms would reach its maximum, that is to say, making a leap of several million leagues in a few days, it would grow from one cubic millimeter to a mass one million times larger than the sun, having at the same time destroyed all the oxygen and all the substances we live on, so that there would no longer be any human race or any animals or even any earth; nor do they reflect, on the other hand, that the mad, ceaseless activity hidden behind the apparent immutability of the sun might bring about an irremediable and entirely possible catastrophe in the ether. They go about their business without giving a thought to either of these two worlds, one of them too minute, and the other too immense, for people to perceive the cosmic menaces they hold imminent all about us. In the same way, the Verdurins (and soon Mme. Verdurin alone, after the death of her husband) gave dinner parties and M. de Charlus went about his pleasures, hardly realising that the Germans were within an hour's automobile ride of Paris — held in check, it is true, by a bloody barrier constantly renewed. But one might say the Verdurins were reminded of this because they had a political salon, where the situation, not only of the armies, but also of the fleets, was discussed every evening. They did, indeed, give a thought to the hecatombs of regiments annihilated, of passengers swallowed up by the sea, but, by two contrary operations, what concerns our well-being is multiplied, and what does not is divided, by a figure so enormous that the death of millions of people whom we do not know barely touches us, and almost less unpleasantly than a current of air. Mme. Verdurin, in distress at not being able to get any *croissants* to dip in her coffee to relieve her headaches, had obtained from Cottard a prescription permitting her to have them made for her in a certain restaurant we have mentioned. This had been almost as difficult to get out of the public authorities as the nomination of a general. Mme. Verdurin resumed her first *croissant* the morning when the newspapers were telling of the sinking of the *Lusitania*. While dipping the *croissant* in her coffee and giving her newspaper a fillip now and then so as to make it lie open without her having to interrupt the dipping process, she exclaimed, "How terrible! It is more awful than the most frightful catastrophes!" But the drowning of all those people must have impressed her with only the millionth part of its real horror, because, even while making these deeply grieved comments with her mouth full of *croissant* and coffee, an expression of sweet contentment suffused her face, due probably to the pleasing savour of the *croissant,* so effective against headaches.

DISINTEGRATION
AND COLLAPSE
Chapter 2

Many conservatives and nationalists in all the belligerent countries hoped that a short war and peace providing annexations and indemnities for the victor would strengthen the domestic social order in their respective countries by deflecting demands for reform. Had the war been short, reformers probably would have lost their momentum, at least in the victorious nations. The last years of the war did bring a shift to the Right in France and England, under the tough leadership of Clemenceau and Lloyd George, but the war was too long and too costly to be stabilizing anywhere, and both victors and losers were compelled to confront the problems of revolutionary turmoil and socioeconomic disruption. Indeed, these problems were never really solved during the two decades following the conflict.

In 1917 the entire character of the war was transformed by events that proved decisive both for the outcome of the war and for the history of the twentieth century. The Russian revolutions of February and October, 1917, and the entry of the United States into the war, as well as the role played by President Woodrow Wilson, introduced into the conflict practical and ideological factors of exceptional moment. Initially, the Russian Revolution in February and America's entry into the war gave a tremendous boost to the Allied cause. They enabled the Allies to pose as the defenders of democracy against Prussian militarism and authoritarianism and to fight, as Wilson said, "to make the world safe for democracy." The government that ruled Russia between February and October, 1917, were committed to the continuation of the war and, it might be added, to the war aims of the tsarist regime. The Bolsheviks, in contrast, repudiated the Allied war aims, accepted a humiliating peace with Germany at Brest-Litovsk, and called upon the workers of all nations to rise up and overthrow their rulers. Wilson's liberal and reformist ideology, initially so useful in the ideological struggle against the Central Powers, was now no less important as a counter to Lenin's revolutionary summons in the enemy and the friendly nations of Europe.

Wilson's Fourteen Points and his highly critical attitude toward the foreign and domestic policies of the Allies provided a rallying point for reformist, nonrevolutionary socialists and liberals throughout Europe. When the German war effort collapsed in the fall of 1918, the defeated nation turned to Wilson in the hope of securing a peace based on the Fourteen Points, without annexations and indemnities. The German revolution of November 9, 1918, which overthrew the monarchy, was made in part because of Wilson's demand that he deal with a government that was truly representative of the German people. The new regime accepted on November 11 an armistice that was tantamount to a capitulation in the hope that Wilson would protect Germany from the ambitions of his rapacious allies.

The Germans considered themselves betrayed when the Treaty of Versailles was imposed on them in June, 1919, and they called the treaty "an injustice without example." Although the Germans had failed to consider the variety of ways in which the Fourteen Points could be interpreted or to remember how much more harsh were the terms they imposed on the Russians at Brest-Litovsk, the treaty could hardly be called mild and did violate both the spirit and the content of the Fourteen Points in many respects. Nevertheless, it must be remembered that the treaty was a compromise derived from incredibly diverse pressures. The political Right demanded a punitive peace, while the Left supported Wilson. Lloyd George needed the Right for domestic support and to counteract Wilson, but he was fearful that a harsh peace would lead to a Bolshevist (Spartacist) revolution in Germany and would exacerbate the chaos in central and eastern Europe. Clemenceau was less concerned about Bolshevism, but he thought that a compromise with Wilson was necessary in order to secure an American guarantee against future German aggression. Wilson was far more of a realist than he has been assumed to be. He understood the pressures on the Allied leaders and recognized the limits of his influence just as he recognized the power of American arms and money. He pinned his hopes on the League of Nations and believed that unsatisfactory features of the treaty could be rectified by the world organization. Finally, he was as convinced as his colleagues of Germany's war guilt. The treaty, then, was the product of great complexity and could hardly lead to a satisfactory solution for the chaos throughout Europe.

The greater tragedy of the peace, perhaps, was that it did not solve the problems later but rather perpetuated them. The American people repudiated Wilson and his internationalist position, and America withdrew into political isolation while remaining Europe's chief creditor. The French, denied the Anglo-American guarantee they had been promised in return for their lenient attitude toward Germany, pursued a harsh and rigid policy with regard to German reparations, culminating in the occupation of the Ruhr in 1923. The Germans, for their part, sought to evade their reparations obligations, whose extent and severity they exaggerated. The reparations issue was particularly damaging because it provided an easy excuse to put off necessary fiscal and economic reforms. The French expected German reparations to solve their problems, while the Germans argued that reform was pointless because the reparations burden was so great. The consequence was the utterly disastrous German inflation of 1922 and 1923, at the height of which one dollar could buy one trillion marks. The French suffered a serious inflation in 1925.

A measure of stability was created by the Dawes Plan, which removed reparations from the political arena by regulating German payments on the basis of Germany's ability to pay. A huge influx of American loans enabled the Germans to rationalize their industrial plant and keep to the Dawes schedule of payments. Unfortunately, however, these economic arrangements were basically unstable. America loaned money to Germany to pay England and France so that they in turn might repay America's war loans. The system depended upon Germany's ability to export enough products to produce the surplus necessary for the system to be more than circular. This was difficult because of general economic problems and trade barriers. Ultimately, the entire structure depended upon American prosperity. When this collapsed in 1929, Europe's shaky recovery went with it. Europeans were subjected to incredible misery and exposed to further radicalization.

The Russian Revolution

Between February and early November in 1917, Russia was ruled under a system of dual power. The provisional government, headed first by the liberal Prince Lvov and then by the moderate socialist Alexander Kerensky, made the fatal mistake of trying to continue the war against Germany. At the same time, it failed to introduce land reform rapidly. The government's power was constantly threatened by the Petrograd Soviet of Workers' and Soldiers' Deputies, the most important of the soviets (councils) that sprang up throughout Russia as instruments of direct democracy. Initially, the Petrograd soviet acted as a watchdog over the provisional government. The Mensheviks and social revolutionaries who dominated the soviet were convinced that Russia had to pass through a bourgeois phase before the socialist revolution could take place, and they refrained from calling for the overthrow of the provisional government. V. I. Lenin transformed the situation, often against the views of the leading members of his own Bolshevik party, by recognizing that the situation was ripe for a socialist revolution in Russia and that the soviets were the ideal instrument for achieving this end. While Kerensky further undermined the credibility of the provisional government by allying himself with such reactionary tsarist generals as Kornilov and Kaledin, Lenin organized the insurrection that overthrew the provisional government in November, 1917. He and his Bolshevik colleagues then rode roughshod over the other socialist parties and implemented the promises of immediate peace and land with which he had won over the masses. His expectation that the rest of Europe would fall prey to revolution was frustrated, but Russia did conclude a unilateral peace with Germany at Brest-Litovsk in March, 1918. John Reed, an American reporter, provided a vivid description of the Bolshevik seizure of power.

Reed's *Ten Days That Shook the World*

It was just 8.40 when a thundering wave of cheers announced the entrance of the presidium, with Lenin — great Lenin — among them. A short, stocky figure, with a big head set down in his shoulders, bald and bulging. Little eyes, a snubbish nose, wide, generous mouth, and heavy chin; clean-shaven now, but already beginning to bristle with the well-known beard of his past and future. Dressed in shabby clothes, his trousers much too long for him. Unimpressive, to be the idol of a mob, loved and revered as perhaps few leaders in history have been. A strange popular leader — a leader purely by virtue of intellect; colourless, humourless, uncompromising and detached, without picturesque idiosyncrasies — but with the power of explaining profound ideas in simple terms, of analysing a concrete situation. And combined with shrewdness, the greatest intellectual audacity.

Kameniev was reading the report of the actions of the Military Revolutionary Committee; abolition of capital punishment in the Army, restoration of the free right of propaganda, release of officers and soldiers arrested for political crimes, orders to arrest Kerensky and confiscation of food supplies in private store-houses. . . . Tremendous applause.

From John Reed, *Ten Days That Shook the World* (© 1934 and 1967 by International Publishers Co., Inc.), (New York: Random House, Modern Library, 1935), pp. 125–35. Reprinted by permission of International Publishers Co., Inc., New York.

Again the representative of the *Bund.* The uncompromising attitude
of the Bolsheviki would mean the crushing of the Revolution; therefore,
the *Bund* delegates must refuse any longer to sit in the Congress. Cries
from the audience, "We thought you walked out last night! How many
more times are you going to walk out?"

Then the representative of the Mensheviki Internationalists. Shouts,
"What! You here still?" The speaker explained that only part of the
Mensheviki Internationalists left the Congress; the rest were going to
stay —

"We consider it dangerous and perhaps even mortal for the Revolution to transfer the power to the Soviets" — Interruptions — "but we feel
it our duty to remain in the Congress and vote against the transfer here!"

Other speakers followed, apparently without any order. A delegate of
the coal-miners of the Don Basin called upon the Congress to take measures against Kaledin, who might cut off coal and food from the capital.
Several soldiers just arrived from the Front brought the enthusiastic
greetings of their regiments. . . . Now Lenin, gripping the edge of the
reading stand, letting his little winking eyes travel over the crowd as he
stood there waiting, apparently oblivious to the long-rolling ovation,
which lasted several minutes. When it finished, he said simply, "We shall
now proceed to construct the Socialist order!" Again that overwhelming
human roar.

"The first thing is the adoption of practical measures to realise peace.
. . . We shall offer peace to the peoples of all the belligerent countries
upon the basis of the Soviet terms — no annexations, no indemnities, and
the right of self-determination of peoples. At the same time, according to
our promise, we shall publish and repudiate the secret treaties. . . . The
question of War and Peace is so clear that I think that I may, without
preamble, read the project of a Proclamation to the Peoples of All the
Belligerent Countries. . . ."

His great mouth, seeming to smile, opened wide as he spoke; his voice
was hoarse — not unpleasantly so, but as if it had hardened that way after
years and years of speaking — and went on monotonously, with the effect
of being able to go on forever. . . . For emphasis he bent forward slightly.
No gestures. And before him, a thousand simple faces looking up in intent adoration.

Proclamation to the Peoples and Governments
of All the Belligerent Nations

The Workers' and Peasants' Government, created by the revolution of November 6th and 7th and based on the Soviets of Workers', Soldiers' and Peasants'
Deputies, proposes to all the belligerent peoples and to their Governments to
begin immediately negotiations for a just and democratic peace.

The Government means by a just and democratic peace, which is desired by the immense majority of the workers and the labouring classes, exhausted and depleted by the war — that peace which the Russian workers and peasants, after having struck down the Tsarist monarchy, have not ceased to demand categorically — immediate peace without annexations (that is to say, without conquest of foreign territory, without forcible annexation of other nationalities), and without indemnities.

The Government of Russia proposes to all the belligerent peoples immediately to conclude such a peace, by showing themselves willing to enter upon the decisive steps of negotiations aiming at such a peace, at once, without the slightest delay, before the definitive ratification of all the conditions of such a peace by the authorised assemblies of the people of all countries and of all nationalities.

By annexation or conquest of foreign territory, the Government means — conformably to the conception of democratic rights in general, and the rights of the working-class in particular — all union to a great and strong State of a small or weak nationality, without the voluntary, clear and precise expression of its consent and desire; whatever be the moment when such an annexation by force was accomplished, whatever be the degree of civilisation of the nation annexed by force or maintained outside the frontiers of another State, no matter if that nation be in Europe or in the far countries across the sea.

If any nation is retained by force within the limits of another State; if, in spite of the desire expressed by it, (it matters little if that desire be expressed by the press, by popular meetings, decisions of political parties, or by disorders and riots against national oppression), that nation is not given the right of deciding by free vote — without the slightest constraint, after the complete departure of the armed forces of the nation which has annexed it or wishes to annex it or is stronger in general — the form of its national and political organisation, such a union constitutes an annexation — that is to say, conquest and an act of violence.

To continue this war in order to permit the strong and rich nations to divide among themselves the weak and conquered nationalities is considered by the Government the greatest possible crime against humanity; and the Government solemnly proclaims its decision to sign a treaty of peace which will put an end to this war upon the above conditions, equally fair for all nationalities without exception.

The Government abolishes secret diplomacy, expressing before the whole country its firm decision to conduct all the negotiations in the light of day before the people, and will proceed immediately to the full publication of all secret treaties confirmed or concluded by the Government of land-owners and capitalists, from March until November 7th, 1917. All the clauses of the secret treaties which, as occur in a majority of cases, have for their object to procure advantages and privileges for Russian capitalists, to maintain or augment the annexations of the Russian imperialists, are denounced by the Government immediately and without discussion.

In proposing to all Governments and all peoples to engage in public negotiations for peace, the Government declares itself ready to carry on these negotiations by telegraph, by post, or by pourparlers between the representatives of the different countries, or at a conference of these representatives. To facilitate these pourparlers, the Government appoints its authorised representatives in the neutral countries.

The Government proposes to all the governments and to the peoples of all the belligerent countries to conclude an immediate armistice, at the same time suggesting that the armistice ought to last three months, during which time it is perfectly possible, not only to hold the necessary pourparlers between the representatives of all the nations and nationalities without exception drawn into the war or forced to take part in it, but also to convoke authorised assemblies of representatives of the people of all countries, for the purpose of the definite acceptance of the conditions of peace.

In addressing this offer of peace to the Governments and to the peoples of all the belligerent countries, the Provisional Workers' and Peasants' Government of Russia addresses equally and in particular the conscious workers of the three nations most devoted to humanity and the three most important nations among those taking part in the present war — England, France, and Germany. The workers of these countries have rendered the greatest services to the cause of progress and of Socialism. The splendid examples of the Chartist movement in England, the series of revolutions, of world-wide historical significance, accomplished by the French proletariat — and finally, in Germany, the historic struggle against the Laws of Exception, an example for the workers of the whole world of prolonged and stubborn action, and the creation of the formidable organisations of German proletarians — all these models of proletarian heroism, these monuments of history, are for us a sure guarantee that the workers of these countries will understand the duty imposed upon them to liberate humanity from the horrors and consequences of war; and that these workers, by decisive, energetic and continued action, will help us to bring to a successful conclusion the cause of peace and at the same time, the cause of the liberation of the exploited working masses from all slavery and all exploitation.

When the grave thunder of applause had died away, Lenin spoke again:

"We propose to the Congress to ratify this declaration. We address ourselves to the Governments as well as to the peoples, for a declaration which would be addressed only to the peoples of the belligerent countries might delay the conclusion of peace. The conditions of peace, drawn up during the armistice, will be ratified by the Constituent Assembly. In fixing the duration of the armistice at three months, we desire to give to the peoples as long a rest as possible after this bloody extermination, and ample time for them to elect their representatives. This proposal of peace will meet with resistance on the part of the imperialist governments — we don't fool ourselves on that score. But we hope that revolution will soon break out in all the belligerent countries; that is why we address ourselves especially to the workers of France, England and Germany. . . .

"The revolution of November 6th and 7th," he ended, "has opened the era of the Social Revolution. . . . The labour movement, in the name of peace and Socialism, shall win, and fulfil its destiny. . . ."

There was something quiet and powerful in all this, which stirred the souls of men. It was understandable why people believed when Lenin spoke. . . .

By crowd vote it was quickly decided that only representatives of political factions should be allowed to speak on the motion and that speakers should be limited to fifteen minutes.

First Karelin for the Left Socialist Revolutionaries. "Our faction had no opportunity to propose amendments to the text of the proclamation; it is a private document of the Bolsheviki. But we will vote for it because we agree with its spirit. . . ."

For the Social Democrats Internationalists Kramarov, long, stoop-shouldered and near-sighted — destined to achieve some notoriety as the Clown of the Opposition. Only a Government composed of all the Social-ist parties, he said, could possess the authority to take such important action. If a Socialist coalition were formed, his faction would support the entire programme; if not, only part of it. As for the proclamation, the Internationalists were in thorough accord with its main points. . . .

Then one after another, amid rising enthusiasm; Ukrainean Social Democracy, support; Lithuanian Social Democracy, support; Populist Socialists, support; Polish Social Democracy, support; Polish Socialists support — but would prefer a Socialist coalition; Lettish Social Democ-racy, support. . . . Something was kindled in these men. One spoke of the "coming World-Revolution, of which we are the advance-guard"; another of "the new age of brotherhood, when all the peoples will be-come one great family. . . ." An individual member claimed the floor. "There is contradiction here," he said. "First you offer peace without annexations and indemnities, and then you say you will consider all peace offers. To consider means to accept. . . ."

Lenin was on his feet. "We want a just peace, but we are not afraid of a revolutionary war. . . . Probably the imperialist Governments will not answer our appeal — but we shall not issue an ultimatum to which it will be easy to say no. . . . If the German proletariat realises that we are ready to consider all offers of peace, that will perhaps be the last drop which overflows the bowl — revolution will break out in Ger-many. . . .

"We consent to examine all conditions of peace, but that doesn't mean that we shall accept them. . . . For some of our terms we shall fight to the end — but possibly for others will find it impossible to continue the war. . . . Above all, we want to finish the war. . . ."

It was exactly 10.35 when Kameniev asked all in favour of the proclamation to hold up their cards. One delegate dared to raise his hand against, but the sudden sharp outburst around him brought it swiftly down. . . . Unanimous.

Suddenly, by common impulse, we found ourselves on our feet, mumbling together into the smooth lifting unison of the *Internationale*. A grizzled old soldier was sobbing like a child. Alexandra Kollontai rapidly winked the tears back. The immense sound rolled through the hall, burst windows and doors and seared into the quiet sky. "The war is ended! The war is ended!" said a young workman near me, his face shining. And when it was over, as we stood there in a kind of awkward hush, some one in the back of the room shouted, "Comrades! Let us remember those who have died for liberty!" So we began to sing the Funeral March, that slow, melancholy and yet triumphant chant, so Russian and so moving. The *Internationale* is an alien air, after all. The Funeral March seemed the very soul of those dark masses whose delegates sat in this hall, building from their obscure visions a new Russia — and perhaps more.

You fell in the fatal fight
For the liberty of the people, for the honour of the people . . .
You gave up your lives and everything dear to you,
You suffered in horrible prisons,
You went to exile in chains. . . .

Without a word you carried your chains because you could not ignore your suffering brothers,
Because you believed that justice is stronger than the sword. . . .
The time will come when your surrendered life will count.
That time is near; when tyranny falls the people will rise, great and free!

Farewell, brothers, you chose a noble path,
You are followed by the new and fresh army ready to die and to suffer. . . .

Farewell, brothers, you chose a noble path,
At your grave we swear to fight, to work for freedom and the people's happiness. . . .

For this did they lie there, the martyrs of March, in their cold Brotherhood Grave on Mars Field; for this thousands and tens of thousands had died in the prisons, in exile, in Siberian mines. It had not come as they expected it would come, nor as the *intelligentzia* desired it; but it had come — rough, strong, impatient of formulas, contemptuous of sentimentalism; *real*. . . .

Peacemaking: Woodrow Wilson, David Lloyd George, and the Versailles Treaty

Revolutionary Russia's summons to peace did not go unheard in the West. The Bolshevik appeal produced significant responses from the Anglo-Saxon powers. The first of these was Woodrow Wilson's Fourteen Points, which he presented to a joint session of Congress on January 8, 1918. Wilson's address was timed to provide the Russians with an alternative to signing the Treaty of Brest-Litovsk and to counter the Bolshevik appeal for revolution. Wilson, like the Bolsheviks, appealed to people over the heads of their leaders, but Wilson's basic goal was democratic reform, not revolution. His Fourteen Points were subject to a variety of interpretations depending upon the political and military situation at the conclusion of peace, and Wilson was aware of their ambiguities. Under Point V, for example, Germany could or could not be allowed to retain its colonies. Similarly, Point X could or could not be interpreted to mean that the Austro-Hungarian Empire would be broken up. Point XIII was not incompatible with a corridor linking Poland to the sea inhabited by indisputably German populations.

Lloyd George too made a significant response to the Bolsheviks during the Paris peace conference. Lloyd George had done much to stir up jingoism at home for political reasons, but revolutionary conditions in eastern and central Europe and labor unrest in Britain, France, and Italy deeply worried him as did the problem of reviving international trade on a sound basis after the war. The high point of his concern was reached in March, 1919, when a Bolshevik regime was established under Bela Kun in Hungary. His response was the Fontainebleau Memorandum of March 25, 1919. Although Wilson and Lloyd George were successful in making the terms of the peace somewhat milder, the Treaty of Versailles was a dictated peace that was punitive and dishonoring as well. The territorial clauses and the reduction of the German army to one hundred thousand men were viewed with outrage, and Germans were particularly incensed by the reparations clauses, especially the intimation of German war guilt in Article 231, the imputation of criminality in Articles 227 and 228, and the provisions for guarantees.

The Fourteen Points

. . . We entered this war because violations of right had occurred which touched us to the quick and made the life of our people impossible unless they were corrected and the world secured once for all against their recurrence. What we demand in this war, therefore, is nothing peculiar to ourselves. It is that the world be made fit and safe to live in; and particularly that it be made safe for every peace-loving nation which, like our own, wishes to live its own life, determine its own institutions, be assured of justice and fair dealing by the other peoples of the world as against force and selfish aggression. All the peoples of the world are in effect partners in this interest, and for our own part we see very clearly that unless justice be done to others it will not be done to us. The programme of the world's peace, therefore, is our programme; and that programme, the only possible programme, as we see it, is this:

I. Open covenants of peace, openly arrived at, after which there shall be no private international understandings of any kind but diplomacy shall proceed always frankly and in the public view.

II. Absolute freedom of navigation upon the seas, outside territorial waters, alike in peace and in war, except as the seas may be closed in whole or in part by international action for the enforcement of international covenants.

III. The removal, so far as possible, of all economic barriers and the establishment of an equality of trade conditions among all the nations consenting to the peace and associating themselves for its maintenance.

IV. Adequate guarantees given and taken that national armaments will be reduced to the lowest point consistent with domestic safety.

V. A free, open-minded, and absolutely impartial adjustment of all colonial claims, based upon a strict observance of the principle that in determining all such questions of sovereignty the interests of the populations concerned must have equal weight with the equitable claims of the government whose title is to be determined.

VI. The evacuation of all Russian territory and such a settlement of all questions affecting Russia as will secure the best and freest co-operation of the other nations of the world in obtaining for her an unhampered and unembarrassed opportunity for the independent determination of her own political development and national policy and assure her of a sincere welcome into the society of free nations under institutions of her own choosing; and, more than a welcome, assistance also of every kind that she may need and may herself desire. The treatment accorded Russia by her sister nations in the months to come will be the acid test of

From U.S. Serial 7443, Document No. 765.

their good will, of their comprehension of her needs as distinguished from their own interests, and of their intelligent and unselfish sympathy.

VII. Belgium, the whole world will agree, must be evacuated and restored, without any attempt to limit the sovereignty which she enjoys in common with all other free nations. No other single act will serve as this will serve to restore confidence among the nations in the laws which they have themselves set and determined for the government of their relations with one another. Without this healing act the whole structure and validity of international law is forever impaired.

VIII. All French territory should be freed and the invaded portions restored, and the wrong done to France by Prussia in 1871 in the matter of Alsace-Lorraine, which has unsettled the peace of the world for nearly fifty years, should be righted, in order that peace may once more be made secure in the interest of all.

IX. A readjustment of the frontiers of Italy should be effected along clearly recognizable lines of nationality.

X. The peoples of Austria-Hungary, whose place among the nations we wish to see safeguarded and assured, should be accorded the freest opportunity of autonomous development.

XI. Rumania, Serbia, and Montenegro should be evacuated; occupied territories restored; Serbia accorded free and secure access to the sea; and the relations of the several Balkan states to one another determined by friendly counsel along historically established lines of allegiance and nationality; and international guarantees of the political and economic independence and territorial integrity of the several Balkan states should be entered into.

XII. The Turkish portions of the present Ottoman Empire should be assured a secure sovereignty, but the other nationalities which are now under Turkish rule should be assured an undoubted security of life and an absolutely unmolested opportunity of autonomous development, and the Dardanelles should be permanently opened as a free passage to the ships and commerce of all nations under international guarantees.

XIII. An independent Polish state should be erected which should include the territories inhabited by indisputably Polish populations, which should be assured a free and secure access to the sea, and whose political and economic independence and territorial integrity should be guaranteed by international covenant.

XIV. A general association of nations must be formed under specific covenants for the purpose of affording mutual guarantees of political independence and territorial integrity to great and small states alike.

The Fontainebleau Memorandum of March 25, 1919

When nations are exhausted by wars in which they have put forth all their strength and which leave them tired, bleeding and broken, it is not difficult to patch up a peace that may last until the generation which experienced the horrors of the war has passed away. Pictures of heroism and triumph only tempt those who know nothing of the sufferings and terrors of war. It is therefore comparatively easy to patch up a peace which will last for 30 years.

What is difficult, however, is to draw up a peace which will not provoke a fresh struggle when those who have had practical experience of what war means have passed away. History has proved that a peace, which has been hailed by a victorious nation as a triumph of diplomatic skill and statesmanship, even of moderation in the long run, has proved itself to be shortsighted and charged with danger to the victor. The peace of 1871 was believed by Germany to ensure not only her security but her permanent supremacy. The facts have shown exactly the contrary. France itself has demonstrated that those who say you can make Germany so feeble that she will never be able to hit back are utterly wrong. Year by year France became numerically weaker in comparison with her victorious neighbour, but in reality she became ever more powerful. She kept watch on Europe; she made alliance with those whom Germany had wronged or menaced; she never ceased to warn the world of its danger and ultimately she was able to secure the overthrow of the far mightier power which had trampled so brutally upon her. You may strip Germany of her colonies, reduce her armaments to a mere police force and her navy to that of a fifth-rate power; all the same in the end if she feels that she has been unjustly treated in the peace of 1919 she will find means of exacting retribution from her conquerors. The impression, the deep impression, made upon the human heart by four years of unexampled slaughter will disappear with the hearts upon which it has been marked by the terrible sword of the great war. The maintenance of peace will then depend upon there being no causes of exasperation constantly stirring up the spirit of patriotism, of justice or of fair play. To achieve redress our terms may be severe, they may be stern and even ruthless, but at the same time they can be so just that the country on which they are imposed will feel in its heart that it has no right to complain. But injustice, arrogance, displayed in the hour of triumph, will never be forgotten or forgiven.

For these reasons I am, therefore, strongly averse to transferring more Germans from German rule to the rule of some other nation than can possibly be helped. I cannot conceive any greater cause of future war

From Great Britain, *State Papers* (1922), Cmd. 1614. Reprinted by permission of Her Majesty's Stationery Office.

than that the German people, who have certainly proved themselves one of the most vigorous and powerful races in the world, should be surrounded by a number of small states, many of them consisting of people who have never previously set up a stable government for themselves, but each of them containing large masses of Germans clamouring for reunion with their native land. The proposal of the Polish Commission that we should place 2,100,000 Germans, under the control of a people which is of a different religion and which has never proved its capacity for stable self-government throughout its history must, in my judgment, lead sooner or later to a new war in the East of Europe. What I have said about the Germans is equally true of the Magyars. There will never be peace in South Eastern Europe if every little state now coming into being is to have a large Magyar Irredenta within its borders. I would therefore take as a guiding principle of the peace that as far as is humanly possible the different races should be allocated to their motherlands, and that this human criterion should have precedence over considerations of strategy or economics or communications, which can usually be adjusted by other means. Secondly, I would say that the duration for the payments of reparation ought to disappear if possible with the generation which made the war.

But there is a consideration in favour of a long-sighted peace which influences me even more than the desire to leave no causes justifying a fresh outbreak 30 years hence. There is one element in the present condition of nations which differentiates it from the situation as it was in 1815. In the Napoleonic war the countries were equally exhausted, but the revolutionary spirit had spent its force in the country of its birth, and Germany had satisfied the legitimate popular demands for the time being by a series of economic changes which were inspired by courage, foresight and high statesmanship. Even in Russia the Czar had effected great reforms which were probably at that time even too advanced for the half savage population. The situation is very different now. The revolution is still in its infancy. The extreme figures of the Terror are still in command in Russia. The whole of Europe is filled with the spirit of revolution. There is a deep sense not only of discontent, but of anger and revolt, amongst the workmen against pre-war conditions. The whole existing order in its political, social and economic aspects is questioned by the masses of the population from one end of Europe to the other. In some countries, like Germany and Russia, the unrest takes the form of open rebellion; in others, like France, Great Britain and Italy, it takes the shape of strikes and of general disinclination to settle down to work — symptoms which are just as much concerned with the desire for political and social change as with wage demands.

Much of this unrest is healthy. We shall never make a lasting peace by attempting to restore the conditions of 1914. But there is a danger that we may throw the masses of the population throughout Europe into the arms of the extremists whose only idea for regenerating mankind is to destroy utterly the whole existing fabric of society. These men have triumphed in Russia. They have done so at a terrible price. Hundreds of thousands of the population have perished. The railways, the roads, the towns, the whole structural organisation of Russia has been almost destroyed, but somehow or other they seem to have managed to keep their hold upon the masses of the Russian people, and what is much more significant, they have succeeded in creating a large army which is apparently well directed and well disciplined, and is, as to a great part of it prepared to die for its ideals. In another year Russia, inspired by a new enthusiasm, may have recovered from her passion for peace and have at her command the only army eager to fight, because it is the only army that believes that it has any cause to fight for.

The greatest danger that I see in the present situation is that Germany may throw in her lot with Bolshevism and place her resources, her brains, her vast organising power at the disposal of the revolutionary fanatics whose dream it is to conquer the world for Bolshevism by force of arms. This danger is no mere chimera. The present Government in Germany is weak; it has no prestige; its authority is challenged; it lingers merely because there is no alternative but the spartacists, and Germany is not ready for spartacism, as yet. But the argument which the spartacists are using with great effect at this very time is that they alone can save Germany from the intolerable conditions which have been bequeathed her by the war. They offer to free the German people from indebtedness to the Allies and indebtedness to their own richer classes. They offer them complete control of their own affairs and the prospect of a new heaven and earth. It is true that the price will be heavy. There will be two or three years of anarchy, perhaps of bloodshed, but at the end the land will remain, the people will remain, the greater part of the houses and the factories will remain, and the railways and the roads will remain, and Germany, having thrown off her burdens, will be able to make a fresh start.

If Germany goes over to the spartacists it is inevitable that she should throw in her lot with the Russian Bolshevists. Once that happens all Eastern Europe will be swept into the orbit of the Bolshevik revolution and within a year we may witness the spectacle of nearly three hundred million people organized into a vast red army under German instructors and German generals equipped with German cannon and German machine guns and prepared for a renewal of the attack on Western Europe. This is a prospect which no one can face with equanimity. Yet the news which came from Hungary yesterday shows only too clearly that this danger is no fantasy. And what are the reasons alleged for this decision? They are mainly the belief that large numbers of Magyars are to be handed over to the control of others. If we are wise, we shall offer to Germany a peace, which, while just, will be preferable for all sensible men to the alternative of Bolshevism. I would, therefore, put it in the forefront of the peace that once she accepts our terms, especially reparation, we will open to her the raw materials and markets of the world on equal terms with ourselves, and will do everything possible to enable the German people to get upon their legs again. We cannot both cripple her and expect her to pay.

Finally, we must offer terms which a responsible Government in Germany can expect to be able to carry out. If we present terms to Germany which are unjust, or excessively onerous, no responsible Government will sign them; certainly the present weak administration will not. If it did, I am told that it would be swept away within 24 hours. Yet if we can find nobody in Germany who will put his hand to a peace treaty, what will be the position? A large army of occupation for an indefinite period is out of the question. Germany would not mind it. A very large number of people in that country would welcome it as it would be the only hope of preserving the existing order of things. The objection would not come from Germany, but from our own countries. Neither the British Empire nor America would agree to occupy Germany. France by itself could not bear the burden of occupation. We should therefore be driven back on the policy of blockading the country. That would inevitably mean spartacism from the Urals to the Rhine, with its inevitable consequence of a huge red army attempting to cross the Rhine. As a matter of fact I am doubtful whether public opinion would allow us deliberately to starve Germany. If the only difference between Germany and ourselves were between onerous terms and moderate terms, I very much doubt if public opinion would tolerate the deliberate condemnation of millions of women and children to death by starvation. If so the Allies would have incurred the moral defeat of having attempted to impose terms on Germany which Germany had successfully resisted.

From every point of view, therefore, it seems to me that we ought to endeavour to draw up a peace settlement as if we were impartial arbiters, forgetful of the passions of the war. This settlement ought to have three ends in view. First of all it must do justice to the Allies by taking into account Germany's responsibility for the origin of the war and for the way in which it was fought. Secondly, it must be a settlement which a responsible German Government can sign in the belief that it can fulfil the obligations it incurs. Thirdly, it must be a settlement which will contain in itself no provocations for future wars, and which will constitute an alternative to Bolshevism, because it will commend itself to all reasonable opinion as a fair settlement of the European problem.

The Treaty of Versailles

ARTICLE 227. The Allied and Associated Powers publicly arraign William II of Hohenzollern, formerly German Emperor, for a supreme offence against international morality and the sanctity of treaties.

A special tribunal will be constituted to try the accused, thereby assuring him the guarantees essential to the right of defence. It will be composed of five judges, one appointed by each of the following Powers: namely, the United States of America, Great Britain, France, Italy and Japan.

In its decision the tribunal will be guided by the highest motives of international policy, with a view to vindicating the solemn obligations of international undertakings and the validity of international morality. It will be its duty to fix the punishment which it considers should be imposed.

The Allied and Associated Powers will address a request to the Government of the Netherlands for the surrender to them of the ex-Emperor in order that he may be put on trial.

ARTICLE 228. The German Government recognises the right of the Allied and Associated Powers to bring before military tribunals persons accused of having committed acts in violation of the laws and customs of war. Such persons shall, if found guilty, be sentenced to punishments laid down by law. This provision will apply notwithstanding any proceedings or prosecution before a tribunal in Germany or in the territory of her allies.

The German Government shall hand over to the Allied and Associated Powers, or to such one of them as shall so request, all persons accused of having committed an act in violation of the laws and customs of war, who are specified either by name or by the rank, office or employment which they held under the German authorities.

ARTICLE 229. Persons guilty of criminal acts against the nationals of one of the Allied and Associated Powers will be brought before the military tribunals of that Power.

Persons guilty of criminal acts against the nationals of more than one of the Allied and Associated Powers will be brought before military tribunals composed of members of the military tribunals of the Powers concerned.

In every case the accused will be entitled to name his own counsel.

ARTICLE 230. The German Government undertakes to furnish all documents and information of every kind, the production of which may be considered necessary to ensure the full knowledge of the incriminating acts, the discovery of offenders and the just appreciation of responsibility.

ARTICLE 231. The Allied and Associated Governments affirm and Ger-

From Great Britain, *State Papers*, vol. 112 (1919), pp. 104 ff. Reprinted by permission of Her Majesty's Stationery Office.

many accepts the responsibility of Germany and her allies for causing all the loss and damage to which the Allied and Associated Governments and their nationals have been subjected as a consequence of the war imposed upon them by the aggression of Germany and her allies.

ARTICLE 232. The Allied and Associated Governments recognise that the resources of Germany are not adequate, after taking into account permanent diminutions of such resources which will result from other provisions of the present Treaty, to make complete reparation for all such loss and damage.

The Allied and Associated Governments, however, require, and Germany undertakes, that she will make compensation for all damage done to the civilian population of the Allied and Associated Powers and to their property during the period of the belligerency of each as an Allied or Associated Power against Germany by such aggression by land, by sea, and from the air, and in general all damage as defined in Annex 1 hereto.

In accordance with Germany's pledges, already given, as to complete restoration for Belgium, Germany undertakes, in addition to the compensation for damage elsewhere in this Part provided for, as a consequence of the violation of the Treaty of 1839, to make reimbursement of all sums which Belgium has borrowed from the Allied and Associated Governments up to November 11, 1918, together with interest at the rate of five per cent. (5 per cent.) per annum on such sums. This amount shall be determined by the Reparation Commission, and the German Government undertakes thereupon forthwith to make a special issue of bearer bonds to an equivalent amount payable in marks gold, on May 1, 1926, or, at the option of the German Government, on May 1 in any year up to 1926. Subject to the foregoing, the form of such bonds shall be handed over to the Reparation Commission, which has authority to take and acknowledge receipt thereof on behalf of Belgium.

ARTICLE 233. The amount of the above damage for which compensation is to be made by Germany shall be determined by an Inter-Allied Commissioned, to be called the *Reparation Commission* and constituted in the form and with the powers set forth hereunder and in Annexes II to VII inclusive hereto.

This Commission shall consider the claims and give to the German Government a just opportunity to be heard.

The findings of the Commission as to the amount of damage defined as above shall be concluded and notified to the German Government on or before May 1, 1921, as representing the extent of that Government's obligations.

The Commission shall concurrently draw up a schedule of payments prescribing the time and manner for securing and discharging the entire obligation within a period of thirty years from May 1, 1921. If, however, within the period mentioned, Germany fails to discharge her obligations, any balance remaining unpaid may, within the discretion of the Commission, be postponed for settlement in subsequent years, or may be handled otherwise in such manner as the Allied and Associated Governments, acting in accordance with the procedure laid down in this Part of the present Treaty, shall determine.

ARTICLE 234. The Reparation Commission shall, after May 1, 1921, from time to time, consider the resources and capacity of Germany, and, after giving her representatives a just opportunity to be heard, shall have discretion to extend the date, and to modify the form of payments, such as are to be provided for in accordance with Article 233; but not to cancel any part, except with the specific authority of the several Governments represented upon the Commission.

.   .   .   .   .

ARTICLE 428. As a guarantee for the execution of the present Treaty by Germany, the German territory situated to the west of the Rhine together with the bridgeheads, will be occupied by Allied and Associated troops for a period of fifteen years from the coming into force of the present Treaty.

ARTICLE 429. If the conditions of the present Treaty are faithfully carried out by Germany, the occupation referred to in Article 428 will be successively restricted as follows:

1. At the expiration of five years there will be evacuated: the bridgehead of Cologne and the territories north of a line running along the Ruhr, then along the railway Jülich, Düren, Euskirchen, Rheinbach, thence along the road Rheinbach to Sinzig, and reaching the Rhine at the confluence with the Ahr; the roads, railways and places mentioned above being excluded from the area evacuated.

2. At the expiration of ten years there will be evacuated: the bridgehead of Coblenz and the territories north of a line to be drawn from the intersection between the frontiers of Belgium, Germany and Holland, running about 4 kilometres south of Aix-la-Chapelle, then to and following the crest of Forst Gemünd, then east of the railway of the Urft Valley, then along Blankenheim, Valdorf, Dreis, Ulmen to and following the Moselle from Bremm to Nehren, then passing by Kappel and Simmern, then following the ridge of the heights between Simmern and the Rhine and reaching this river at Bacharach; all the places, valleys, roads and railways mentioned above being excluded from the area evacuated.

3. At the expiration of fifteen years there will be evacuated: the bridgehead of Mainz, the bridgehead of Kehl and the remainder of the German territory under occupation.

If at that date the guarantees against unprovoked aggression by Germany are not considered sufficient by the Allied and Associated Governments, the evacuation of the occupying troops may be delayed to the extent regarded as necessary for the purpose of obtaining the required guarantees.

ARTICLE 430. In case either during the occupation or after the expiration of the fifteen years referred to above the Reparation Commission finds that Germany refuses to observe the whole or part of her obligations under the present Treaty with regard to reparation, the whole or part of the areas specified in Article 429 will be re-occupied immediately by the Allied and Associated forces.

ARTICLE 431. If before the expiration of the period of fifteen years Germany complies with all the undertakings resulting from the present Treaty, the occupying forces will be withdrawn immediately.

War Debts and Reparations

The most outstanding and effective critic of the Treaty of Versailles was the great British economist John Maynard Keynes (1883–1946). Keynes resigned from the British delegation to the peace conference in protest over the reparations question, and his Economic Consequences of the Peace *(1919) was a widely read and devastating criticism of the treaty. Keynes probably exaggerated Germany's inability to pay reparations, but his emphasis upon the need for economic reconstruction and for a responsible American role in the economic life of Europe and the world was quite to the point. Keynes's work was of major importance in England's moral retreat from the Versailles Treaty and thus helped pave the way for its revision. Keynes's attention to the problem of the relationship between war debts and reparations and his plea for American cancellation of war debts have received less attention from historians. Keynes's approach to the general problems of the world economy after the war were quite far-ranging.*

Keynes: War Debts and the United States

CANCELLATION (1921)

Who believes that the Allies will, over a period of one or two generations, exert adequate force over the German Government, or that the German Government can exert adequate authority over its subjects, to extract continuing fruits on a vast scale from forced labour? No one believes it in his heart; no one at all. There is not the faintest possibility of our persisting with this affair to the end. But if this is so, then, most

From John Maynard Keynes, *Essays in Persuasion* (New York: Norton, 1963), pp. 52–58, 61–62. Reprinted by permission of R. F. Kahn, Esq., trustee of the estate of Lord Keynes.

certainly, it will not be worth our while to disorder our export trades and disturb the equilibrium of our industry for two or three years; much less to endanger the peace of Europe.

The same principles apply with one modification to the United States and to the exaction by her of the debts which the Allied Governments owe. The industries of the United States would suffer, not so much from the competition of cheap goods from the Allies in their endeavours to pay their debts, as from the inability of the Allies to purchase from America their usual proportion of her exports. The Allies would have to find the money to pay America, not so much by selling more as by buying less. The farmers of the United States would suffer more than the manufacturers; if only because increased imports can be kept out by a tariff, whilst there is no such easy way of stimulating diminished exports. It is, however, a curious fact that whilst Wall Street and the manufacturing East are prepared to consider a modification of the debts, the Middle West and South is reported (I write ignorantly) to be dead against it. For two years Germany was not required to pay cash to the Allies, and during that period the manufacturers of Great Britain were quite blind to what the consequences would be to themselves when the payments actually began. The Allies have not yet been required to begin to pay cash to the United States, and the farmers of the latter are still as blind as were the British manufacturers to the injuries they will suffer if the Allies ever try seriously to pay in full.

The decisive argument, however, for the United States, as for Great Britain, is not the damage to particular interests (which would diminish with time), but the unlikelihood of permanence in the exaction of the debts, even if they were paid for a short period. I say this, not only because I doubt the ability of the European Allies to pay, but because of the great difficulty of the problem which the United States has before her in any case in balancing her commercial account with the Old World.

American economists have examined somewhat carefully the statistical measure of the change from the pre-war position. According to their estimates, America is now owed more interest on foreign investments than is due from her, quite apart from the interest on the debts of the Allied Governments; and her mercantile marine now earns from foreigners more than she owes them for similar services. Her excess of exports of commodities over imports approaches $3000 million a year; whilst, on the other side of the balance, payments, mainly to Europe, in respect of tourists and of immigrant remittances are estimated at not above $1000 million a year. Thus, in order to balance the account as it now stands, the United States must lend to the rest of the world, in one shape or another, not less than $2000 million a year, to which interest and sinking fund on the European Governmental War Debts would, if they were paid, add about $600 million.

Recently, therefore, the United States must have been lending to the rest of the world, mainly Europe, something like $2000 million a year. Fortunately for Europe, a fair proportion of this was by way of speculative purchases of depreciated paper currencies. From 1919 to 1921 the losses of American speculators fed Europe; but this source of income can scarcely be reckoned on permanently. For a time the policy of loans can meet the situation; but, as the interest on past loans mounts up, it must in the long run aggravate it.

Mercantile nations have always employed large funds in overseas trade. But the practice of foreign investment, as we know it now, is a very modern contrivance, a very unstable one, and only suited to peculiar circumstances. An old country can in this way develop a new one at a time when the latter could not possibly do so with its own resources alone; the arrangement may be mutually advantageous, and out of abundant profits the lender may hope to be repaid. But the position cannot be reversed. If European bonds are issued in America on the analogy of the American bonds issued in Europe during the nineteenth century, the analogy will be a false one; because, taken in the aggregate, there is no natural increase, no *real* sinking fund, out of which they can be repaid. The interest will be furnished out of new loans, so long as these are obtainable, and the financial structure will mount always higher, until it is not worth while to maintain any longer the illusion that it has foundations. The unwillingness of American investors to buy European bonds is based on common sense.

At the end of 1919 I advocated (in *The Economic Consequences of the Peace*) a reconstruction loan from America to Europe, conditioned, however, on Europe's putting her own house in order. In the past two years America, in spite of European complaints to the contrary, has, in fact, made *very large* loans, much larger than the sum I contemplated, though not mainly in the form of regular, dollar-bond issues. No particular conditions were attached to these loans, and much of the money has been lost. Though wasted in part, they have helped Europe through the critical days of the post-Armistice period. But a continuance of them cannot provide a solution for the existing dis-equilibrium in the balance of indebtedness.

In part the adjustment may be effected by the United States taking the place hitherto held by England, France, and (on a small scale) Germany in providing capital for those new parts of the world less developed than herself — the British Dominions and South America. The Russian Empire, too, in Europe and Asia, is to be regarded as virgin soil, which may at a later date provide a suitable outlet for foreign capital. The American investor will lend more wisely to these countries, on the lines on which British and French investors used to lend to them, than direct to the old countries of Europe. But it is not likely that the whole gap can be bridged thus. Ultimately, and probably soon, there must be a readjustment of the balance of exports and imports. America must buy more and sell less. This is the only alternative to her making to Europe an annual present. Either American prices must rise faster than European (which will be the case if the Federal Reserve Board allows the gold influx to produce its natural consequences), or, failing this, the same result must be brought about by a further depreciation of the European exchanges, until Europe, by inability to buy, has reduced her purchases to articles of necessity. At first the American exporter, unable to scrap all at once the processes of production for export, may meet the situation by lowering his prices; but when these have continued, say for two years, below his cost of production, he will be driven inevitably to curtail or abandon his business.

It is useless for the United States to suppose that an equilibrium position can be reached on the basis of her exporting at least as much as at present, and at the same time restricting her imports by a tariff. Just as the Allies demand vast payments from Germany, and then exercise their ingenuity to prevent her paying them, so the American Administration devises, with one hand, schemes for financing exports, and, with the other, tariffs which will make it as difficult as possible for such credits to be repaid. Great nations can often act with a degree of folly which we should not excuse in an individual.   .

By the shipment to the United States of all the bullion in the world, and the erection there of a sky-scraping golden calf, a short postponement may be gained. But a point may even come when the United States will refuse gold, yet still demand to be paid — a new Midas vainly asking more succulent fare than the barren metal of her own contract.

In any case the readjustment will be severe, and injurious to important interests. If, in addition, the United States exacts payment of the Allied debts, the position will be intolerable. If she persevered to the bitter end, scrapped her export industries and diverted to other uses the capital now employed in them, and if her former European associates decided to meet their obligations at whatever cost to themselves, I do not deny that the final result might be to America's material interest. But the project is utterly chimerical. It will not happen. Nothing is more certain than that America will not pursue such a policy to its conclusion; she will abandon it as soon as she experiences its first consequences. Nor, if she did, would the Allies pay the money. The position is exactly parallel to that of German Reparation. America will not carry through to a conclusion the collection of Allied debt, any more than the Allies will carry through the collection of their present Reparation demands. Neither, in the long run, is serious politics. Nearly all well-informed persons admit this in private conversation. But we live in a curious age when utterances in the press are deliberately designed to be in conformity with the worst-informed, instead of with the best-informed, opinion, because the former is the wider spread; so that for comparatively long periods there can be discrepancies, laughable or monstrous, between the written and the spoken word.

If this is so, it is not good business for America to embitter her relations with Europe, and to disorder her export industries for two years, in pursuance of a policy which she is certain to abandon before it has profited her. . . .

The average American, I fancy, would like to see the European nations approaching him with a pathetic light in their eyes and the cash in their hands, saying, "America, we owe to you our liberty and our life; here we bring what we can in grateful thanks, money not wrung by grievous taxation from the widow and orphan, but saved, the best fruits of victory, out of the abolition of armaments, militarism, Empire, and internal strife, made possible by the help you freely gave us." And then the average American would reply: "I honour you for your integrity. It is what I expected. But I did not enter the war for profit or to invest my money well. I have had my reward in the words you have just uttered. The loans are forgiven. Return to your homes and use the resources I release to uplift the poor and the unfortunate." And it would be an essential part of the little scene that his reply should come as a complete and overwhelming surprise.

Alas for the wickedness of the world! It is not in international affairs that we can secure the sentimental satisfactions which we all love. For only individuals are good, and all nations are dishonourable, cruel, and designing. And whilst the various Prime Ministers will telegraph something suitable, drafted by their private secretaries, to the effect that America's action makes the moment of writing the most important in the history of the world and proves that Americans are the noblest creatures living, America must not expect adequate or appropriate thanks.

The Depression

Although a more economically responsible approach to Europe's problems was taken after 1924, it was too little and too late. The depression that hit America and Europe after 1929 was devastating both socioeconomically and politically. It is most difficult to recapture, however, the extent of the human disaster. The German novelist Hans Fallada provided a personal depiction of the depression in his story of a young couple, Johannes Pinneberg and his wife Bunny. Pinneberg is unsuccessful in his efforts to hold a job in Berlin during the depression, and, like so many of his contemporaries, he is torn between the Communists and the Nazis in his politics.

Fallada's *Little Man, What Now?*

Pinneberg put the baby on the floor, gave him a paper to look at, and prepared to clear up the room. It was a very large newspaper for such a small child, and it lasted quite a while, until the baby had spread it all over the floor. The room was very small, only nine feet by nine. It contained a bed, two chairs, a table, and the dressing-table.

The baby had discovered the pictures on the inner pages of the paper and was chuckling with delight. "Yes," said Pinneberg encouragingly. "Those are pictures, baby." Whatever the baby took for a man, he called "Da-Da," and the women were all "Ma-Ma." He was delighted because there were so many people in the paper.

Pinneberg hung the mattresses out of the window to air, tidied the room and went into the kitchen. This was just a strip cut off the other room, nine feet long, and four and a half feet wide, the stove was about the smallest ever made, with only one oven. It was Bunny's greatest affliction. Here too Pinneberg tidied and washed up and swept the floor, all of which he was happy to do. But his next occupation he did not enjoy at all; he set himself to peel potatoes and scrape carrots for dinner.

After a while Pinneberg had finished all he had to do. He went for a few moments into the garden and surveyed the landscape. The hut with its little glass-roofed porch seemed so tiny, the plot of land so large — almost a thousand square meters. But the soil looked in poor condition, no work had been done on it since Heilbutt had inherited the place, now three years ago. Perhaps the strawberries could still be saved, but a terrific amount of digging would be needed. The place was thick with weeds, couchgrass and thistles.

After the rain of the morning the sky had cleared, and there was a crisp feeling in the air. It would be good for the baby to get out.

Pinneberg went in again. "Now, baby, we'll go for a ride," he said, put on the child's woollen sweater and his gray waterproof leggings, and set his little white cap on his head.

"Ka-Ka! Ka-Ka!" came the child's eager cry. Pinneberg put the cigarette box with the playing cards into the baby's hand: he always had to hold something. On the porch stood the little cart which they had exchanged for the carriage that summer. "All aboard," said Pinneberg, and the baby got in.

Slowly they set forth. Pinneberg did not go the usual way, he did not want to pass Krymna's hut just then, there would only have been a quarrel which he was only too glad to avoid. But sometimes you couldn't sidestep it. On these three thousand little plots of land hardly fifty per-

From Hans Fallada, "Man as Woman: A Matter of Six Marks," *Little Man, What Now?* (© 1933 by Simon & Schuster, Inc.), (New York: Simon and Schuster, 1933), pp. 345–52. Reprinted by permission of Simon & Schuster, Inc., and Mrs. Emma Hey representing the estate of Hans Fallada.

sons were left this winter; anyone who could raise the money for a room, or get himself taken in by relatives, had fled to the city to escape the cold and dirt and solitude.

Those that stayed, the poorest, the most enduring and courageous, felt somehow that they ought to hang together, but unluckily they did not hang together at all. They were either Communists or Nazis, and thus involved in constant quarrels and conflicts.

Pinneberg had never been able to make up his mind one way or the other; he had thought that this would be an easy way out of the dilemma, but it often appeared to be the hardest.

On some of the plots there was much sawing and chopping going on — these were the Communists who had been on the night expedition with Krymna. They quickly reduced the wood to kindling, so that when the forest-guard came along he would find no evidence. When Pinneberg politely said "Good-day," they growled a brusque "G'day" in answer. Pinneberg felt uneasy.

Finally they reached a respectable district of long sidewalks and rows of little villas. Pinneberg unhitched the straps of the cart. "Out with you!"

The baby looked at his father; in his blue eyes danced a little rogue.

"Out with you," said Pinneberg again, "and push your cart."

The baby surveyed his father, put a leg out of the cart, smiled, drew it back. Then he lay back as though about to fall asleep.

"Da-Da will go by himself."

The baby blinked.

Slowly Pinneberg went on, leaving cart and baby behind him. He walked on for ten paces, twenty paces: not a movement. He walked another ten paces, very slowly.

"Da-Da! Da-Da!"

Pinneberg turned: the child had got out of the cart but still made no attempt to follow his father, he held out the straps to be tied round him.

Pinneberg went back and tied the straps. This done, the child's sense of order was satisfied, and for quite a while he pushed the cart alongside his father. Soon they reached a bridge, beneath which a broad swift stream flowed across a meadow. After the rain the stream was full, and the turbid water surged along in swirling eddies.

Pinneberg left the cart standing above, and with the child's hand in his, walked down to the edge of the stream. They surveyed the speeding water. After a while Pinneberg said: "That's water, baby, nice water."

The child uttered a faint small sound of applause. Pinneberg repeated his words several times, to the baby's never-failing enjoyment.

It seemed to Pinneberg unfair that he should stand up so tall beside his boy, imparting information; so he crouched down on his heels.

The child, thinking this the right thing to do, imitated him. Thus they both sat for a while, and watched the water. Then they went on.

The child was tired of pushing his cart; he walked by himself, first for a while beside his father and the cart; then he began to notice things and stop — chickens, or a shop-window, or the grating of a drain that caught his eye in the expanse of pavement.

Pinneberg waited a while; then he walked slowly on, stopped again, called and waved to the child who pattered on for a few short steps, laughed at his father, turned, and went back again to his grating.

This happened a few times, until Pinneberg was quite a distance in front, much too far — so the child thought. There the boy stood, shifting from one small leg to another, a very earnest look on his little face. He snatched at the edge of his woolly cap, and pulled it down over his face, so that he could no longer see. Then he called out: "Da-Da!"

Pinneberg looked around. There stood his little son in the middle of the street, his face quite covered with his cap, swaying on his little legs as though at any moment he might fall. Pinneberg rushed back to him, his heart pounding against his chest. He thought: That's pretty cute for one and a half: covering his eyes so that I'd have to go back for him.

He pulled the cap off the child's face. It beamed up at him. "Well, you are a little rascal and no mistake," said he.

Pinneberg said it over and over again, and the tears stood in his eyes.

Then they turned down the Gartenstrasse, towards the house of Rusch the manufacturer, whose wife had owed Bunny six marks for three weeks. Pinneberg repeated to himself his promise that he would not make a scene.

The villa stood in a garden, a little way back from the street; it was a large and pleasant villa with a large pleasant orchard behind it. It looked very good to Pinneberg.

Slowly he became aware that no one had answered his ring. He tried it again.

A window was flung up, and a woman called out: "Nothing for beggars."

"My wife did some mending in your house," said Pinneberg. "I have come to get the six marks."

"Come again tomorrow." The woman slammed the window.

Pinneberg stood for a while considering how much scope was left to him by his promise to Bunny. The baby was sitting quietly in his cart as if aware that his father was angry.

Pinneberg recollected the drudgery of eighteen hours of darning and mending. He pressed his thumb firmly against the bell-button. Several people passed and looked at him. The baby did not utter a sound.

The window was flung open again. "If you don't get away from the bell at once I'll call the police."

Pinneberg removed his thumb and shouted back: "I wish you would. And I'll tell the policeman."

But the window was down again, and Pinneberg began to ring once more. He had always been a quiet and peaceable man, but these virtues had begun to collapse. As a matter of fact, he would have been in a very awkward position if a policeman had in fact appeared. But he did not care. It was very cold, too, for the baby to sit so long in his cart, but of that he did not think. Here stood the little man, Pinneberg, ringing the bell at the house of Rusch the manufacturer. He wanted his six marks and he intended to get them.

The hall door opened and the woman came out. She was wild with rage. She had two dogs on a leash, a black and a gray. The beasts had understood that here was an enemy, they tugged and growled ominously.

"I'll set the dogs on you if you don't go away at once."

"I want six marks from you."

The woman grew more furious when she saw the dogs were no help, as she could not really let them loose. They would have been over the railings in an instant and would have torn him to pieces. Pinneberg knew that as well as she did.

"You must be used to waiting," she said.

"I am," said Pinneberg, without moving.

"You're one of the unemployed," said the woman contemptuously; "I can see that quite well. I'll put the police on you for not reporting your wife's earnings."

"All right," said Pinneberg.

"And I'll take the taxes and sick insurance off your wife's six marks."

"If you do," said Pinneberg. "I'll come along tomorrow and make you show me the receipts."

"You wait until your wife comes and asks for some work!" shouted the woman.

"Six marks please," said Pinneberg.

"You impertinent ruffian!" said the woman. "If my husband was here . . ."

"Yes, but he isn't," said Pinneberg.

Here at last were the six marks. There they lay, two three mark pieces, on the top of the railing. Pinneberg could not pick them up at once, the woman had first to take the dogs back to the house.

"Thank you very much," he said, taking off his hat.

The baby gurgled something. "Yes, money," cried Pinneberg. "Money, little one. And now it's home for us!"

He did not once look back at the woman and the villa, he slowly trundled off with the little cart; he felt dizzy and tired and sad.

The baby chattered and gurgled.

From time to time the father answered, but his voice now sounded different. Finally the baby, too, was silent.

LIBERAL ATTEMPTS
AT RECONSTRUCTION
Chapter 3

The efforts of the Western democracies to restore stability domestically and internationally took place under unpropitious circumstances. The limited success of these efforts may be measured by the fact that in 1940 Europe was once again at war, and the only remaining free liberal democracies were Great Britain and the United States. Nevertheless, the period between the wars was not without its hopeful starts and promising moments, and the historian would be remiss if he neglected them, just as he would be misleading if he did not notice their limitations.

The effectiveness of the League of Nations, certainly the most idealistic institution created during the postwar period, was badly hampered by America's refusal to join, Germany's exclusion until 1926, and the organization's limited powers. The League was dominated by England and France and functioned best in the mediation of minor disputes. The peace of Europe and the world continued to depend upon the willingness of the great powers to maintain it because it was in their interest.

It is no accident, therefore, that the period of relative economic stability and prosperity between 1924 and 1929 coincided with a stabilization of international relations. The end of France's occupation of the Ruhr and the acceptance of the Dawes Plan marked the restoration of a measure of common sense in both the economic and the political spheres. The devastating inflation had destroyed, temporarily at least, the adventuresomeness of the Germans. German businessmen in particular needed a restoration of international trade, and they were prepared to support moderate statesmen such as Gustav Stresemann, German foreign minister from 1924 to 1929. His policy of "fulfillment" and peaceful restoration of Germany's prestige made sense within the context of American loans and reasonable chances of economic reconstruction. The French, no longer confident that German reparations would solve their economic problems, were fighting off inflation.

In France too businessmen and other important segments of the public turned away from hard-liners such as Poincaré and supported the conciliatory policies of Aristide Briand. Finally, the British under Austen Chamberlain were most anxious to restore order in Europe and, if at all possible, include Germany in a European system of collective security. This constellation of personalities and powers was responsible for the "Locarno spirit" and the 1925 treaties by which Germany accepted western borders with France and Belgium, and Britain guaranteed them against aggression from either side. Germany was admitted to the League of Nations in 1926. These arrangements did leave important questions open, above all Germany's eastern borders, which Stresemann refused to accept as permanent. Ultimately, the Locarno spirit lasted as long as the prosperity of which it was a symptom. The depression and the high tariff policies that accompanied it chilled the international atmosphere, and Adolf Hitler's rise to power after 1933 made permanent the aggressive and stubborn line that German diplomacy took after Stresemann's death in 1929.

Domestic politics in the leading countries of the Western world paralleled the international political situation in many respects. Those who had hoped that the end of the war would mark an era of major social reconstruction were bitterly disappointed. There was no significant socialization in Germany, and the ideas of worker control in the plants that sprang up throughout Europe between 1918 and 1921 came to naught. Political life resumed an all-too-normal course. The Weimar Republic was hated by the Right, which perpetrated the legend that the socialists had stabbed the army in the back in 1918, and the first years of the new regime were filled with putsches from both the Right and the Left. After 1924, conditions stabilized somewhat, but the country continued to be ruled by fragile coalition governments. After the September, 1930, elections, it became impossible to form viable majority governments, and President Hindenburg and his chancellors ruled by decree, a practice that contributed to Hitler's seizure of power in January, 1933.

France too suffered from chronic political and social instability, which reached a dangerous culmination in right-wing riots in June, 1934. The fear of a fascist takeover forced the radicals, socialists and, in a more passive sense, the Communists to produce a Popular Front government in 1936 under the socialist Léon Blum. This short-lived experiment was completely over by 1938, when politics returned to normal once again. France paid the price of stagnation in 1940.

Britain was spared the extreme political instability from which the Continental powers suffered, but it was not spared the social turmoil that afflicted all industrial societies in this period. A great general strike in 1926 intensified the conflict between organized labor and the more conservative elements of the population, and the Conservative governments ruling Britain between 1924 and 1929 accomplished little. Unfortunately, the same must be said for the Labor government of Ramsay MacDonald, which took over in 1929. It was singularly lacking in ideas for handling the depression and finally formed a coalition with the Conservatives and pursued a traditional deflationary policy. Indeed, with the exception of Blum in France and Franklin Roosevelt in the United States, the leaders of the liberal democracies were inept and unimaginative in handling the depression, and their deflationary policies only exacerbated the situation. Although such policies conformed to the economic wisdom of the period, imaginative politicians such as Blum, Roosevelt, and, unhappily, Hitler demonstrated that an inflationary policy involving public expenditure and social benefits was more useful in relieving the situation and restoring confidence.

The German Republic on Paper

The framers of the Weimar Constitution sought to combine the best of the German liberal tradition with a measure of continuity with Germany's imperial past. At the same time, they created a constitution that was peculiarly modern in many respects. Thus they chose the colors of the 1848 revolutionaries for the flag, vested sovereignty in the people, made the parliament exceptionally powerful, strengthened the power of the central government over the states, and included basic rights within the document itself. Yet, with traditional German suspicion of partisan politics and a yearning for a strong executive, they created a president whose direct election by the people would ensure that he was "above politics" and who had important powers, especially in times of emergency (Article 48). The document is particularly remarkable for its economic provisions, which attempted to deal with the issues of a modern industrial society directly.

Unfortunately, the realities of German political life served to distort the high purposes of the Constitution. Unstable parliamentary coalitions made governing difficult, and Article 48 was used excessively even by the first president, the socialist Friedrich Ebert. Direct election of the president proved disastrous when Field Marshal Paul von Hindenburg was elected in 1925. Surprisingly, he was faithful to the Con-

stitution initially despite his monarchist sentiments, but he used and abused Article 48 by turning it into a substitute for parliamentary government in the crisis lasting from 1930 to 1933. Similarly, the provisions for tenure of civil servants and judges, though acceptable and desirable under normal circumstances, often placed the people at the mercy of holdovers from the old regime who used their positions to sabotage reforms. These conditions made it difficult to implement the progressive features of the constitution effectively.

The Weimar Constitution, August 11, 1919

This Constitution has been framed by the united German people, inspired by the determination to restore and establish their Federation upon a basis of liberty and justice, to be of service to the cause of peace both at home and abroad, and to promote social progress.

PART I. CONSTRUCTION AND DUTIES OF THE FEDERATION

SECTION I. FEDERATION AND STATES

ART. 1. The German Federation is a republic.

The supreme power proceeds from the people.

2. The Federal territory consists of the territories of the German States. Other territories may, by Federal law, be admitted within the Federation, if desired by their population, in virtue of the right of self-determination.

3. The Federal colours are black, red and gold. The commercial flag is black, white and red, with the Federal colours in the upper inside corner.

4. The universally recognised rules of International Law are valid as binding constituent parts of German Federal law.

5. The executive power is exercised in Federal affairs through the institutions of the Federation, in virtue of the Federal Constitution, and in State affairs by the officials of the States, in virtue of the Constitutions of the States. . . .

13. Federal law overrides State law. Where there exists any doubt or difference of opinion as to whether a regulation of State law is compatible with Federal law, an appeal may be made by the competent Federal or State authorities to the decision of the highest tribunal of the Federation for a more exact interpretation of the Federal law. . . .

17. Each State must have a republican constitution. The representatives of the people must be elected by the universal, equal, direct and

From *British and Foreign State Papers,* vol. 112 (1919), pp. 1063–64, 1066, 1068, 1071–72, 1081–83, 1085–86. Reprinted by permission of Her Majesty's Stationery Office.

secret suffrage of all men and women of the German Federation, upon the principles of proportional representation. The State Government requires the confidence of the people's representatives.

The principles underlying elections of the people's representatives apply also to municipal elections. By a State law the qualification for a vote may, however, be declared conditional upon a year's residence in the district. . . .

21. The deputies are representatives of the whole people. They are subject to their conscience only, and not bound by any mandates.

22. The deputies are elected by the universal, equal, direct and secret suffrage of all men and women above the age of 20, upon the principles of proportional representation. Elections must take place on a Sunday or a public holiday.

Details are determined by the Federal election law.

23. The Reichstag is elected for four years. The general election must take place not later than sixty days after dissolution. The Reichstag must assemble not less than thirty days after the election. . . .

25. The President of the Federation may dissolve the Reichstag, but only once for any one reason. The general election will take place not later than sixty days after the dissolution. . . .

SECTION III. THE PRESIDENT OF THE FEDERATION
AND THE FEDERAL GOVERNMENT

41. The President of the Federation is elected by the whole German people.

Every German who has completed his 35th year is eligible.

Details are determined by a Federal law.

42. The President of the Federation when entering upon his office in the Reichstag, takes the following oath:

"I swear to dedicate my powers to the welfare of the German people, to enlarge their sphere of usefulness, to guard them from injury, to observe the Constitution and the laws of the Federation, to fulfil my duties conscientiously, and to do justice to every man."

The addition of a religious asseveration is permissible.

43. The President of the Federation remains in office for seven years. Re-election is permissible.

Before the expiration of the set term, the President of the Federation may, upon the motion of the Reichstag, be removed from office by the vote of the people. The decision of the Reichstag requires a two-thirds majority. By such a decision, the President of the Federation is prevented from the further exercise of his office. The refusal to remove him from office, expressed by the vote of the people, is equivalent to re-election, and involves the dissolution of the Reichstag.

Penal proceedings may not be taken against the President of the Federation without the consent of the Reichstag.

44. The President of the Federation cannot at the same time be a member of the Reichstag.

45. The President of the Federation represents the Federation in international relations. He concludes alliances and other treaties with foreign Powers in the name of the Federation. He accredits and receives Ambassadors.

The declaration of war and the conclusion of peace are dependent upon the passing of a Federal law.

Alliances and treaties with foreign States, which refer to subjects of Federal legislation, require the consent of the Reichstag.

46. The President of the Federation appoints and dismisses Federal officials and officers, where no other system is determined by law. He may depute these powers to other authorities.

47. The President of the Federation has supreme command over all the armed forces of the Federation.

48. In the case of a State not fulfilling the duties imposed on it by the Federal Constitution or the Federal laws, the President of the Federation may enforce their fulfilment with the help of the armed forces.

Where public security and order are seriously disturbed or endangered within the Federation, the President of the Federation may take the measures necessary for their restoration, intervening in case of need with the help of armed forces. For this purpose he is permitted, for the time being, to abrogate, either wholly or partially, the fundamental laws laid down in Articles 114, 115, 117, 118, 123, 124 and 153.

The President of the Federation must, without delay, inform the Reichstag of any measures taken in accordance with paragraphs 1 or 2 of this Article. Such measures shall be withdrawn upon the demand of the Reichstag.

Where there is danger in delay, the State Government may take provisional measures of the kind described in paragraph 2, for its own territory. Such measures shall be withdrawn upon the demand of the President of the Federation or the Reichstag. . . .

SECTION VII. ADMINISTRATION OF JUSTICE

102. Judges are independent and subject only to the law.

103. The regular jurisdiction is exercised by the Federal High Court of Justice, and the Courts of Justice of the States.

104. The judges of the regular jurisdiction are appointed for life. They may be removed from the office permanently or temporarily only by the authority of a judicial decision, and only upon the grounds and by the methods of procedure fixed by the laws; the same applies to

change of post or superannuation. Age limits may be fixed by legislation, upon reaching which judges shall retire. . . .

PART II. FUNDAMENTAL RIGHTS AND DUTIES OF GERMANS

SECTION I. THE INDIVIDUAL

109. All Germans are equal before the law.

Men and women have in principle equal civic rights and duties.

Public and legal privileges or disadvantages of birth or rank are to be abolished. Titles of nobility simply form a part of the name, and may no longer be conferred.

Titles may be conferred only when they indicate an office or calling, academical degrees not being hereby affected.

Orders and badges of honour may not be conferred by the State.

No German is permitted to accept a title or order from a foreign Government.

110. Nationality in the Federation and the States is acquired and lost according to the provisions of a Federal law. Every subject of a State is also a subject of the Federation.

Every German has the same rights and duties in any State of the Federation as the subjects of that State.

111. All Germans enjoy the right of change of domicile within the whole Federation. Everyone has the right to stop in any part of the Federation that he chooses, to settle there, acquire real estate and pursue any means of livelihood. Restrictions can be imposed by Federal law only.

112. Every German is entitled to emigrate to countries outside the Federation. Emigration can be restricted by Federal law only.

All citizens of the Federation within and beyond its territory are entitled to claim the protection of the Federation in relation to a foreign Power.

No German may be handed over to a foreign Government for prosecution or punishment.

113. Sections of the population of the Federation speaking a foreign language may not be restricted, by means of legislation and administration, in their free, national development; this applies especially to the use of their mother-tongue in education, as well as in questions of internal administration and courts of law.

114. Personal liberty is inviolable. No encroachment on, or deprivation of, personal liberty by public authority is permissible, unless supported by law.

Persons who have been deprived of their liberty shall be informed — at the latest on the following day — by what authority and on what grounds the deprivation of liberty has been ordered; opportunity shall be given them without delay to make objections against such deprivation.

115. The residence of every German is a sanctuary for him, and inviolable; exceptions are admissible only in virtue of laws.

116. Punishment may only be inflicted for any action if the penalty for such action has been legally determined, before it took place.

117. The secrecy of correspondence, as well as of the postal, telegraph and telephone services, is inviolable. Exceptions may be admitted only by Federal law.

118. Every German has the right, within the limits of general laws, to express his opinion freely by word, writing, printed matter or picture, or in any other manner. This right must not be affected by any conditions of his work or appointment, and no one is permitted to injure him on account of his making use of such right.

There is no censorship in force, but various regulations may be introduced by law in reference to cinematograph entertainments. Legal measures are also admissible for the purpose of combating bad and obscene literature, as well as for the protection of youth in public representations and performances. . . .

SECTION III. RELIGION AND RELIGIOUS BODIES

135. All inhabitants of the Federation enjoy full liberty of faith and conscience. The undisturbed practice of religion is guaranteed by the Constitution, and is under State protection. The general laws of the State remain unaffected hereby.

136. Civil and political rights and duties are neither dependent upon nor restricted by the practice of religious freedom.

The enjoyment of civil and political rights, as well as admission to official posts, are independent of religious creed.

No one is bound to disclose his religious convictions. The authorities have the right to make enquiries as to membership of a religious body only when rights and duties depend upon it, or when the collection of statistics ordered by law requires it.

No one may be compelled to take part in any ecclesiastical act or ceremony, or to participate in religious practices, or to make use of any religious form of oath.

137. There is no State Church. . . .

SECTION IV. EDUCATION AND SCHOOLS

142. Art, science, and the teaching of both, are free.

The State guarantees their protection and participates in furthering them.

143. Provision shall be made for the education of the young by means

of public institutions. The Federal Government, the States and all communities, shall co-operate in their organisation.

The training of teachers shall be regulated in a uniform manner for the whole Federation, in accordance with the principles generally applying to higher education.

Teachers in public schools have the rights and duties of State officials.

144. The whole system of education is under the supervision of the State, which may assign a share in such work to the communities. School inspection is carried out by chief officials who are trained experts.

145. School attendance is compulsory for all. This is provided for by elementary schools, with at least an eight years' course, followed by the continuation schools, with a course extending to the completion of the eighteenth year.

Instruction and all accessories are free of charge in the elementary and continuation schools.

146. The public system of education shall be thoroughly organised. Upon the basis of elementary schools common to all is constructed the system of secondary and higher education. The leading consideration for the complete organisation is the multiplicity of possible employments, and as regards the admission of a child into any particular school, its capacities and inclination, not the economic and social standing or the religious creed of its parents.

Upon the proposition of those entitled to education, however, elementary schools in accordance with their religious creed or philosophic views may be established within the communities so far as this does not lead to any restriction of regular school management, especially as regards the general sense of the first paragraph of this Article. The will of those entitled to education shall be taken into consideration as far as possible. The State Legislature determines further particulars, in accordance with the principles of a Federal law.

Public provision shall be made by the Federation, States and communities, for the admission of persons of small means to secondary and advanced courses; in particular, there shall be educational grants for the parents of children who are considered suitable for training in secondary and higher schools, up to the termination of such training. . . .

Section V. Economic life

151. The organisation of economic life must correspond to the principles of justice, with the aim of ensuring for all conditions worthy of a human being. Within these limits the economic freedom of the individual must be guaranteed.

Legal compulsion is permissible only for the realisation of threatened rights, or in support of the superior demands of public welfare.

Freedom of trade and industry is guaranteed in accordance with the provisions of Federal law. . . .

153. Property is guaranteed by the Constitution. Its extent and limits are defined by the laws.

Expropriation may be effected only for the benefit of the whole community and upon the basis of law. It is accompanied by due compensation, unless otherwise determined by Federal law. In case of dispute with regard to the amount of compensation, the course of law in the regular Courts of Justice shall be available, unless otherwise determined by Federal laws. Expropriation by the Federation in respect of States, communities and associations of public utility must be accompanied by compensation.

Property implies duties, and the use to which it is put should be of service to the welfare of all. . . .

156. The Federation may, by means of law, without prejudice to compensation and with appropriate application of decisions in force for expropriation, convert into public property private economic concerns and unions which are suitable for association. It may itself assign to the States or communities a share in the administration of economic concerns or unions, or otherwise assure to itself decisive influence.

Further, the Federation may, by law, in case of pressing necessity and for objects of public economic interest, combine economic concerns and unions on the basis of self-government, with the aim of ensuring the co-operation of all sections of productive workers, and of interesting employers and employees in the administration. A further aim would be the regulation, upon the principles of public economy, of production, collection, distribution, employment and valuation, together with import and export of all economic articles.

Industrial and co-operative societies, and their unions, shall upon their request and with due regard to their constitution and special characteristics, be incorporated into the public economic system.

157. Labour is under the special protection of the Federation. . . .

159. Freedom of association for the preservation and improvement of labour and economic conditions is guaranteed to everyone and for all occupations. All agreements and measures tending to restrict or prevent such freedom are contrary to law.

160. Anyone in the position of an employee or workman has a right to the necessary free time to avail himself of his political rights, and, so far as his business will not suffer seriously thereby, for the exercise of public honorary posts entrusted to him. The law decides as to how far his claim for compensation can be maintained.

161. The Federal Government will, with the co-operation of insured persons, draw up a comprehensive scheme of insurance for the maintenance of health and fitness for work, the protection of motherhood, and provision for the economic consequences of old age, weakness and the vicissitudes of life.

162. The Federation will intervene for the purpose of obtaining an

international regulation of the legal conditions of the workers, with the aim of securing for the working-class of the whole world a universal minimum of social rights.

163. It is the moral duty of every German, without prejudice to his personal liberty, to make such use of his mental and bodily powers as shall be for the welfare of the whole community.

It must be possible for every German to gain his livelihood by economic labour. Where no suitable opportunity of work can be found for him, provision shall be made for his support. Details shall be determined by special Federal laws.

164. The interests of the independent middle-class in agriculture, industry and commerce shall be advanced in legislation and administration, and its members shall be protected against excessive taxation and oppression.

165. Workmen and employees are called upon, with equal rights in common with the employers, to co-operate in the regulation of wage and labour conditions, as well as in the whole economic development of production. The organisations on both sides, and their agreements, are recognised.

For the protection of their social and economic interests, workmen and employees are legally represented in the Trades Workmen's Councils, as well as in the District Workmen's Councils formed in connection with economic districts, and in a Federal Workmen's Council.

The District Workmen's Councils and the Federal Workmen's Council meet, for the accomplishment of all economic tasks and for co-operation in the execution of social laws, with the representatives of the employers and other sections of the nation concerned to form District Economic Councils and a Federal Economic Council. These Economic Councils shall be so constituted as to represent all important groups of occupations, in proportion to their economic and social importance.

Drafts of laws of fundamental importance, involving social and economic policy, shall be submitted by the Federal Government to the Federal Economic Council for approval before they are actually brought forward. The latter has the right of proposing such Bills itself. Should the Federal Government not approve of them, it must nevertheless introduce them into the Reichstag, with a statement of its own views. The Federal Economic Council may present its proposals to the Reichstag by one of its members.

Powers of control and administration in questions assigned to them may be transferred to Workmen's and Economic Councils.

It is exclusively the business of the Federal Government to regulate the constitution and spheres of action of Workmen's and Economic Councils, as well as their relation to other self-governing bodies.

Gustav Stresemann and
the Policy of "Fulfillment"

The best and most successful years of the Weimar Republic were 1924 through 1929, when Gustav Stresemann served as foreign minister. Stresemann had been one of the leaders of the National Liberal party under the empire, and he founded and led its successor, the German People's party, after 1918. An ardent nationalist and supporter of annexations during the war, Stresemann's willingness to undertake a policy of "fulfillment" and conciliation was often misinterpreted as a conversion to new ideals. Indeed, he received the Nobel Peace Prize for his work at Locarno. In reality, he remained a nationalist as he became much more of a realist. He saw no purpose in refusing to recognize Germany's western borders since Germany was in no military position to change them, and he was convinced that the restoration of Germany's position by economic and political means would pave the way for a revision of the Versailles Treaty in the east. Stresemann met with little understanding from right-wing nationalist elements in Germany, who were distrustful of his approach and impatient with its limited results. His speech, delivered in Berlin to the Central Association of Provincial Organizations on December 14, 1925, illustrates his efforts to convince his right-wing critics. Stresemann hoped that his foreign policy successes would promote political stability at home, and he literally drove himself to death trying to persuade his countrymen to accept the Young Plan reparations settlement in 1929.

Stresemann's Speech to the Central Association
of Provincial Organizations, Berlin,
December 14, 1925

The publicity given to our negotiations at Locarno was in certain regards unfortunate. We had decided that our negotiations should be absolutely confidential, which was sensible; no worse nonsense has been talked lately than that about the abolition of secret diplomacy. Every man has his own secret diplomacy. Every merchant who has some new scheme in view for the coming year does not proclaim it in an announce-

From *Gustav Stresemann, His Diaries, Letters, and Papers*, vol. 2, ed. and trans. Eric Sutton (New York: Macmillan, 1937), pp. 215–16, 220–25, 227–29; published in the United States by The Macmillan Company. Reprinted by permission of The Macmillan Company and Macmillan and Company Ltd.

ment in a Berlin newspaper, so that any competitor may see what is coming and take measures accordingly. We perhaps rather overdid secret diplomacy. In the art of saying nothing in our *communiqués,* we really had no rivals. But the Press representatives had to telegraph a thousand lines a day, and they naturally telegraphed a great deal of nonsense. People must have thought that we were behaving like small children. We read a description of the Chancellor stroking a cat. That cat existed only in the imagination of the reporter. There were stories of marvellous trips on Lago Maggiore in a boat that was picturesquely named the *Orange Blossom,* and the German citizen thought to himself that we were having a very good time indeed. The fact was that on this marvellous trip we spent more than five hours in the cabin; the first two and a half hours were occupied in a discussion of Article 16 of the League Covenant, and the remaining two and a half hours were taken up with the French guarantee regarding the Eastern European treaties. I have never been so tired and done up as I was on that occasion. And the discussions were so acrimonious that I wished the minutes of them could have been published afterwards. You would then see how the former Entente and Germany contended together until the finish, and with what openness we spoke our minds at this conference. I fancy that most of the attacks upon us would be silenced if the minutes of the meeting were published at which we discussed German disarmament, and in the face of Briand, Chamberlain, and Vandervelde, rejected the charge of War Guilt. I tell you that you are not to conceive matters as though, under the sunshine of Locarno, we had stumbled into a fresh alliance of friendship. There were problems of such importance still unsolved before the conference, that one might well have been doubtful whether it could ever have been held.

The main question was: What of the German frontiers in the East? At Locarno the word went forth: insistence on a surrender of the guarantee would be an insult to the honour of France. That was the first outcry we had to face when we stated that we could not accept this guarantee in Article 6 of the treaty, and Article 6 was struck out, in spite of what had been said. But for days it was doubtful how things would go. . . .

As touching Eastern European questions, where the principle of national self-determination has been so grievously violated, I have no notions of decisions to be reached by war. What I have in mind is that when conditions arise which indicate that European peace or the economic consolidation of Europe is threatened by developments in the East, and when it is realized that this entire non-consolidation of Europe appears to have its origin in impossible frontier-lines in the East, that Germany might succeed with her claims, if she had previously effected a political understanding with all the world Powers who would have to decide the matter, and established a common economic interest with her opponents. That, in my opinion, is the only practicable policy. That we should not recognize the frontier in the East, I made clear, to the disgust of the Polish Government, in a public speech before the Foreign Committee of the Reichstag, when I stated in my opinion that no German Government, from the German Nationals to the Communists, would ever recognize this frontier. And I shall never shrink from repeating this declaration.

I see the importance in another connection of this security for peace between ourselves and France. It is true that these are all matters that lie in the future; a nation must not adopt the attitude of a child that writes a list of its wants on Christmas Eve, which contains everything that the child will need for the next fifteen years. The parents would not be in a position to give it all this. In foreign politics I often have the feeling that I am being confronted with such a list, and that it is forgotten that history advances merely step by step, and Nature not by leaps and bounds. But what stands in the way of a strengthening of Germany? What stands in the way of a recovery of German soil, or a junction with Austria? What stands in our way is the eternal anxiety that if this 60-million nation becomes a 70-million nation, we are threatened by France, and we cannot so far endanger our vital political interests. The moment the incessant threat of war on our western frontier ceases to exist, this argument is no longer valid. As a consequence, our prospects in this connection are entirely favourable. . . .

On the Rhineland question criticism has been very intense. If this crticism is to succeed it must attack the Government for not looking far enough ahead. That may be so; we did not ask for the evacuation of the Second and Third Zones before the conclusion of the treaty. We did not do it, because I said to myself that we ourselves should not do anything of the sort if we were in the position of the other side, and because I always tell myself that policy is the art of what is possible, in so far as one side does not demand of the other more than can be granted without loss of prestige. What we asked was, that after the treaty had come into force, the evacuation of the Second and Third Zones might take place at an earlier date, and a year later I shall be very ready to stand before you and answer the question whether any progress has been made in this direction. We were left in no doubt that evacuation would not take place earlier, and equally in no doubt that the matter would be discussed after the treaty. On this point too I find myself regretting the crassness of our Press. When the English Foreign Minister said a few days ago: No one supposes that we shall stay ten years longer in the Rhineland — that, from his point of view, since he is by no means devoted to Germany, means in the first instance a recognition in principle that the dates at present current cannot stand. And the *Lokal-Anzeiger* reports: "Contemptuous words from Chamberlain." If anyone imagines that this kind of thing makes foreign politics any easier, he is mistaken.

One thing more. It is to the interest of Germans abroad that we should once again take a large place in world history, or at least present some appearance of doing so. Until the last occasion the German Ambassador has never been present at the Lord Mayor's banquet at the Guild Hall. He did refuse this time for reasons which I will not mention, but which were connected with the former hostility of Londoners towards the Germans. But he was again invited. He was begged to come, not merely by the Lord Mayor but also by the Foreign Office. He went, and as he walked from the entrance of the hall to his place, the company rose from their seats and applauded until he had sat down. His place was beside the Foreign Minister, and when, by an old English tradition, the latter raised the so-called loving-cup, drank to him, and said, "I thank the Lord Mayor for giving me an opportunity of expressing my feelings of respect and friendship for Germany," there is no need to offer any special acknowledgment; but the German Press should not talk about Herr Chamberlain's poisoned goblet. The man did not deserve this. Such a scene is cabled all over the world; people read it in Capetown, in Rio, in Shanghai, and they say to themselves: What is happening in Germany? The Germans must be becoming a great nation again if they are honoured in this fashion. . . .

On one occasion, in a very heated discussion, Briand described to me the political situation in which he was placed at home and all the difficulties in which he found himself; he then launched into a wonderful description of conditions in Germany, and I must say it was very difficult to answer him. He said: "I know the German people, and I know that the great majority of the German people desire peace, of that I have no doubt; another section of the nation will rightly protest against the charge that Germany wants war. But you have something in your public life that I might call the policy of German mysticism; there are men among you who are not interested in such a peace pact at the present time, because they believe in something marvellous that is going to happen in the future. If you ask them what this marvel is, they will not be able to tell you; but the idea that a miracle may happen makes them look forward into a nebulous future and judge events from that standpoint, so that they have no eyes for what is immediately before them." He added: "You are not to imagine, however, that you have a monopoly of such visionaries; they are to be found everywhere, and while your people gaze into the future and believe in miracles, there are people in my country who gaze into the past and remember that we once held the Palatinate, that Mainz was once French, and that the Rhine policy was once the historic policy of France; and I must fight against these people in France just as you have to contend against such moods in Germany."

The policy that we have inaugurated, we have always and at least contemplated as a policy of security for the German Rhineland against French Rhine policy, and as we cannot safeguard it by force, we must do so by treaties.

If it be said that England will at any given moment do what serves her interests, and will not adopt a standpoint of pure justice, I am prepared to accept that contention. But England has no interest in a French hegemony in Europe. It is not to England's interest to be thrust out of Continental affairs, as has lately been the case. If England showed such extraordinary respect for her Foreign Minister in the matter of this treaty, that is because England has again become the arbitrator of Europe. But I ask myself which would be better: the exclusion of England, and a French hegemony and Poincarism, or, at the least, the institution of an arbitrator whose interest was the suppression of the French hegemony. If I am told that I pursue a policy friendly to England, I do not do so from any love of England, but because in this question German interests coincide with those of England, and because we must find someone who helps us to shake off the strangle-hold upon our throat. . . .

One word about the ratification of the treaty, and the League of Nations. As regards the latter, it may be asked whether it is better for Germany to remain outside or to join it. The League was in its origin directed against us. Its proceedings were hostile to us. It is responsible for the verdict that, in the Upper Silesian question, transferred to Poland cities in which 92 per cent of the inhabitants had voted for Germany. We had, from our point of view, no cause to be very sympathetic to the League. But in the present state of affairs I do not ask whether people are sympathetic to me or not; I ask whether a thing is to my advantage, or otherwise. Now I look at the situation in the following way. Everything that most deeply affects the German people, all the unsolved problems arising out of the World War, can there be most suitably brought forward. All the awkward questions, which we cannot after all leave alone, may be dealt with by that assembly. We asked at Locarno that Disarmament should be introduced into the programme of the League. This was done. Yesterday we received the invitation to take part in the conference, and it would be faint-hearted to believe that nothing will be achieved. In the background stands the will of the United States to disarm, and in the economic sphere, Coolidge's attitude that no more loans would be granted to Europe, as they were turned to powder for her armies. And if I myself have no army and cannot equip it, I must demand that the others should disarm, so that we may meet on reasonable terms.

The most important question is that of minorities. On this point the Covenant of the League was altered before we joined that body, whence I assume that the other members were nervous of our collaboration. But this alteration does not prevent us from interceding in favour of minorities. There exists a committee of three to deal with minority questions. Kindred nations may not belong to it — in other words, Germany; for we are akin to so many nations. But this committee of three may not take any decision unless the Council of the League agrees; and as the Council may only take unanimous decisions, the veto of our representative will be enough to make a decision against a German minority ineffective and to bring it before the League. Moreover every Power represented on the Council has the right to remove any question that it regards as important in principle from the competence of the committee of three and bring it direct before the League Council. If I were to represent Germany at Geneva I would make it my business to bring every question before the Council, so that these gentlemen might see the result of altering the Covenant.

Now a last word on the subject of the Danzig problems. In this matter decisions were taken that we must regard as unsatisfactory, but not, according to reports that have reached me from Danzig, to the extent that has been represented. Here, too, I must ask the question: Has not Germany great possibilities before her in the League, in two directions? This city, and the minorities, will feel quite differently if they can approach the German representatives at Geneva, instead of sitting in the anterooms of foreign Powers and waiting their turn to state their pleas. Ask the Saar deputation. When they waited on Beneš, as I was informed at Locarno that they did, what sort of a situation was that compared with the one occupied by Germany at Locarno, where we played the first part and the others were of small account? There, Herren Beneš and Skrzynski had to sit in a neighbouring room until we let them in. Such was the situation of the States which had been so pampered until then, because they were the servants of the others, but were dropped the moment there seemed a prospect of coming to an understanding with Germany. Germans abroad, moreover, must look towards their motherland. We shall not of course succeed everywhere. But we can begin by countering everything that is hostile to Germany; for without our vote no decision can be taken on the League Council, and later on we can pass over from the negative to the positive.

Thus I see in the entire movement of affairs a step forward, not as the result of any affection for us from outside, but as a consequence of this whole inner complex that I have described. In this I see the only possible policy that will get us forward. I do not know whether it will lead us wholly to success; for in these days of world revolution, whoever presumes to say what will happen in the next year is to be envied for his imagination. I frankly declare that it is to-day not possible to lay out a programme of policy, because in certain circumstances events dash onward like a torrent, and in others, barely trickle forward at all. I do not resent criticism; it is always of some service, and it has often made me think. But every criticism must have a positive sense. In 1849 Bismarck wrote to his friend, von Gerlach: "I am ready to discuss any other plan which would achieve our object better; but a criticism that does not suggest any other plan, would bring our foreign policy into a state of passive purposelessness which would be particularly impracticable for a State like Germany, situated as we are in the centre of Europe." These words, I think, apply equally to-day. Activity may go too far; a policy may be wrong. But I should like to make this one claim for myself: I believe that it is always better to live under a foreign policy with ideas, even when they are sometimes wrong, than under a policy that is merely passive instead of trying to set a course. And for my part I think that in one thing at least we have succeeded — in making a little progress towards a better future for Germany.

Léon Blum and the Popular Front

Léon Blum (1872–1950) was a humanist intellectual as well as a socialist, and although he espoused militant socialism, he rejected the Communists for their undemocratic practices. When he assumed leadership of the Popular Front government in May, 1936, he recognized from the start that there were limits to what he could accomplish. His Radical partners were prepared to support the Republic against fascism, but they were suspicious of economic experimentation. The Communists refused to take any direct responsibility by joining the government. At the same time, the workers often entertained the illusion they were one step away from social revolution and engaged in massive sitdown strikes. Blum sought to deal with France's problems by a comprehensive program of reforms within the framework of a capitalist society, a repudiation of retrenchment and the stagnation that came with it, and an insistence that the employers recognize the trade unions. The last demand led to the conclusion of the Matignon Accords. Although these measures paved the way for the French welfare state of the future, they were often not enough for the workers, particularly when the Radicals took a more conservative stance. The Popular Front also lost much of its élan because of its failure to intervene on the republican side in the Spanish Civil War. Blum, a Jew and left-winger, was hated by the Right, some of whose members took up the slogan "Better Hitler Than Blum," and he was imprisoned and tried by the collaborationist Vichy regime in 1942. His defense reveals his conception of the role he sought to play as leader of the Popular Front.

Ministerial Declaration of the Popular Front, June, 1936

Gentlemen, the government comes before you following general elections in which universal suffrage, the judge and master of us all, delivered its judgment with greater force and clarity than at any other moment in the history of the Republic.

The French people have indicated their resolute determination to preserve against violent and cunning attacks the democratic liberties they created and which remain their heritage. They have voiced their determination to seek new remedies for the crisis which crushes them, relief from the suffering and agony which has been made even crueler by long duration, and to return to active, healthy and confident life. Finally, they have proclaimed the desire for peace which animates them all. . . .

The government does not need to formulate its program. Its program is the common program accepted by all the parties making up the majority, and the sole problem will be to translate it into law. These laws will be presented in rapid succession, for the government believes that the moral and material changes demanded by the country will be achieved through their combined effect.

From the beginning of the next week, we shall bring before the Chamber a group of bills which we shall ask the two Houses to act upon before adjournment. These bills will deal with:

A political amnesty; the forty-hour week; collective bargaining contracts; paid vacations; a public works program to provide facilities for public health, science, sports and tourism; the nationalization of armament production; a wheat office which will serve as a model price support system for other agricultural products such as wine, meat and milk; the extension of the years of [compulsory] schooling; a reform in the organization of the Bank of France that will guarantee the predominance of national interests in its management; a first revision of the decree laws in favor of the most severely affected categories of public service employees and of veterans.

As soon as these measures are disposed of, we shall present to parliament a second series of bills dealing with national unemployment insurance, insurance against agricultural disasters, the regulation of agricultural debts, and a pension system guaranteeing the aged workers in the city and on the land protection against misery.

In a short time we shall present a comprehensive system of fiscal simplification and relief in order to ease the condition of industry and commerce, and, above all, to permit general recovery. The measures will

From *Economic History of Europe: Twentieth Century*, ed. Shepard B. Clough, Thomas Moodie, and Carol Moodie (New York: Harper & Row, 1968), pp. 256–57. Reprinted by permission of Harper & Row.

require no new revenues, except out of wealth acquired through repression and fraud.

While we shall strive, with your full cooperation, thus to revitalize the French economy, to absorb the unemployed, to increase disposable income in general, and to provide well-being and security for those whose labor creates true riches, we must govern the country. We shall govern as republicans; we shall assure the republican order. We shall apply the laws of republican defense with quiet firmness. We shall show that we intend to instill the republican spirit throughout the entire administration and public services. If democratic institutions are attacked, we shall assure their integrity with the means appropriate to the danger or the resistance.

The government misapprehends neither the nature nor the seriousness of the difficulties that await it. As it has not deceived itself, neither will it deceive the country. In a few days it will present publicly a report on the economic and financial situation as it exists at the beginning of this legislative session. It realizes that for a country like France, accustomed by long usage to political liberty, one can speak the truth without fear, and that frankness of governments assures rather than impairs the necessary confidence of the nation. As for us, the immensity of the task we face, far from discouraging us, only increases our determination. . . .

Repudiation of Retrenchment

Gentlemen, an examination of the consequences of the decree laws of the Doumergue and Laval Governments regarding veterans, war victims, and public servants shows that the laws have worsened the living conditions of an important segment of the population. Disabled veterans whose injuries were minor and therefore did not entitle them to full disability benefits, have been particularly affected, and there are many unemployed among them. Lesser officials, whose previously inadequate salaries were reduced by the decree laws, find themselves in a very difficult situation. Moreover, private industry, emulating the example of the State, has taken advantage of this situation by imposing on their employees new and important wage reductions.

This reduction of the purchasing power of wage earners has had disastrous consequences for small and medium merchants. Businesses fail more and more frequently, and farmers find the market price for agricultural products considerably reduced. As a result, the sale of government bonds has diminished, making budget estimates less reliable and thus putting the Treasury in difficulties.

From *Economic History of Europe: Twentieth Century*, ed. Shepard B. Clough, Thomas Moodie, and Carol Moodie (New York: Harper & Row, 1968), pp. 257–58. Reprinted by permission of Harper & Row.

In view of the fact that justice demands the restoration of the salaries of state and public service employees, and that to do so would be in the best interests of the entire country, we have the honor to propose the following resolution:

The Chamber requests the Government immediately to formulate a bill providing for:

1. Restoration of full rights to veterans and war victims by the suspension of the reductions adopted after June 1, 1932;

2. Annulment of the reductions made after June 1, 1932, in payments for public health and child care, as well as in welfare and social security payments;

3. Immediate suspension of all reductions in pension payments resulting from measures taken after June 1, 1932, and complete reorganization of the pension system so as to allow all the retired, both civilian and military, treatment that is equitable and that accords all categories satisfaction of their legitimate claims;

4. For all employees of the State, the departments, municipalities, public services, of Algeria, the colonies, protectorates and mandated territories, abolition of the salary reductions effected after June 1, 1932;

5. Restoration of the 10 per cent cut in interest imposed on government bonds held by small investors by the decree law of July 16, 1935.

The Matignon Accords

ARTICLE 1. The representatives of the employers accept the immediate establishment of collective labor contracts.

ARTICLE 2. These contracts are specifically to include Articles 3 and 5 following.

ARTICLE 3. Observance of the law being the duty of all citizens, the employers acknowledge the freedom of opinion of workers as well as their right freely to join and belong to trade unions established in accordance with Book 3 of the Labor Code.

Employers undertake not to allow the fact of membership or nonmembership in a union to affect their decisions in matters of hiring, the conduct or the distribution of labor, disciplinary measures, or dismissal.

If one of the parties to the contract contests the motive for dismissal of a worker as having been in violation of the rights of organized labor indicated above, both parties will seek to gather the facts and in disputed cases to arrive at an equitable solution.

This action does not prejudice the right of the parties to obtain

From *Economic History of Europe: Twentieth Century*, ed. Shepard B. Clough, Thomas Moodie, and Carol Moodie (New York: Harper & Row, 1968), pp. 259–60. Reprinted by permission of Harper & Row.

through the courts compensation for damages caused. The exercise of the rights of organized labor ought not to result in acts contrary to law.

ARTICLE 4. The real wages paid to all workers on May 25, 1936, will be, when work is resumed, raised on a descending scale beginning at 15 per cent for the lowest wages and declining to 7 per cent for the highest.

The total wages bill of any establishment must not in any case increase by more than 12 per cent. Wage increases agreed to after the above date are to be included in the adjustments specified. However, increases that exceed the above adjustments will remain.

The negotiations for collective contracts fixing minimum wages by region and by category, which are to begin immediately, ought to be concerned particularly with necessary adjustments in abnormally low wages.

The representatives of the employers pledge to proceed with any adjustments necessary to maintain a normal relationship between the earnings of wage earners and salaried employees.

ARTICLE 5. Except for particular cases already regulated by law, in each establishment employing more than ten workers, after agreement with trade-union organizations or, in their absence, among the interested parties, there will be designated two (head) or several (head and assistant) workers' delegates according to the size of the establishment. These delegates are responsible for presenting to the management individual complaints not expressly met concerning the application of the laws, decrees, regulations of the Labor Code, the rates of wages, and measures of hygiene and safety.

All workers, male and female, above eighteen years of age, provided they have been employed in the establishment at least three months and that they have not been deprived of their civic rights, are qualified voters [for the workers' delegates].

Eligible [as delegates] are the voters as defined above who are French citizens, at least twenty-five years of age and who have been employed in the establishment continuously for one year, with the reservation that the duration of employment may be shortened if it reduces the number of those eligible to five.

Workers engaged in the retail trade, of whatever nature, whether conducted by themselves or by their spouses, are not eligible.

ARTICLE 6. The employers' representatives undertake not to employ sanctions against workers [now] on strike.

ARTICLE 7. The representatives of the labor confederation will request that striking workers return to the job as soon as the management of the establishment has accepted the general agreement arrived at, and as soon as discussions concerning its application have begun between management and labor in the establishment.

80

Blum's Defense at the Riom Trials, March 12, 1943

I see — you will excuse me — the good I have been able to do, I see how I smoothed out great social conflicts, I see that for the first time I secured unanimous support for war credits; I see that I prepared the minds of the people for this conception of French unity which was surely as splendid as in the early months of the war of 1914, for it was a spectacle which those who saw it will never forget. I see what I have done. I see the good I have been able to do, that I have been fortunate enough to do. What is the wrong which even involuntarily, even in spite of my good-will and good intentions which nobody I think can doubt, what is the wrong I have done? Is it my crime, as poisoner and traitor, that I have, as is asserted, ruined the authority of the employers and destroyed the pillars of discipline? I do not think so, for, if it were so, my Collective Agreements Act would have been impeached. It was this Collective Agreements Act which introduced democracy into the factories, it is this Act which balks the employer of the right, perhaps essential, linked up as it is to a certain extent with his right of property, of discussing conditions of labour with each of his employees or workers individually. It is this act which makes Collective Agreements the subject of discussion upon a basis of equality of parity, between workers and employers, between the workers as a group and the employers as a group.

If ever there was a law which modified the employers' authority, it is this law. However, it is not in the charge. I am not one of those who have tried to ruin the authority of the industrial chiefs. Too often, alas, the employers have themselves been responsible for doing that. I believe that, in a Labour democracy, as in a political democracy, authority is necessary, and the leader gains this authority by an example of competence, industry, justice and goodness But, on the other hand, one form of employers' authority has, I believe, disappeared and will not be seen again; the form of authority of which during that difficult period some employers seemed to retain a rather painful memory. The divine right of employers is dead.

Gentlemen, I retract nothing of what I have said. I do not think there is one single argument which I have not supplied. I have told you why repression, regret for the non-employment of which seems to be expressed in some of the evidence, appeared impossible to me, for had it been possible it would have been the worst of mistakes, the worst of crimes, against our country.

From *Léon Blum Before His Judges*, at the Supreme Court of Riom, March 11th and 12th, 1942, trans. Christian Howie, foreword by the Right Hon. Clement R. Attlee, M.P., introduction by Felix Gouin (London: Routledge & Kegan Paul, 1943), pp. 154–55. Reprinted by permission of Routledge & Kegan Paul Ltd.

But, suppose I did what they appeared to ask me, what certain witnesses at least seemed to want me to do, what they seem to regret that I did not do. Let us suppose I had made a blood-bath for the workers, that I had been the cause of more days like those of June, for that is where historically, the most probable analogy may be found. I agree that I would have established order, material order. Do you think I would have established it for long? Don't you know that in this country there exists an underlying generosity of feeling to which the use and abuse of force is repugnant? Don't you know that after a certain time in any movement of this kind, however blameworthy it may appear, in the end public sympathy always goes to the victims? I played a rôle for which I would almost venture to say I was destined, the rôle of conciliator. Had I done otherwise, had I been the arm that strikes, the arm that avenges so many fears, and had I used force, the order which I should have restored would have been but a fragile and precarious thing for I should have wounded the deepest, most sensitive, and most generous feelings in the heart of this country. In the Chamber, Briand, in an inspired moment, once said: "Look at my hands; not a drop of blood." He responded to this deep popular sentiment. Yesterday evening in my cell I was reading Michelet's *French Revolution,* and, as if by chance, just as so often happens in opening the Bible to look up a text, I lit upon this sentence: "My heart bleeds to see French blood flowing." The sentence was in inverted commas. Who said it? Joan of Arc.

Franklin D. Roosevelt and the New Deal

Franklin D. Roosevelt, like Blum, repudiated the deflationary policies of his predecessor, Herbert Hoover, just as he rejected the policy of letting business have its own way as practiced by the Republican administrations of Harding, Coolidge, and Hoover. Although Roosevelt was often accused of dictatorial aspirations by anxious conservatives with their eyes on Germany, he was deeply committed to the American democratic and liberal traditions. Furthermore, he was not antagonistic to capitalism and free enterprise. Above all, he was a pragmatist. He was prepared to experiment and intervene where such actions became necessary. His philosophy and the spirit of his administration are perhaps best summed up in his campaign speech at the Commonwealth Club in San Francisco on September 23, 1932.

Address by Governor Roosevelt, San Francisco, September 22, 1932

. . . A glance at the situation today only too clearly indicates that equality of opportunity as we have known it no longer exists. Our industrial plant is built; the problem just now is whether under existing conditions it is not overbuilt. Our last frontier has long since been reached, and there is practically no more free land. More than half of our people do not live on the farms or on lands and cannot derive a living by cultivating their own property. There is no safety valve in the form of a Western prairie to which those thrown out of work by the Eastern economic machines can go for a new start. We are not able to invite the immigration from Europe to share our endless plenty. We are now providing a drab living for our own people.

Our system of constantly rising tariffs has at last reacted against us to the point of closing our Canadian frontier on the north, our European markets on the east, many of our Latin American markets to the south, and a goodly proportion of our Pacific markets on the west, through the retaliatory tariffs of those countries. It has forced many of our great industrial institutions who exported their surplus production to such countries, to establish plants in such countries, within the tariff walls. This has resulted in the reduction of the operation of their American plants, and opportunity for employment.

Just as freedom to farm has ceased, so also the opportunity in business has narrowed. It still is true that men can start small enterprises, trusting to native shrewdness and ability to keep abreast of competitors; but area after area has been preempted altogether by the great corporations, and even in the fields which still have no great concerns, the small man starts under a handicap. The unfeeling statistics of the past three decades show that the independent business man is running a losing race. Perhaps he is forced to the wall; perhaps he cannot command credit; perhaps he is "squeezed out," in Mr. Wilson's words, by highly organized corporate competitors, as your corner grocery man can tell you. Recently a careful study was made of the concentration of business in the United States. It showed that our economic life was dominated by some six hundred odd corporations who controlled two-thirds of American industry. Ten million small business men divided the other third. More striking still, it appeared that if the process of concentration goes on at the same rate, at the end of another century we shall have all American industry controlled by a dozen corporations, and run by perhaps a hundred men. Put plainly, we are steering a steady course toward economic oligarchy, if we are not there already.

Mimeographed release by Franklin D. Roosevelt's Press Representative, M. H. McIntyre.

Clearly, all this calls for a re-appraisal of values. A mere builder of more industrial plants, a creator of more railroad systems, an organizer of more corporations, is as likely to be a danger as a help. The day of the great promoter or the financial Titan, to whom we granted anything if only he would build, or develop, is over. Our task now is not discovery or exploitation of natural resources, or necessarily producing more goods. It is the soberer, less dramatic business of administering resources and plants already in hand, of seeking to reestablish foreign markets for our surplus production, of meeting the problem of underconsumption, of adjusting production to consumption, of distributing wealth and products to the service of the people. The day of enlightened administration has come.

Just as in older times the central government was first a haven of refuge, and then a threat, so now in a closer economic system the central and ambitious financial unit is no longer a servant of national desire, but a danger. I would draw the parallel one step farther. We did not think because national government had become a threat in the 18th century that therefore we should abandon the principle of national government. Nor today should we abandon the principle of strong economic units called corporations, merely because their power is susceptible of easy abuse. In other times we dealt with the problem of an unduly ambitious central government by modifying it gradually into a constitutional democratic government. So today we are modifying and controlling our economic units.

As I see it, the task of government in its relation to business is to assist the development of an economic declaration of rights, an economic constitutional order. This is the common task of statesman and business man. It is the minimum requirement of a more permanently safe order of things. . . .

Every man has a right to life; and this means that he has also a right to make a comfortable living. He may by sloth or crime decline to exercise that right; but it may not be denied him. We have no actual famine or dearth; our industrial and agricultural mechanism can produce enough and to spare. Our government formal and informal, political and economic, owes to every one an avenue to possess himself of a portion of that plenty sufficient for his needs, through his own work.

Every man has a right to his own property; which means a right to be assured, to the fullest extent attainable, in the safety of his savings. By no other means can men carry the burdens of those parts of life which, in the nature of things, afford no chance of labor; childhood, sickness, old age. In all thought of property, this right is paramount; all other property rights must yield to it. If, in accord with this principle, we must restrict the operations of the speculator, the manipulator, even the financier, I believe we must accept the restriction as needful, not to hamper individualism but to protect it.

These two requirements must be satisfied, in the main, by the individuals who claim and hold control of the great industrial and financial combinations which dominate so large a part of our industrial life. They have undertaken to be, not business men, but princes — princes of property. I am not prepared to say that the system which produces them is wrong. I am very clear that they must fearlessly and competently assume the responsibility which goes with the power. So many enlightened business men know this that the statement would be little more than a platitude, were it not for an added implication.

This implication is, briefly, that the responsible heads of finance and industry instead of acting each for himself, must work together to achieve the common end. They must, where necessary, sacrifice this or that private advantage; and in reciprocal self-denial must seek a general advantage. It is here that formed government — political government, if you choose, comes in. Whenever in the pursuit of this objective the lone wolf, the unethical competitor, the reckless promoter, the Ishmael or Insull whose hand is against every man's, declines to join in achieving an end recognized as being for the public welfare, and threatens to drag the industry back to a state of anarchy, the government may properly be asked to apply restraint. Likewise, should the group ever use its collective power contrary to the public welfare, the government must be swift to enter and protect the public interest.

The government should assume the function of economic regulation only as a last resort, to be tried only when private initiative, inspired by high responsibility, with such assistance and balance as government can give, has finally failed. As yet there has been no final failure, because there has been no attempt; and I decline to assume that this nation is unable to meet the situation.

The final terms of the high contract was for liberty and the pursuit of happiness. We have learnt a great deal of both in the past century. We know that individual liberty and individual happiness mean nothing unless both are ordered in the sense that one man's meat is not another man's poison. We know that the old "rights of personal competency" — the right to read, to think, to speak, to choose and live a mode of life, must be respected at all hazards. We know that liberty to do anything which deprives others of those elemental rights is outside the protection of any compact; and that government in this regard is the maintenance of a balance, within which every individual may have a place if he will take it; in which every individual may find safety if he wishes it; in which every individual may attain such power as his ability permits, consistent with his assuming the accompanying responsibility. . . .

Faith in America, faith in our tradition of personal responsibility, faith in our institutions, faith in ourselves demands that we recognize the new terms of the old social contract. We shall fulfill them, as we fulfilled the obligation of the apparent Utopia which Jefferson imagined for us in 1776, and which Jefferson, Roosevelt and Wilson sought to bring to realization. We must do so, lest a rising tide of misery engendered by our common failure, engulf us all. But failure is not an American habit; and in the strength of great hope we must all shoulder our common load.

AUTHORITARIAN ATTEMPTS AT RECONSTRUCTION

Chapter 4

Liberal democracy and democratic socialism faced serious competition from both Communism and fascism during the interwar period. Of the two movements, Communism was by far more organized and more international at the time of the depression, but it suffered from two serious deficiencies when it came to gaining adherents. It had a narrow class orientation, limiting its appeal largely to workers and scattered intellectuals, and the international Communist movement was dominated by the Soviet Union and its special interests and was ill attuned to the specific national interests of the countries it sought to infiltrate. Fascism, in contrast, had a wider social base and was peculiarly national. It could combine the promise of social amelioration, concern for status anxieties, and nationalist sentiments in a manner precluded by the character and ideology of Communism. In the 1930's, however, Communism and fascism did offer one thing in common: totalitarianism. Dictatorial rule by one leader in a state utilizing secret police and propaganda and employing the instruments of modern technology to impose conformity as well as obedience were common to Communist Russia, fascist Italy, and Nazi Germany.

Historians continue to debate whether Stalinist rule was a necessary and logical outcome of the ideology and system of government established by Lenin and his colleagues. Lenin did differ from Stalin in being more tolerant of and humane toward opponents within the movement, and, again in contrast to Stalin, he believed that the success of the revolution in the advanced industrial societies was essential to the ultimate success of Communism within Russia itself. At the same time, however, the elitist position that Lenin gave to the party, his insistence upon ideological conformity both within the Russian Communist party and within the Third International, and his ruthless suppression of opposition to Bolshevik rule pointed in the direction of later practices.

Joseph Stalin, who succeeded Lenin upon his death in 1924, took four years to consolidate his power and emerge as de facto dictator of the Soviet Union in 1928. Stalin skillfully capitalized upon the war weariness and economic exhaustion of Russia to defeat his chief competitor, Leon Trotsky, who tended to subordinate Russian interests to those of the world revolution and who wished to implement Communist economic doctrines more rigorously in Russia. Stalin supported the New Economic Policy of concessions to private enterprise so long as it suited the immediate goal of economic recovery, and he consistently subordinated the International to Russian needs so that the policy of the International often did little more than reflect political shifts within the Kremlin.

By 1928, Stalin had consolidated his position and determined on a change of course. He promoted the rapid and ruthless industrialization of Russia by a program of forced collectivization and five-year plans in an effort to build "socialism in one country." As Stalin eliminated his domestic competitors and made increasingly greater demands on his people, he became more suspicious and paranoid. These tendencies culminated in the great purges of the 1930's in which millions lost their lives or were imprisoned. At the same time, however, the growing threat from Nazi Germany caused Stalin to abandon his disastrous policy of viewing the western European socialists as "social fascists" and to order the International to support popular fronts. A democratic veneer was given to the Soviet Union by its constitution of 1936, but the ruthless purges that followed the promulgation of the constitution were hardly reassuring to those trying to distinguish between Stalin and Hitler.

Fascism presented itself quite deliberately as an alternative to both liberalism and Communism. Its birthplace was Italy, where Benito Mussolini, an ex-socialist of considerable intellectual ability and oratorical skill, combined his radical activism with a nationalist appeal and organized the new movement after the First World War. Mussolini capitalized on nationalist discontent with the Versailles Treaty, bourgeois anxieties over workers and peasant strikes in 1920 and 1921, and miserable economic conditions to persuade conservatives and members of the lower middle class that fascism offered a viable alternative. His words were backed by the actions of radical gangs of veterans and youths who terrorized the country. After the march on Rome in October, 1922, Mussolini became prime minister of a coalition government. It took him some time before he decided to establish an open dictatorship. Militant demands from within his own movement combined with an unwillingness to accept opposition from the old parties led to the termination of the parliamentary façade in 1924.

Although action and propaganda were the most important aspects of the fascist movement, Mussolini did encourage the development of a fascist ideology and experimented with corporatist ideas and institutions that created harmony between the social classes in theory while serving the interests of big business and the landowners in practice.

Nazism, the German variety of fascism, was much more demonic and ruthless than its Italian counterpart, but it combined many of the same forces and owed its success to many of the same causes. National Socialism was an attempt to combine the two chief forces contained in its name. It capitalized on both national and social resentments, and it employed the services of paramilitary organizations such as the S.A. and S.S., which were composed of veterans and young people. The movement had a strong appeal to groups in society who suffered from industrialization: craftsmen, white collar workers, retailers, peasants, and small businessmen. These groups suffered badly in the inflation of 1922–1923 and the depression of 1929–1933, and they resented the power of organized labor and big business. The movement had a special appeal for young people who craved action.

Adolf Hitler, the leader of the movement, was an Austrian of lower-middle-class origins. His political philosophy, set down in *Mein Kampf (My Struggle)* in 1924, was a remarkably arid combination of the anti-Semitic and Social Darwinist ideas developed by nationalist and pan-German thinkers and politicians. Hitler, however, was a brilliant politician and spellbinding orator with an uncanny ability to seize every opportunity that offered itself. After the abortive Munich Putsch of 1923, he resolved to take power legally because he recognized that he had to have the support, or at least the acceptance, of the army and conservative groups if he was to achieve power. The Nazis never received a majority in any of the elections between 1930 and 1933, but they did manage to become the largest party in the Reichstag in the July, 1932, elections. Military and conservative circles around President Hindenburg could not neglect the movement and deluded themselves into thinking they could tame it and use Hitler as a "drummer" for a nationalist and military revival. As a consequence of a series of intrigues, Hitler became chancellor of a right-wing coalition government in January, 1933. By July, 1933, he had eliminated his conservative allies from the cabinet, and one year later he was *Führer* of the Third Reich.

Purification of
the Socialist Movement

The failure of the Second International to prevent the outbreak of World War I or to employ the war for purposes of bringing about world revolution had wrecked that organization. The Bolsheviks were convinced that a new International, which rejected all compromise with the bourgeois order and supported the kind of political and organizational discipline that had enabled the Bolsheviks to succeed in Russia, was needed. The Third International was founded in 1919 and was composed of the oppositional socialist parties. After the defeat of the Hungarian Communist-Socialist regime, Lenin and the head of the Comintern, Zinoviev, became convinced that world revolution would never succeed if the revolutionary socialists continued to tolerate reformists ("opportunists") and permitted breaches of party discipline. The twenty-one conditions, passed at the Second Comintern Congress in 1920, were deliberately designed to split the socialist movement in Europe and purify it. The split did take place, but the conditions ultimately served to impose ideological conformity and inflexibility and were used by the Russian leaders of the Comintern to serve the interests of Russia rather than the cause of world revolution.

The Twenty-One Conditions for Admission
to the Third International, August 6, 1920

The second congress of the Communist International puts forward the following conditions of adherence to the Communist International:

1. *All propaganda and agitation* must be of a genuinely communist character and in conformity with the programme and decisions of the Communist International. The entire party press must be run by reliable communists who have proved their devotion to the cause of the proletariat. The dictatorship of the proletariat is to be treated not simply as a current formula learnt by rote; it must be advocated in a way which makes its necessity comprehensible to every ordinary working man and woman, every soldier and peasant, from the facts of their daily life, which must be systematically noted in our press and made use of every day.

The periodical press and other publications, and all party publishing houses, must be completely subordinated to the party presidium, re-

From *The Communist International, 1919–1943*, ed. Jane Degras, vol. 1 (London: Oxford University Press, 1956), pp. 168–72. Published under the auspices of the Royal Institute of International Affairs. Reprinted by permission of Oxford University Press.

gardless of whether the party as a whole is at the given moment legal or illegal. Publishing houses must not be allowed to abuse their independence and pursue a policy which is not wholly in accordance with the policy of the party.

In the columns of the press, at popular meetings, the trade unions and co-operatives, wherever the adherents of the Communist International have an entry, it is necessary to denounce, systematically and unrelentingly, not only the bourgeoisie, but also their assistants, the reformists of all shades.

2. Every organization which wishes to join the Communist International must, in an orderly and planned fashion, remove reformists and centrists from all responsible positions in the workers' movement (party organizations, editorial boards, trade unions, parliamentary fractions, co-operatives, local government bodies) and replace them by tried communists, even if, particularly at the beginning, 'experienced' opportunists have to be replaced by ordinary rank and file workers.

3. In practically every country of Europe and America the class struggle is entering the phase of civil war. In these circumstances communists can have no confidence in bourgeois legality. They are obliged everywhere to create a parallel illegal organization which at the decisive moment will help the party to do its duty to the revolution. In all those countries where, because of a state of siege or of emergency laws, communists are unable to do all their work legally, it is absolutely essential to combine legal and illegal work.

4. The obligation to spread communist ideas includes the special obligation to carry on systematic and energetic propaganda in the army. Where such agitation is prevented by emergency laws, it must be carried on illegally. Refusal to undertake such work would be tantamount to a dereliction of revolutionary duty and is incompatible with membership of the Communist International.

5. Systematic and well-planned agitation must be carried on in the countryside. The working class cannot consolidate its victory if it has not by its policy assured itself of the support of at least part of the rural proletariat and the poorest peasants, and of the neutrality of part of the rest of the rural population. At the present time communist work in rural areas is acquiring first-rate importance. It should be conducted primarily with the help of revolutionary communist urban and rural workers who have close connexions with the countryside. To neglect this work or to leave it in unreliable semi-reformist hands, is tantamount to renouncing the proletarian revolution.

6. Every party which wishes to join the Communist International is obliged to expose not only avowed social-patriotism, but also the insincerity and hypocrisy of social-pacifism; to bring home to the workers systematically that without the revolutionary overthrow of capitalism no international court of arbitration, no agreement to limit armaments, no

'democratic' reorganization of the League of Nations, will be able to prevent new imperialist wars.

7. Parties which wish to join the Communist International are obliged to recognize the necessity for a complete and absolute break with reformism and with the policy of the 'centre,' and to advocate this break as widely as possible among their members. Without that no consistent communist policy is possible.

The Communist International demands unconditionally and categorically that this break be effected as quickly as possible. The Communist International is unable to agree that notorious opportunists, such as Turati, Modigliani, Kautsky, Hilferding, Hilquit, Longuet, MacDonald, etc., shall have the right to appear as members of the Communist International. That could only lead to the Communist International becoming in many respects similar to the Second International, which has gone to pieces.

8. A particularly explicit and clear attitude on the question of the colonies and the oppressed peoples is necessary for the parties in those countries where the bourgeoisie possess colonies and oppress other nations. Every party which wishes to join the Communist International is obliged to expose the tricks and dodges of 'its' imperialists in the colonies, to support every colonial liberation movement not merely in words but in deeds, to demand the expulsion of their own imperialists from these colonies, to inculcate among the workers of their country a genuinely fraternal attitude to the working people of the colonies and the oppressed nations, and to carry on systematic agitation among the troops of their country against any oppression of the colonial peoples.

9. Every party which wishes to join the Communist International must carry on systematic and persistent communist activity inside the trade unions, the workers' councils and factory committees, the co-operatives, and other mass workers' organizations. Within these organizations communist cells must be organized which shall by persistent and unflagging work win the trade unions, etc., for the communist cause. In their daily work the cells must everywhere expose the treachery of the social-patriots and the instability of the 'centre.' The communist cells must be completely subordinate to the party as a whole.

10. Every party belonging to the Communist International is obliged to wage an unyielding struggle against the Amsterdam 'International' of the yellow trade unions. It must conduct the most vigorous propaganda among trade unionists for the necessity of a break with the yellow Amsterdam International. It must do all it can to support the international association of red trade unions, adhering to the Communist International, which is being formed.

11. Parties which wish to join the Communist International are obliged to review the personnel of their parliamentary fractions and remove all unreliable elements, to make these fractions not only verbally

but in fact subordinate to the party presidium, requiring of each individual communist member of parliament that he subordinate his entire activity to the interests of genuinely revolutionary propaganda and agitation.

12. Parties belonging to the Communist International must be based on the principle of *democratic centralism*. In the present epoch of acute civil war the communist party will be able to fulfil its duty only if its organization is as centralized as possible, if iron discipline prevails, and if the party centre, upheld by the confidence of the party membership, has strength and authority and is equipped with the most comprehensive powers.

13. Communist parties in those countries where communists carry on their work legally must from time to time undertake cleansing (re-registration) of the membership of the party in order to get rid of any petty-bourgeois elements which have crept in.

14. Every party which wishes to join the Communist International is obliged to give unconditional support to any Soviet republic in its struggle against counter-revolutionary forces. Communist parties must carry on unambiguous propaganda to prevent the dispatch of munitions transports to the enemies of the Soviet republics; they must also carry on propaganda by every means, legal or illegal, among the troops sent to strangle workers' republics.

15. Parties which still retain their old social-democratic programmes are obliged to revise them as quickly as possible, and to draw up, in accordance with the special conditions of their country, a new communist programme in conformity with the decisions of the Communist International. As a rule the programme of every party belonging to the Communist International must be ratified by the regular congress of the Communist International or by the Executive Committee. Should the programme of a party not be ratified by the ECCI, the party concerned has the right to appeal to the congress of the Communist International.

16. All the decisions of the congresses of the Communist International, as well as the decisions of its Executive Committee, are binding on all parties belonging to the Communist International. The Communist International, working in conditions of acute civil war, must be far more centralized in its structure than was the Second International. Consideration must of course be given by the Communist International and its Executive Committee in all their activities to the varying conditions in which the individual parties have to fight and work, and they must take decisions of general validity only when such decisions are possible.

17. In this connexion, all parties which wish to join the Communist International must change their names. Every party which wishes to join the Communist International must be called: *Communist* party of such and such a country (section of the Communist International). This question of name is not merely a formal matter, but essentially a politi-

cal question of great importance. The Communist International has declared war on the entire bourgeois world and on all yellow social-democratic parties. The difference between the communist parties and the old official 'social-democratic' or 'socialist' parties, which have betrayed the banner of the working class, must be brought home to every ordinary worker.

18. All leading party press organs in all countries are obliged to publish all important official documents of the Executive Committee of the Communist International.

19. All parties belonging to the Communist International and those which have applied for admission, are obliged to convene an extraordinary congress as soon as possible, and in any case not later than four months after the second congress of the Communist International, to examine all these conditions of admission. In this connexion all party centres must see that the decisions of the second congress of the Communist International are made known to all local organizations.

20. Those parties which now wish to join the Communist International, but which have not radically changed their former tactics, must see to it that, before entering the Communist International, not less than two-thirds of the members of their central committee and of all their leading central bodies consist of comrades who publicly and unambiguously advocated the entry of their party into the Communist International before its second congress. Exceptions can be made with the consent of the Executive Committee of the Communist International. The ECCI also has the right to make exceptions in the case of representatives of the centre mentioned in paragraph 7.

21. Those members of the party who reject in principle the conditions and theses put forward by the Communist International are to be expelled from the party.

The same applies in particular to delegates to the extraordinary congresses.

The Soviet Constitution of 1936

On November 25, 1936, Stalin reported to the Special Eighth All-Union Congress of Soviets on the new constitution, which replaced that of 1924. The new constitution was supposed to be more democratic than its predecessor. It contained a long bill of rights and opened the ballot to all citizens, not just workers and peasants. It also confirmed the existence of only one political party. Stalin justified the extension of the ballot on the grounds that his collectivization and other policies had eliminated kulaks (independent peasants allowed to own land under the New Economic Policy) and other "exploiters." The federal character of the Soviet Union was confirmed, and the various nationalities received important cultural and administrative rights. Politically and economically, however, the system remained as centralized as ever. The value of the constitution seems to have been mainly propagandistic. As Stalin's speech shows, it was used to demonstrate that his policies had brought the Soviet Union to a higher stage of development where a more advanced type of constitution became both necessary and justifiable. At the same time, the constitution was a useful propaganda weapon in the arsenal against fascism.

Stalin: On the Draft Constitution

What changes in the life of the U.S.S.R. have been brought about in the period from 1924 to 1936 which the Constitution Commission was to reflect in its Draft Constitution?

What is the essence of these changes?

What was the situation in 1924?

This was the first period of the New Economic Policy, when the Soviet government permitted some revival of capitalism while taking all measures to develop socialism; when it calculated, in the course of competition between the two systems of economy — the capitalist system and the socialist system — on securing the preponderance of the socialist system over the capitalist system. The task was, in the course of this competition, to consolidate the position of socialism, to achieve the liquidation of the capitalist elements and to consummate the victory of the socialist system as the fundamental system of national economy.

Our industry presented an unenviable picture at that time, particularly heavy industry. True, it was being gradually restored, but it had not yet raised its output to anywhere near the pre-war level. It was based on the old, backward and poorly equipped technique. Of course, it was developing in the direction of socialism. The proportion of the socialist sector of our industry at that time represented about 80 per cent of the whole. But the capitalist sector still controlled no less than 20 per cent of industry.

Our agriculture presented a still more unsightly picture. True, the landlord class had already been liquidated, but, on the other hand, the agricultural capitalist class, the kulak class, still represented a fairly considerable force. On the whole, agriculture at that time resembled a boundless ocean of small individual peasant farms with backward, medi-

From Joseph Stalin, *On the New Soviet Constitution,* pp. 3–6, 9–17, 19–20, 22–23. Reprinted by permission of International Publishers Co., Inc.

aeval technical equipment. In this ocean, like small dots and islands, were the collective farms and state farms, which strictly speaking, did not yet have any serious significance in our national economy. The collective farms and state farms were weak, while the kulak was still strong. At that time we spoke not of liquidating the kulaks, but of restricting them.

The same must be said about trade in the country. The socialist sector in trade represented some 50 or 60 per cent, not more, while all the rest of the field was occupied by merchants, profiteers and other private traders.

Such was the picture our economy presented in 1924.

What is the situation now, in 1936?

At that time we were in the first period of the New Economic Policy, the beginning of the New Economic Policy, the period of some revival of capitalism; now, however, we are in the last period of the New Economic Policy, the end of the New Economic Policy, the period of the complete liquidation of capitalism in all spheres of national economy.

To begin with, there is, say, the fact that during this period our industry has grown into a gigantic force. Now it can no longer be described as weak and technically ill-equipped. On the contrary, it is now based on new, rich, modern technical equipment, with a powerfully developed heavy industry and an even more developed machine building industry. But the most important thing is that capitalism has been banished entirely from the sphere of our industry, while the socialist form of production is now the system which has undivided sway in the sphere of our industry. The fact that as regards volume of output our present socialist industry exceeds that of pre-war industry more than sevenfold cannot be regarded as a trifle.

In the sphere of agriculture, instead of the ocean of small individual peasant farms with their poor technical equipment and strong kulak influence, we now have mechanized production, conducted on a scale larger than anywhere else in the world, with up-to-date technical equipment, in the form of an all-embracing system of collective farms and state farms. Everybody knows that the kulak class has been liquidated in agriculture, while the sector of small individual peasant farms, with its backward, mediaeval technical equipment, now occupies an insignificant place; and its proportion in agriculture as regards area of cultivation does not amount to more than two or three per cent. We must not overlook the fact that the collective farms now have at their disposal 316,000 tractors with a total of 5,700,000 horse power, and, together with the state farms, a total of over 400,000 tractors of 7,580,000 horse power.

As for trade in the country, the merchants and profiteers have been banished entirely from this sphere. All trade is now in the hands of the state, the cooperative societies and the collective farms. A new, Soviet trade, trade without profiteers, trade without capitalists has arisen and developed.

Thus the complete victory of the socialist system in all spheres of national economy is now a fact.

And what does this mean?

It means that the exploitation of man by man has been abolished, liquidated, while the socialist ownership of the implements and means of production has been established as the unshakable foundation of our Soviet society. [*Prolonged applause.*]

As a result of all these changes in the sphere of the national economy of the U.S.S.R., we now have a new, socialist economy, which knows neither crises nor unemployment, which knows neither poverty nor ruin, and which provides citizens with every opportunity to lead a prosperous and cultured life. . . .

What do these changes signify?

Firstly, they signify that the dividing line between the working class and the peasantry, and between these classes and the intelligentsia, is being obliterated, while the old class exclusiveness is disappearing. This means that the distance between these social groups is steadily diminishing.

Secondly, they signify that the economic contradictions between these social groups are subsiding, are becoming obliterated.

And lastly, they signify that the political contradictions between them are also subsiding and becoming obliterated.

Such is the position in regard to the changes in the sphere of the *class structure* of the U.S.S.R.

The picture of the changes in the social life of the U.S.S.R. would be incomplete if a few words were not said about the changes in yet another sphere. I refer to the sphere of *national* relationships in the U.S.S.R. As you know, within the Soviet Union there are about sixty nations, national groups and nationalities. The Soviet state is a multi-national state. Clearly, the question of the relations between the peoples of the U.S.S.R. cannot but be one of first rate importance for us. . . .

By the absence of exploiting classes, which are the principal organizers of strife between nations; the absence of exploitation, which cultivates mutual distrust and kindles nationalist passions; the fact that power is in the hands of the working class, which is an enemy of all enslavement and the true vehicle of the ideas of internationalism; the actual practice of mutual aid among the peoples in all spheres of economic and social life; and, finally, the flourishing national culture of the peoples of the U.S.S.R., culture which is national in form and socialist in content — all these and similar factors have brought about a radical change in the aspect of the peoples of the U.S.S.R.; their feeling of mutual distrust has disappeared, a feeling of mutual friendship has developed among them, and thus, real fraternal cooperation between the peoples was established within the system of a single federated state.

As a result, we now have a fully formed multi-national socialist state, which has stood all tests, and the stability of which might well be envied by any national state in any part of the world. [*Loud applause.*]

Such are the changes which have taken place during this period in the sphere of *national relations* in the U.S.S.R.

Such is the sum total of changes which have taken place in the sphere of the economic and social-political life in the U.S.S.R. in the period from 1924 to 1936. . . .

How are all these changes in the life of the U.S.S.R. reflected in the draft of the new Constitution?

In other words: What are the principal specific features of the Draft Constitution that is submitted for consideration to the present Congress?

The Constitution Commission was instructed to amend the text of the Constitution of 1924. The work of the Constitution Commission has resulted in a new text of the Constitution, a draft of a new Constitution of the U.S.S.R. In drafting the new Constitution, the Constitution Commission proceeded from the assumption that a Constitution must not be confused with a program. This means that there is an essential difference between a program and a Constitution. While a program speaks of what does not yet exist, of what has yet to be achieved and won in the future, a Constitution, on the contrary, must speak of what already exists, of what has already been achieved and won now, at the present time. A program deals mainly with the future, a Constitution with the present.

Two examples by way of illustration.

Our Soviet society has already, in the main, succeeded in achieving socialism; it has created a socialist system, *i.e.*, it has brought about what Marxists in other words call the first, or lower phase of communism. Hence, in the main, we have already achieved the first phase of communism, socialism. [*Prolonged applause.*] The fundamental principle of this phase of communism is, as you know, the formula: "From each according to his ability, to each according to his work." Should our Constitution reflect this fact, the fact that socialism has been achieved? Should it be based on this achievement? Undoubtedly, it should. It should, because for the U.S.S.R., socialism is something already achieved and won.

But Soviet society has not yet reached the higher phase of communism, in which the ruling principle will be the formula: "From each according to his ability, to each according to his needs," although it sets itself the aim of achieving the higher phase of communism in the future. Can our Constitution be based on the higher phase of communism, which does not yet exist and which has still to be achieved? No, it cannot, because for the U.S.S.R. the higher phase of communism is something that has not yet been achieved, and which has to be achieved in the future. It cannot, if it is not to be converted into a program or a declaration of future achievements.

Such are the limits of our Constitution at the present historical moment.

Thus the draft of the new Constitution is a summary of the path that has been traversed, a summary of the gains already achieved. Consequently, it is the registration and legislative consolidation of what has already been achieved and won in actual fact. [*Loud applause.*]

This is the first specific feature of the draft of the new Constitution of the U.S.S.R.

Further. The constitutions of bourgeois countries usually proceed from the conviction that the capitalist system is immutable. The main foundation of these constitutions consists of the principles of capitalism, of its main pillars: the private ownership of the land, forests, factories, works and other implements and means of production; the exploitation of man by man and the existence of exploiters and exploited; insecurity for the toiling majority at one pole of society, and luxury for the non-toiling but secured minority at the other pole, etc., etc. They rest on these and similar pillars of capitalism. They reflect them, they give them legislative consolidation.

Unlike these, the draft of the new Constitution of the U.S.S.R. proceeds from the fact that the capitalist system has been liquidated, from the fact that the socialist system is victorious in the U.S.S.R. The main foundation of the draft of the new Constitution of the U.S.S.R. consists of the principles of socialism, its main pillars, which have already been won and achieved: the socialist ownership of the land, forests, factories, works and other implements and means of production; the abolition of exploitation and of exploiting classes; the abolition of poverty for the majority and of luxury for the minority; the abolition of unemployment; work as an obligation and honourable duty for every able-bodied citizen, in accordance with the formula: "He who does not work, neither shall he eat." The right to work, *i.e.*, the right of every citizen to receive guaranteed employment; the right to rest and leisure; the right to education, etc., etc. The draft of the new Constitution rests on these and similar pillars of socialism. It reflects them, it gives them legislative consolidation.

Such is the second specific feature of the draft of the new Constitution.

Further. Bourgeois constitutions tacitly proceed from the premise that society consists of antagonistic classes, of classes which own wealth and classes which do not own wealth, that no matter what party comes into power the guidance of society by the state (the dictatorship) must be in the hands of the bourgeoisie, that a Constitution is needed for the purpose of consolidating a social order desired by and beneficial to the propertied classes.

Unlike bourgeois constitutions, the draft of the new Constitution of the U.S.S.R. proceeds from the fact that there are no longer any antagonistic classes in society, that society consists of two friendly classes, of workers and peasants, that it is these classes, the toiling classes, that are in power, that the guidance of society by the state (the dictatorship) is in the hands of the working class, the most advanced class in society, that a Constitution is needed for the purpose of consolidating a social order desired by and beneficial to the toilers.

Such is the third specific feature of the draft of the new Constitution.

Further. Bourgeois constitutions tacitly proceed from the premise that nations and races cannot have equal rights, that there are nations with full rights and nations without full rights, and that, in addition, there is a third category of nations or races, for example in the colonies, which have even fewer rights than the nations without full rights. This means that, at bottom, all these constitutions are nationalistic, *i.e.*, constitutions of ruling nations.

Unlike these constitutions, the draft of the new Constitution of the U.S.S.R. is, on the contrary, profoundly internationalistic. It proceeds from the fact that all nations and races have equal rights. It proceeds from the fact that neither difference in colour or language, cultural level or level of political development, nor any other difference between nations and races, can serve as grounds for justifying national inequality of rights. It proceeds from the fact that all nations and races, irrespective of their past and present position, irrespective of their strength or weakness, must enjoy equal rights in all spheres of the economic, social, political and cultural life of society.

Such is the fourth specific feature of the draft of the new Constitution.

The fifth specific feature of the draft of the new Constitution is its consistent and thoroughgoing democracy. From the standpoint of democracy bourgeois constitutions may be divided into two groups: one group of constitutions openly denies, or actually nullifies, the equality of rights of citizens and democratic liberties. The other group of constitutions readily accepts and even advertises democratic principles, but at the same time it makes reservations and limitations which utterly mutilate democratic rights and liberties. They speak of equal suffrage for all citizens, but in the same breath limit it by residential, educational and even property qualifications. They speak of equal rights for citizens, but in the same breath they make the reservation that this does not apply to women or only partly applies to them. And so on and so forth.

The specific feature of the draft of the new Constitution of the U.S.S.R. is that it is free from such reservations and limitations. For it, active and passive citizens do not exist; for it, all citizens are active. It does not recognize any difference in rights as between men and women, "residents" and "non-residents," propertied and propertyless, educated and uneducated. For it, all citizens have equal rights. It is not property status, not national origin, not sex, not office that determines the position of every citizen in society, but personal ability and personal labour.

Lastly, there is still one other specific feature of the draft of the new Constitution. Bourgeois constitutions usually confine themselves to fixing the formal rights of citizens without bothering about the conditions for exercising these rights, about the possibility of exercising them, about the means by which they can be exercised. They speak of the equality of citizens, but forget that there cannot be real equality between master and workman, between landlord and peasant, if the former possess wealth and political weight in society while the latter are deprived of both, if the former are exploiters while the latter are exploited. Or again: they speak of freedom of speech, assembly and the press, but forget that all these liberties may be merely a hollow sound for the working class if the latter cannot have access to suitable premises for meetings, good print-shops, a sufficient quantity of printing paper, etc.

The specific feature of the draft of the new Constitution is that it does not confine itself to fixing the formal rights of citizens, but shifts the centre of gravity to the guarantees of these rights, to the means by which these rights can be exercised. It does not simply proclaim equality of rights for citizens, but ensures it by the legislative consolidation of the fact that the regime of exploitation has been abolished, of the fact that the citizens have been emancipated from all exploitation. It does not simply proclaim the right to work, but ensures it by the legislative consolidation of the fact that crises do not exist in Soviet society, of the fact that unemployment has been abolished. It does not simply proclaim democratic liberties but legislatively ensures them by providing definite material resources. It is clear, therefore, that democracy in the draft of the new Constitution is not the "ordinary" and "universally recognized" democracy in general, but *socialist* democracy.

Such are the principal specific features of the draft of the new Constitution of the U.S.S.R.

Such is the reflection in the draft of the new Constitution of the progress and changes that have been brought about in the economic and social-political life of the U.S.S.R. in the period from 1924 to 1936.

The *second* group of critics admits that there really is such a thing as a Draft Constitution but considers that the draft is not of much interest because it is really not a Draft Constitution but a scrap of paper, an empty promise, calculated, by performing a certain manoeuvre, to deceive the people. . . .

In 1917 the peoples of the U.S.S.R. overthrew the bourgeoisie and established the dictatorship of the proletariat, established a Soviet government. This is a fact, not a promise.

Further, the Soviet government liquidated the landlord class and transferred to the peasants over 150,000,000 hectares of former landlord, government and monasterial lands, and this over and above the lands which were already in the possession of the peasants. This is a fact, not a promise.

Further, the Soviet government expropriated the capitalist class, took away their banks, factories, railways and other implements and means of production, declared them to be socialist property and placed at the head of these enterprises the best members of the working class. This is a fact, not a promise. [*Prolonged applause.*]

Further, having organized industry and agriculture on new, socialist lines, with a new technical base, the Soviet government has today attained the position where agriculture in the U.S.S.R. is producing one and a half times as much as was produced in pre-war times, that industry is producing seven times more than was produced in pre-war times and that the national income has increased fourfold compared with pre-war times. All these are facts, not promises. [*Prolonged applause.*]

Further, the Soviet government abolished unemployment, introduced the right to work, the right to rest and leisure, the right to education, provided better material and cultural conditions for the workers, peasants and intelligentsia and ensured the introduction of universal, direct and equal suffrage with secret ballots for its citizens. All these are facts, not promises. [*Prolonged applause.*]

Finally, the U.S.S.R. produced the draft of a new Constitution which is not a promise but the registration and legislative consolidation of these generally known facts, the registration and legislative consolidation of what has already been achieved and won. . . .

Finally, there is yet another group of crtics. While the last-mentioned group accuses the Draft Constitution of abandoning the dictatorship of the working class, this group, on the contrary, accuses it of not changing anything in the present situation in the U.S.S.R., of leaving the dictatorship of the working class intact, of not granting freedom to political parties and of preserving the present leading position of the Communist Party in the U.S.S.R. And this group of critics believes that the absence of freedom for parties in the U.S.S.R. is a symptom of the violation of the principles of democracy.

I must admit that the draft of the new Constitution really does preserve the regime of the dictatorship of the working class, just as it also preserves unchanged the present leading position of the Communist Party of the U.S.S.R. [*Loud applause.*] If our esteemed critics regard this as a flaw in the Draft Constitution, it is only to be regretted. We Bolsheviks regard it as a merit of the Draft Constitution. [*Loud applause.*]

As to freedom for various political parties, we adhere to somewhat different views. A party is a part of a class, its foremost part. Several parties, and, consequently, freedom for parties, can exist only in a society in which there are antagonistic classes whose interests are mutually hostile and irreconcilable, in which there are, say, capitalists and workers, landlords and peasants, kulaks and poor peasants, etc. But in the U.S.S.R. there are no longer such classes as capitalists, landlords, kulaks, etc. In the U.S.S.R. there are only two classes, workers and peasants, whose interests are not only not mutually hostile, but, on the contrary, are friendly. Consequently, in the U.S.S.R. there is no ground for the existence of several parties, and, consequently, for freedom for these parties. In the U.S.S.R. there is ground only for one party, the Communist Party. In the U.S.S.R. only one party can exist, the Communist Party, which courageously defends the interests of the workers and peasants to the very end. And that it defends the interests of these classes not at all badly is a matter about which there can hardly be any doubt. [*Loud applause.*]

They talk about democracy. But what is democracy? Democracy in capitalist countries, where there are antagonistic classes, is, in the last analysis, democracy for the strong, democracy for the propertied minority. In the U.S.S.R., on the contrary, democracy is democracy for the toilers, *i.e.,* democracy for all. But from this it follows that the principles of democracy are violated, not by the draft of the new Constitution of the U.S.S.R., but by the bourgeois constitutions. That is why I think that the Constitution of the U.S.S.R. is the only thoroughly democratic Constitution in the world.

Such is the position with regard to the bourgeois criticism of the draft of the new Constitution of the U.S.S.R. . . .

Benito Mussolini
and Fascism

An official exposition of the Italian fascist doctrine did not appear until 1932, which indicates that action was given primacy by Mussolini and his colleagues. The first part of "The Doctrine of Fascism" was written by Mussolini for the Enciclopedia Italiana. *It demonstrates the extent to which fascism was a reaction against liberalism and socialism, indeed against the values and ideals of the French Revolution as they became translated into nineteenth-century thought and practice. The positive aspects of the doctrine, in contrast, are quite vague, emphasizing "personality," "spirit," "unity," and "the nation."*

Mussolini's "Doctrine of Fascism"

1. Like every sound political conception, Fascism is both practice and thought; action in which a doctrine is immanent, and a doctrine which, arising out of a given system of historical forces, remains embedded in

From *The Social and Political Doctrine of Contemporary Europe,* ed. Michael Oakeshott (Cambridge: Cambridge University Press, 1939), pp. 164–68. Reprinted by permission of Cambridge University Press.

them and works there from within. Hence it has a form correlative to the contingencies of place and time, but it has also a content of thought which raises it to a formula of truth in the higher level of the history of thought. In the world one does not act spiritually as a human will dominating other wills without a conception of the transient and particular reality under which it is necessary to act, and of the permanent and universal reality in which the first has its being and its life. In order to know men it is necessary to know man; and in order to know man it is necessary to know reality and its laws. There is no concept of the State which is not fundamentally a concept of life: philosophy or intuition, a system of ideas which develops logically or is gathered up into a vision or into a faith, but which is always, at least virtually, an organic conception of the world.

2. Thus Fascism could not be understood in many of its practical manifestations as a party organization, as a system of education, as a discipline, if it were not always looked at in the light of its whole way of conceiving life, a spiritualized way. The world seen through Fascism is not this material world which appears on the surface, in which man is an individual separated from all others and standing by himself, and in which he is governed by a natural law that makes him instinctively live a life of selfish and momentary pleasure. The man of Fascism is an individual who is nation and fatherland, which is a moral law, binding together individuals and the generations into a tradition and a mission, suppressing the instinct for a life enclosed within the brief round of pleasure in order to restore within duty a higher life free from the limits of time and space: a life in which the individual, through the denial of himself, through the sacrifice of his own private interests, through death itself, realizes that completely spiritual existence in which his value as a man lies.

3. Therefore it is a spiritualized conception, itself the result of the general reaction of modern times against the flabby materialistic positivism of the nineteenth century. Anti-positivistic, but positive: not sceptical, nor agnostic, nor pessimistic, nor passively optimistic, as are, in general, the doctrines (all negative) that put the centre of life outside man, who with his free will can and must create his own world. Fascism desires an active man, one engaged in activity with all his energies: it desires a man virilely conscious of the difficulties that exist in action and ready to face them. It conceives of life as a struggle, considering that it behoves man to conquer for himself that life truly worthy of him, creating first of all in himself the instrument (physical, moral, intellectual) in order to construct it. Thus for the single individual, thus for the nation, thus for humanity. Hence the high value of culture in all its forms (art, religion, science), and the enormous importance of education. Hence also the essential value of work, with which man conquers nature and creates the human world (economic, political, moral, intellectual).

4. This positive conception of life is clearly an ethical conception. It covers the whole of reality, not merely the human activity which controls it. No action can be divorced from moral judgement; there is nothing in the world which can be deprived of the value which belongs to everything in its relation to moral ends. Life, therefore, as conceived by the Fascist, is serious, austere, religious: the whole of it is poised in a world supported by the moral and responsible forces of the spirit. The Fascist disdains the "comfortable" life.

5. Fascism is a religious conception in which man is seen in his immanent relationship with a superior law and with an objective Will that transcends the particular individual and raises him to conscious membership of a spiritual society. Whoever has seen in the religious politics of the Fascist regime nothing but mere opportunism has not understood that Fascism besides being a system of government is also, and above all, a system of thought.

6. Fascism is an historical conception, in which man is what he is only in so far as he works with the spiritual process in which he finds himself, in the family or social group, in the nation and in the history in which all nations collaborate. From this follows the great value of tradition, in memories, in language, in customs, in the standards of social life. Outside history man is nothing. Consequently Fascism is opposed to all the individualistic abstractions of a materialistic nature like those of the eighteenth century; and it is opposed to all Jacobin utopias and innovations. It does not consider that "happiness" is possible upon earth, as it appeared to be in the desire of the economic literature of the eighteenth century, and hence it rejects all teleological theories according to which mankind would reach a definitive stabilized condition at a certain period in history. This implies putting oneself outside history and life, which is a continual change and coming to be. Politically, Fascism wishes to be a realistic doctrine; practically, it aspires to solve only the problems which arise historically of themselves and that of themselves find or suggest their own solution. To act among men, as to act in the natural world, it is necessary to enter into the process of reality and to master the already operating forces.

7. Against individualism, the Fascist conception is for the State; and it is for the individual in so far as he coincides with the State, which is the conscience and universal will of man in his historical existence. It is opposed to classical Liberalism, which arose from the necessity of reacting against absolutism, and which brought its historical purpose to an end when the State was transformed into the conscience and will of the people. Liberalism denied the State in the interests of the particular individual; Fascism reaffirms the State as the true reality of the individual. And if liberty is to be the attribute of the real man, and not of that abstract puppet envisaged by individualistic Liberalism, Fascism is for liberty. And for the only liberty which can be a real thing, the liberty of

the State and of the individual within the State. Therefore, for the Fascist, everything is in the State, and nothing human or spiritual exists, much less has value, outside the State. In this sense Fascism is totalitarian, and the Fascist State, the synthesis and unity of all values, interprets, develops and gives strength to the whole life of the people.

8. Outside the State there can be neither individuals nor groups (political parties, associations, syndicates, classes). Therefore Fascism is opposed to Socialism, which confines the movement of history within the class struggle and ignores the unity of classes established in one economic and moral reality in the State; and analogously it is opposed to class syndicalism. Fascism recognizes the real exigencies for which the socialist and syndicalist movement arose, but while recognizing them wishes to bring them under the control of the State and give them a purpose within the corporative system of interests reconciled within the unity of the State.

9. Individuals form classes according to the similarity of their interests, they form syndicates according to differentiated economic activities within these interests; but they form first, and above all, the State, which is not to be thought of numerically as the sum-total of individuals forming the majority of a nation. And consequently Fascism is opposed to Democracy, which equates the nation to the majority, lowering it to the level of that majority; nevertheless it is the purest form of democracy if the nation is conceived, as it should be, qualitatively and not quantitatively, as the most powerful idea (most powerful because most moral, most coherent, most true) which acts within the nation as the conscience and the will of a few, even of One, which ideal tends to become active within the conscience and the will of all — that is to say, of all those who rightly constitute a nation by reason of nature, history or race, and have set out upon the same line of development and spiritual formation as one conscience and one sole will. Not a race, nor a geographically determined region, but as a community historically perpetuating itself, a multitude unified by a single idea, which is the will to existence and to power: consciousness of itself, personality.

10. This higher personality is truly the nation in so far as it is the State. It is not the nation that generates the State, as according to the old naturalistic concept which served as the basis of the political theories of the national States of the nineteenth century. Rather the nation is created by the State, which gives to the people, conscious of its own moral unity, a will and therefore an effective existence. The right of a nation to independence derives not from a literary and ideal consciousness of its own being, still less from a more or less unconscious and inert acceptance of a *de facto* situation, but from an active consciousness, from a political will in action and ready to demonstrate its own rights: that is to say, from a state already coming into being. The State, in fact, as the universal ethical will, is the creator of right.

11. The nation as the State is an ethical reality which exists and lives in so far as it develops. To arrest its development is to kill it. Therefore the State is not only the authority which governs and gives the form of laws and the value of spiritual life to the wills of individuals, but it is also a power that makes its will felt abroad, making it known and respected, in other words, demonstrating the fact of its universality in all the necessary directions of its development. It is consequently organization and expansion, at least virtually. Thus it can be likened to the human will which knows no limits to its development and realizes itself in testing its own limitlessness.

12. The Fascist State, the highest and most powerful form of personality, is a force, but a spiritual force, which takes over all the forms of the moral and intellectual life of man. It cannot therefore confine itself simply to the functions of order and supervision as Liberalism desired. It is not simply a mechanism which limits the sphere of the supposed liberties of the individual. It is the form, the inner standard and the discipline of the whole person; it saturates the will as well as the intelligence. Its principle, the central inspiration of the human personality living in the civil community, pierces into the depths and makes its home in the heart of the man of action as well as of the thinker, of the artist as well as of the scientist: it is the soul of the soul.

13. Fascism, in short, is not only the giver of laws and the founder of institutions, but the educator and promoter of spiritual life. It wants to remake, not the forms of human life, but its content, man, character, faith. And to this end it requires discipline and authority that can enter into the spirits of men and there govern unopposed. Its sign, therefore, is the Lictors' rods, the symbol of unity, of strength and justice.

Nazism

Hitler was working as a right-wing agitator and propagandist for the army in Munich when he came upon the National Socialist German Workers' party, one of many extreme nationalist and racist groups that had established themselves in Munich in 1919. Hitler joined and speedily became leader of this then obscure organization. The program of the party, written by Gottfried Feder, an engineer and economic crank, reflected the peculiar mixture of antimodern, extreme nationalist, and anti-Semitic views of the party's lower-middle-class membership. Hitler cared little about the program, which he subsequently declared unalterable, but some aspects of it caused him embarrassment, as did the revolutionary slogans and violence of the S.A., in his efforts to win support from the army and conservative social groups.

Businessmen were particularly suspicious and often compared the Nazis to the Communists. On January 27, 1932, Hitler addressed the Düsseldorf Industry Club, an organization comparable in the wealth and importance of its members to the Commonwealth Club that Roosevelt addressed nine months later. The speech was one of Hitler's most brilliant performances and demonstrates how he managed to reassure and even render conservatives enthusiastic. In contrast to Stresemann, Hitler was convinced that internal stability could not be created by a successful foreign policy, but rather that a successful domestic policy would pave the way for the solution of Germany's international problems. He assured his listeners of his belief in individualism and achievement, played upon their fear of communism, and in a crescendo at the end appealed to their nationalistic sentiments. He modestly accepted the role of a "drummer" in a higher cause and thus fed the conservative delusion that he could be tamed.

The Nazi Program, Munich, February 24, 1920

The programme of the German Workers' Party is limited as to period. The leaders have no intention, once the aims announced in it have been achieved, of setting up fresh ones, so as to ensure the continued existence of the Party by the artificially increased discontent of the masses.

1. We demand, on the basis of the right of national self-determination, the union of all Germans to form one Great Germany.

2. We demand juridical equality for the German people in its dealings with other nations, and the abolition of the Peace Treaties of Versailles and St Germain.

3. We demand territory and soil (colonies) for the nourishment of our people and for settling our surplus population.

4. None but members of the nation may be citizens of the State. None but those of German blood, whatever their creed, may be members of the nation. No Jew, therefore, may be considered a member of the nation.

5. Anyone who is not a citizen of the State may live in Germany only as a guest and must be regarded as subject to the laws governing aliens.

6. The right to determine the leadership and laws of the State is to be enjoyed by the citizens of the State alone. We demand, therefore, that all official appointments of whatever kind, whether in the Reich, in the one or other of the federal states, or in the municipalities, shall be held by citizens of the State alone.

We oppose the corrupt Parliamentary custom of filling public offices

From *The Social and Political Doctrine of Contemporary Europe*, ed. Michael Oakeshott (Cambridge: Cambridge University Press, 1939), pp. 190–93. Reprinted by permission of Cambridge University Press.

merely with a view to party considerations, and without reference to character or capacity.

7. We demand that the State shall make it one of its chief duties to provide work and the means of livelihood for the citizens of the State. If it is not possible to provide for the entire population living within the confines of the State, foreign nationals (non-citizens of the State) must be excluded (expatriated).

8. All further non-German immigration must be prevented. We demand that all non-Germans who have entered Germany subsequently to 2 August 1914 shall be required forthwith to depart from the Reich.

9. All citizens of the State shall be equal as regards rights and duties.

10. It must be the first duty of every citizen of the State to work with his mind or with his body. The activities of the individual must not clash with the interests of the whole, but must be pursued within the framework of the national activity and must be for the general good.

11. We demand, therefore, the abolition of incomes unearned by work, and emancipation from the slavery of interest charges.

12. Because of the enormous sacrifice of life and property demanded of a nation by every war, personal profit through war must be regarded as a crime against the nation. We demand, therefore, the complete confiscation of all war profits.

13. We demand the nationalization of all business combines (trusts).

14. We demand that the great industries shall be organized on a profit-sharing basis.

15. We demand an extensive development of provision for old age.

16. We demand the creation and maintenance of a healthy middle class; the immediate communalization of the big department stores and the lease of the various departments at a low rate to small traders, and that the greatest consideration shall be shown to all small traders supplying goods to the State, the federal states or the municipalities.

17. We demand a programme of land reform suitable to our national requirements, the enactment of a law for confiscation without compensation of land for communal purposes, the abolition of ground rents, and the prohibition of all speculation in land.

18. We demand a ruthless campaign against all whose activities are injurious to the common interest. Oppressors of the nation, usurers, profiteers, etc., must be punished with death, whatever their creed or race.

19. We demand that the Roman Code, which serves the materialistic world order, shall be replaced by a system of German Common Law.

20. The State must undertake a thorough reconstruction of our national system of education, with the aim of giving to every capable and industrious German the benefits of a higher education and therewith the capacity to take his place in the leadership of the nation. The curricula of all educational establishments must be brought into line with the

necessities of practical life. With the first dawn of intelligence, the schools must aim at teaching the pupil to know what the State stands for (instruction in citizenship). We demand educational facilities for specially gifted children of poor parents, whatever their class or occupation, at the expense of the State.

21. The State must concern itself with raising the standard of health in the nation by exercising its guardianship over mothers and infants, by prohibiting child labour, and by increasing bodily efficiency by legally obligatory gymnastics and sports, and by the extensive support of clubs engaged in the physical training of the young.

22. We demand the abolition of a paid army and the foundation of a national army.

23. We demand legal measures against intentional political lies and their dissemination in the Press. In order to facilitate the creation of a German national Press, we demand:

(a) that all editors of newspapers and all contributors, employing the German language, shall be members of the nation;

(b) that special permission from the State shall be necessary before non-German newspapers may appear. These must not be printed in the German language;

(c) that non-Germans shall be prohibited by law from participation financially in, or from influencing German newspapers, and that the penalty for contravention of this law shall be suppression of any such newspaper and the immediate deportation of the non-German concerned in it.

It must be forbidden to publish newspapers which do not conduce to the national welfare. We demand the legal prosecution of all tendencies in art and literature of a kind calculated to disintegrate our national life, and the suppression of institutions which militate against the above-mentioned requirements.

24. We demand liberty for all religious denominations in the State, in so far as they are not a danger to it and do not militate against the moral sense of the German race.

The Party, as such, stands for a positive Christianity, but does not bind itself in the matter of creed to any particular confession. It is strenuously opposed to the Jewish-materialist spirit within and without the Party, and is convinced that our nation can only achieve permanent well-being from within on the principle of placing the common interests before self-interest.

25. That all the foregoing demands may be realized, we demand the creation of a strong central power of the Reich; the unconditional authority of the central Parliament over the entire Reich and its organization; the formation of Diets and vocational Chambers for the purpose of administering in the various federal States the general laws promulgated by the Reich.

The leaders of the Party swear to proceed regardless of consequences — if necessary to sacrifice their lives — in securing the fulfilment of the foregoing points.

Hitler's Speech to the Düsseldorf Industry Club, January 27, 1932

If to-day the National Socialist Movement is regarded amongst widespread circles in Germany as being hostile to our business life, I believe the reason for this view is to be found in the fact that we adopted towards the events which determined the development leading to our present position an attitude which differed from that of all the other organizations which are of any importance in our public life. Even now our outlook differs in many points from that of our opponents.

Our conviction is that our present distress has not its final and deepest cause in general world-happenings which would therefore from the outset more or less exclude any possibility for a single people to better its position. If it were true that the cause of distress in Germany is to be found solely in a so-called world-crisis from which none can escape — a world-crisis on the course of which we as a people could naturally exercise no influence or at best only an infinitesimal influence — then we should be forced to characterize Germany's future as hopeless. How should a state of affairs be altered for which no one is directly responsible? In my judgement the view that the world-crisis is solely responsible must as its result lead to a dangerous pessimism. It is but natural that the more the causes of a particular state of affairs are withdrawn from any possibility of improvement through the efforts of individuals, the more the individual will despair of ever being able to alter such a state of affairs. And the consequence must gradually be a certain lethargy, an indifference, and in the end perhaps despair.

I regard it as of the first importance to break once and for all with the view that our destiny is conditioned by world-events. It is not true that our distress has its final cause in a world-crisis, in a world-catastrophe: the true view is that we have reached a state of general crisis, because from the first certain mistakes were made. I must not say "According to the general view the Peace Treaty of Versailles is the cause of our misfortune." What is the Peace Treaty of Versailles but the work of men? It is not a burden which has been imposed or laid upon us by Providence. It is the work of men for which, it goes without saying, once again men with their merits or their feelings must be held responsible.

From *The Speeches of Adolf Hitler, April 1922–August 1939*, vol. 2, ed. Norman H. Baynes (Oxford: Oxford University Press, 1942), pp. 777–88, 826–29. Published under the auspices of the Royal Institute of International Affairs. Reprinted by permission of Oxford University Press.

If this were not so, how should men ever be able to set aside this work at all? I am of the opinion that there is nothing which has been produced by the will of man which cannot in its turn be altered by another human will.

Both the Peace Treaty of Versailles together with all the consequences of that Treaty have been the result of a policy which perhaps fifteen, fourteen, or thirteen years ago was regarded as the right policy, at least in the enemy-States, but which from our point of view was bound to be regarded as fatal when ten or less years ago its true character was disclosed to millions of Germans and now to-day stands revealed in its utter impossibility. I am bound therefore to assert that there must of necessity have been in Germany, too, some responsibility for these happenings if I am to have any belief that the German people can exercise some influence towards changing these conditions.

It is also in my view false to say that life in Germany to-day is solely determined by considerations of foreign policy, that the primacy of foreign policy governs to-day the whole of our domestic life. Certainly a people can reach the point when foreign relations influence and determine completely its domestic life. But let no one say that such a condition is from the first either natural or desirable. Rather the important thing is that a people should create the conditions for a change in this state of affairs.

If anyone says to me that its foreign politics is primarily decisive for the life of a people, then I must first ask: what then is the meaning of the term "Politics"? There is a whole series of definitions. Frederick the Great said "Politics is the art of serving one's State with every means." Bismarck's explanation was that "Politics is the Art of the Possible," starting from the conception that advantage should be taken of every possibility to serve the State — and, in the later transformation of the idea of the State into the idea of nationalities, the Nation. Another considers that this service rendered to the people can be effected by military as well as peaceful action: for Clausewitz says that war is the continuation of politics though with different means. Conversely, Clemenceau considers that to-day peace is nothing but the continuation of war and the pursuing of the war-aim, though again with other means. To put it briefly: politics is nothing else and can be nothing else than the safeguarding of a people's vital interests and the practical waging of its life-battle with every means. Thus it is quite clear that this life-battle from the first has its starting-point in the people itself and that at the same time the people is the object — the real thing of value — which has to be preserved. All functions of this body formed by the people must in the last resort fulfil only one purpose — to secure in the future the maintenance of this body which is the people. I can therefore say neither that foreign policy nor economic policy is of primary significance. Of course a people needs the business world in order to live. But business

is but one of the functions of this body-politic whereby its existence is
assured. But primarily the essential thing is the starting-point and that is
the people itself.

One must not say that foreign politics is the factor which decisively
determines a people's path, but one must rather say that it is primarily
the people which itself, through its inner value, through its organization,
and through its education into this inner value, marks out its own path
within the world by which it is surrounded. I must not say that foreign
politics could ever alter in essentials the value of a people: rather I must
say: every people has to wage the battle for the safeguarding of its interests that can wage that battle only which corresponds to its most
essential character, its value, its capacities, the effectiveness of its organization, &c. Naturally foreign relations will also once more react upon
a people. But we know from experience what a difference there is in the
way individual peoples react to foreign relations! The reaction is determined through the inner disposition, the inner value, through the
inborn talents and capacities of each people. I am therefore able to state
that even when the fundamental value of a nation remains unchanged,
alterations in the inner organization of the life of this nation can of
themselves lead to a change in its attitude to foreign relations.

It is therefore false to say that foreign politics shapes a people: rather,
peoples order their relations to the world about them in correspondence
with their inborn forces according to the measure in which their education enables them to bring those forces into play. We may be quite convinced that if in the place of the Germany of to-day there had stood a
different Germany, the attitude towards the rest of the world would also
have been different, and then presumably the influences exercised by the
rest of the world would have taken a different form. To deny this would
mean that Germany's destiny can no longer be changed no matter what
Government rules in Germany. If such a view is held, one can immediately find its root and its explanation: assertions that a people's
fate is solely determined by foreign Powers have always formed the shifts
of bad Governments. Weak and bad Governments have at all times
made play with this argument in order thus to excuse and explain their
own failure and that of their predecessors, the failure of their whole
stereotyped and traditional mode of thought: their plea has always been,
"Anyone else in our position could not have done otherwise": for what
could he begin to do with his people in the face of conditions which are
fixed once for all and have their roots in the world beyond Germany's
frontiers — so long as, quite naturally, he regards his people, too, as a
factor whose value cannot change?

And as against this conception I am the champion of another standpoint: three factors, I hold, essentially determine a people's political
life:

First, the inner value of a people which as an inherited sum and possession is transmitted again and again through the generations, a value which suffers any change when the people, the custodian of this inherited possession, changes itself in its inner blood-conditioned composition. It is beyond question that certain traits of character, certain virtues, and certain vices always recur in peoples so long as their inner nature — their blood-conditioned composition — has not essentially altered. I can already trace the virtues and vices of our German people in the writers of Rome just as clearly as I see them to-day. This inner value which determines the life of a people can be destroyed by nothing save only through a change in the blood causing a change in substance. Temporarily an illogical form of organization of life or unintelligent education may prejudice it. But in that case, though its effective action may be hindered, the fundamental value in itself is still present as it was before. And it is this value which is the great source of all hopes for a people's revival, it is this which justifies the belief that a people which in the course of thousands of years has furnished countless examples of the highest inner value cannot suddenly have lost overnight this inborn inherited value, but that one day this people will once again bring this value into action. If this were not the case, then the faith of millions of men in a better future — the mystic hope for a new Germany — would be incomprehensible. It would be incomprehensible how it was that this German people, at the end of the Thirty Years War, when its population had shrunk from 18 to 13½ millions, could ever have once more formed the hope through work, through industry, and capacity to rise again, how in this completely crushed people hundreds of thousands and finally millions should have been seized with the longing for a re-formation of their State. It would be inconceivable had it not been that in all these individuals, unconsciously, there was some trace of the conviction that there was present an essential value which ever and again had been evidenced through the millennia, which many a time had been repressed and hindered in its effective action through bad leadership, through bad education, through a bad State-form, but which ever in the end had triumphed, had ever presented to the world the wonderful spectacle of a new revival of our people.

I said that this value can be destroyed. There are indeed in especial two other closely related factors which we can time and again trace in periods of national decline: the one is that for the conception of the value of personality there is substituted a levelling idea of the supremacy of mere numbers — democracy — and the other is the negation of the value of a people, the denial of any difference in the inborn capacity, the achievement, &c., of individual peoples. Thus both factors condition one another or at least influence each other in the course of their development. Internationalism and democracy are inseparable conceptions. It is but logical that democracy, which within a people denies the special value of the individual and puts in its place a value which represents the sum of all individualities — a purely numerical value — should proceed in precisely the same way in the life of peoples and should in that sphere result in internationalism. Broadly it is maintained: peoples have no inborn values, but, at the most, there can be admitted perhaps temporary differences in education. Between negroes, Aryans, Mongolians, and Redskins there is no essential difference in value. This view which forms the basis of the whole of the international thought-world of to-day and in its effects is carried to such lengths that in the end a negro can sit as president in the sessions of the League of Nations leads necessarily as a further consequence to the point that in a similar way within a people differences in value between individual members of this people are denied. And thus naturally every special capacity, every fundamental value of a people, can practically be made of no effect. For the greatness of a people is the result not of the sum of all its achievements but in the last resort of the sum of its outstanding achievements. Let no one say that the picture produced as a first impression of human civilization is the impression of its achievement as a whole. The whole edifice of civilization is in its foundations and in all its stones nothing else than the result of the creative capacity, the achievement, the intelligence, the industry of individuals: in its greatest triumphs it represents the great crowning achievement of individual God-favoured geniuses, in its average accomplishment the achievement of men of average capacity, and in its sum doubtless the result of the use of human labour-force in order to turn to account the creations of genius and of talent. So it is only natural that when the capable intelligences of a nation, which are always in a minority, are regarded only as of the same value as all the rest, then genius, capacity, the value of personality are slowly subjected to the majority and this process is then falsely named the rule of the people. For this is not the rule of the people, but in reality the rule of stupidity, of mediocrity, of half-heartedness, of cowardice, of weakness, and of inadequacy. Rule of the people means rather that a people should allow itself to be governed and led by its most capable individuals, those who are born to the task, and not that a chance majority which of necessity is alien to these tasks should be permitted to administer all spheres of life.

Thus democracy will in practice lead to the destruction of a people's true values. And this also serves to explain how it is that peoples with a great past from the time when they surrender themselves to the unlimited, democratic rule of the masses slowly lose their former position; for the outstanding achievements of individuals which they still possess or which could be produced in all spheres of life are now rendered practically ineffective through the oppression of mere numbers. And thus in these conditions a people will gradually lose its importance not merely in the cultural and economic spheres but altogether; in a comparatively short time it will no longer, within the setting of the other peoples of the world, maintain its former value. And that will also of necessity mean a change in its power to safeguard its own interests as against the rest of the world. It is not, for example, a matter of indifference whether a people enters on such a period as the years from 1807 to 1813 under the leadership of its most capable intelligences, men to whom an extraordinary authority is granted, or whether it marches into a similar period, such as the years 1918 to 1921, under the leadership of parliamentary mass-madness. In the one case one can see the result of the internal building-up of the nation's life the highest achievements — which, though founded doubtless on the pre-existent value of the people, could only in this way reach their full effect — while in the other case the value which was already there could no longer find any opportunity for manifesting its presence. Indeed, things can then reach such a pass that an unquestionably industrious people in whose whole life there had hardly been any apparent change — especially so far as concerns the efforts of individuals — can lose so much in the sum of its achievement that it no longer counts for anything in the eyes of the world.

And to this there must be added a third factor: namely, the view that life in this world, after the denial of the value of personality and of the special value of a people, is not to be maintained through conflict. That is a conception which could perhaps be disregarded if it fixed itself only in the heads of individuals, but yet has appalling consequences because it slowly poisons an entire people. And it is not as if such general changes in men's outlook on the world remained only on the surface or were confined to their effects on men's minds. No, in course of time they exercise a profound influence and affect all expressions of a people's life.

I may cite an example: you maintain, gentlemen, that German business life must be constructed on a basis of private property. Now such a conception as that of private property you can defend only if in some way or another it appears to have a logical foundation. This conception must deduce its ethical justification from an insight into the necessity which Nature dictates. It cannot simply be upheld by saying: "It has always been so and therefore it must continue to be so." For in periods of great upheavals within States, of movements of peoples and changes in thought, institutions and systems cannot remain untouched because they have previously been preserved without change. It is the characteristic feature of all really great revolutionary epochs in the history of mankind that they pay astonishingly little regard for forms which are hallowed only by age or which are apparently only so consecrated. It is thus necessary to give foundations to traditional forms which are to be preserved that they can be regarded as absolutely essential, as logical and right. And then I am bound to say that private property can be morally and ethically justified only if I admit that men's achievements are different, the results of those achievements are also different. But if the results of those achievements are different, then it is reasonable to leave to men the administration of those results to a corresponding degree. It would not be logical to entrust the administration of the result of an achievement which was bound up with a personality either to the next best but less capable person or to a community which, through the mere fact that it had not performed the achievement, has proved that it is not capable of administering the result of that achievement. Thus it must be admitted that in the economic sphere, from the start, in all branches men are not of equal value or of equal importance. And once this is admitted it is madness to say: in the economic sphere there are undoubtedly differences in value, but that is not true in the political sphere. It is absurd to build up economic life on the conceptions of achievement, of the value of personality, and therefore in practice on the authority of personality, but in the political sphere to deny the authority of personality and to thrust into its place the law of the greater number — democracy. In that case there must slowly arise a cleavage between the economic and the political point of view, and to bridge that cleavage an attempt will be made to assimilate the former to the latter — indeed the attempt has been made, for this cleavage has not remained bare pale theory. The conception of the equality of values has already, not only in politics but in economics also, been raised to a system, and that not merely in abstract theory: no! this economic system is alive in gigantic organizations and it has already today inspired a State which rules over immense areas.

But I cannot regard it as possible that the life of a people should in the long run be based upon two fundamental conceptions. If the view is right that there are differences in human achievement, then it must also be true that the value of men in respect of the production of certain achievements is different. It is then absurd to allow this principle to hold good only in one sphere — the sphere of economic life and its leadership — and to refuse to acknowledge its validity in the sphere of the whole life-struggle of a people — the sphere of politics. Rather the logical course is that if I recognize without qualification in the economic sphere the fact of special achievements as forming the condition of all higher culture, then in the same way I should recognize special achievement in the sphere of politics and that means that I am bound to put in the forefront the authority of personality. If, on the contrary, it is asserted — and that too by those engaged in business — that in the political sphere special capacities are not necessary but that here an absolute equality in achievement reigns, then one day this same theory will be transferred from politics and applied to economic life. But in the economic sphere Communism is analogous to democracy in the political sphere. We find ourselves to-day in a period in which these two fundamental principles are at grips in all spheres which come into contact with each other; already they are invading economics. . . .

If I speak to you to-day it is not to ask for your votes or to induce you on my account to do this or that for the Party. No, I am here to expound a point of view, and I am convinced that the victory of this point of view would mean the only possible starting-point for a German recovery; it is indeed the last item standing to the credit of the German people. I hear it said so often by our opponents, "You, too, will be unable to master the present crisis." Supposing, gentlemen, that they are right, what would that mean? It would mean that we should be facing a ghastly period and that we should have to meet it with no other defences than a purely materialistic outlook on every side. And then the distress would, simply in its material aspect, be a thousandfold harder to bear, if one had failed to restore to the people any ideal whatsoever.

People say to me so often: "You are only the drummer of national Germany." And supposing that I were only the drummer? It would to-day be a far more statesmanlike achievement to drum once more into this German people a new faith than gradually to squander the only faith they have. Take the case of a fortress, imagine that it is reduced to extreme privations: as long as the garrison sees a possible salvation, be-lieves in it, hopes for it, so long they can bear the reduced ration. But take from the hearts of men their last belief in the possibility of salva-tion, in a better future — take that completely from them, and you will see how these men suddenly regard their reduced rations as the most im-portant thing in life. The more you bring it home to their consciousness that they are only objects for men to bargain with, that they are only prisoners of world-politics, the more will they, like all prisoners, concen-trate their thoughts on purely material interests. On the other hand, the more you bring back a people into the sphere of faith, of ideals, the more will it cease to regard material distress as the one and only thing which counts. And the weightiest evidence for the truth of that statement is our own German people. We would not ever forget that the German people waged wars of religion for 150 years with prodigious devotion, that hun-dreds of thousands of men once left their plot of land, their property, and their belongings simply for an ideal, simply for a conviction. We would never forget that during those 150 years there was no trace of even an ounce of material interests. Then you will understand how mighty is the force of an idea, of an ideal. Only so can you comprehend how it is that in our Movement to-day hundreds of thousands of young men are prepared at the risk of their lives to withstand our opponents. I know quite well, gentlemen, that when National Socialists march through the streets and suddenly in the evening there arise a tumult and commotion, then the *bourgeois* draws back the window-curtain, looks out, and says: Once more my night's rest disturbed: no more sleep for me. Why must the Nazis always be so provocative and run about the place at night? Gentlemen, if everyone thought like that, then no one's sleep at nights would be disturbed, it is true, but then the *bourgeois* to-day could not venture into the street. If everyone thought in that way, if these young folk had no ideal to move them and drive them forward, then certainly they would gladly be rid of these nocturnal fights. But remember that it means sacrifice when to-day many hundred thousands of SA and SS men of the National Socialist Movement every day have to mount on their lorries, protect meetings, undertake marches, sacrifice themselves night after night and then come back in the grey dawn either to workshop and factory or as unemployed to take the pittance of the dole: it means sacrifice when from the little which they possess they have further to buy their uniforms, their shirts, their badges, yes, and even pay their own fares. Believe me, there is already in all this the force of an ideal — a great ideal! And if the whole German nation to-day had the same faith in its vocation as these hundred thousands, if the whole nation possessed this idealism, Germany would stand in the eyes of the world otherwise than she stands now! (*Loud applause.*) For our situation in the world in its fatal effects is but the result of our own underestimate of German strength. (*Very true!*) Only when we have once more changed this fatal valuation of ourselves can Germany take advantage of the political possi-bilities which, if we look far enough into the future, can place German life once more upon a natural and secure basis — and that means either new living-space (*Lebensraum*) and the development of a great internal market or protection of German economic life against the world without and utilization of all the concentrated strength of Germany. The labour resources of our people, the capacities, we have them already: no one can deny that we are industrious. But we must first refashion the political pre-conditions: without that, industry and capacity, diligence and econ-omy are in the last resort of no avail, for an oppressed nation will not be able to spend on its own welfare even the fruits of its own economy but must sacrifice them on the altar of exactions and of tribute.

And so in contrast to our own official Government I cannot see any hope for the resurrection of Germany if we regard the foreign politics of Germany as the primary factor: the primary necessity is the restoration of a sound national German body-politic armed to strike. In order to realize this end I founded thirteen years ago the National Socialist Movement: that Movement I have led during the last twelve years, and I hope that one day it will accomplish this task and that, as the fairest result of its struggle, it will leave behind it a German body-politic com-pletely renewed internally, intolerant of anyone who sins against the nation and its interests, intolerant against anyone who will not acknowl-edge its vital interests or who opposes them, intolerant and pitiless against anyone who shall attempt once more to destroy or disintegrate this body-politic, and yet ready for friendship and peace with anyone who has a wish for peace and friendship. (*Long and tumultuous ap-plause.*)

THE SECOND WORLD WAR
Chapter 5

The origins of Hitler's diplomatic successes are similar to those of Hitler's domestic success in Germany. Hitler combined a steady and rigid adherence to basic goals with great tactical skill and flexibility in achieving them. He knew his enemies, and they did not know — or did not want to know — him. With each "Sunday surprise," came the reassurance that this was his last demand in Europe. The Western Allies, above all Great Britain, deluded themselves into thinking that this was the truth and that Hitler would become "reasonable" once his "just claims" were met. Underlying this policy of appeasement was the feeling that many of Hitler's claims were indeed justified. Germany could not be disarmed forever; the Rhineland was German and demilitarization was too humiliating to last forever; Austria was German; much of the Sudetenland population was German. Not only the moral retreat from Versailles, however, but an understandable horror of war and a no less understandable, albeit shortsighted, distrust of the Soviet Union and distaste for Communism promoted appeasement. Indeed, when the appeasers could not escape the increasingly clear evidence that Hitler could be stopped only by force, they argued that delay was necessary in order to catch up with the Germans and be prepared. At the same time, they disparaged the Soviet Union's military strength and pointed to the fact that Stalin had wiped out his officer corps in the purges. In reality, the Germans were never "armed in depth" until the middle of the war, and the Allies had greater potential for stopping Hitler earlier than later.

The critical matter, however, was that the Western democracies had lost the initiative to the more dynamic and ruthless totalitarian powers. This was first made evident in the failure of the League, Great Britain, and the United States to prevent Japanese aggression against China, first in Manchuria in 1931 and then more overtly in an undeclared war beginning in 1937. The Western reaction to Italy's aggression against Ethiopia in 1935 was incompetent as well as morally reprehensible. The League first voted sanctions and then withdrew them after it became clear that Britain would not make them effective by closing the Suez Canal to Italian shipping and that the League's timid actions merely served to drive Mussolini into alliance with Hitler.

The most gruesome and tragic prelude to the war, however, was the Spanish Civil War, which lasted from 1936 to 1939. While Britain and France sought to evade domestic conflict and international complications by pursuing a policy of nonintervention and arms embargo, Italy and Germany, on one side, and the Soviet Union, on the other, intervened with material assistance and "volunteers" and turned the war into a contest between fascism and its opponents. It gave Mussolini the opportunity to win cheap victories, Hitler a chance to try out new weapons and techniques, and Stalin a chance to make propaganda at the expense of the Spaniards. Ultimately, it was the Spaniards who paid the price of the war and of the victory of General Franco's authoritarian cause. The war further diminished the credibility of the Western democracies.

The greatest damage, however, was done by the appeasement of Hitler. Britain and France stood by while Germany broke the Versailles Treaty by unilaterally rearming in 1935, remilitarizing the Rhineland in 1936, and annexing Austria in 1938. The Western powers then actively participated in the aggression against Czechoslovakia by accepting Hitler's demands at the Munich conference in September, 1938. Only after Hitler's violation of the Munich agreement by his occupation of Prague in March, 1939, did Britain and France determine to resist any new German acts of aggression and give unilateral assurances to Germany's next victim, Poland. Hitler had hoped either to come to terms with the Poles and then join with them in war against Russia or to smash the Poles first without interference from Britain. Both plans were frustrated, but Hitler and Stalin did surprise the world by concluding a Nonaggression Pact in August, 1939, and attacking Poland together.

As in diplomacy, so in military affairs, the initiative lay with the totalitarian states, especially Germany. Hitler's lightning wars (*Blitzkrieg*) against Poland and France were based on the massive use of tanks and airplanes and made a mockery of the paper matériel and manpower superiority that the Allies had over the Germans. Hitler finally went down to defeat because of the utter irrationality of his aims and the fundamental barbarism that lay at their roots. Instead of concentrating on the defeat of England by pursuing the promising possibilities of the African campaign, Hitler turned to the basic goal that had driven him to all his acts of aggression in the first place, the winning of "living space" (*Lebensraum*) in the east. Despite its initial successes, the *Blitzkrieg* was not enough to conquer the vast spaces of Russia, and the battle of Stalingrad in the winter of 1942–1943 marked the turning point of the war. As Hitler pursued his twin goals of win-

ning living space and "solving" the Jewish problem with increasing
ferocity, the flexibility and cunning that had earned him so many
victories seemed to desert him, and he became more and more rigid in
his insistence upon a policy of nonretreat and total victory. Although
the Germans, largely thanks to the brilliant organizing abilities of
Albert Speer, did a spectacular job of increasing weapons and munitions production during the last two and a half years of the war, the
superiority of the Allies in men and matériel, particularly after America's entry in December, 1941, the fundamental chaos of the Nazi system, the complete absence of coordination among the Axis powers,
and the ceaseless bombardment of Germany, doomed Hitler's efforts.
The fundamental question after Hitler's defeat was whether the Allies
could correct the conditions in Germany and in their own countries
that had made Hitler's success possible in the first place.

Civil War in Spain

*One of the most moving and revealing accounts of the Spanish Civil
War was written by the British writer George Orwell. Thousands of
western European and American intellectuals went to Spain in a spirit
of idealism to fight against fascism and escape the apathy and inaction
they found at home. Orwell was one of them, and, like them, he was
attracted to Communism for its egalitarian ideals and its militant actions against fascism. His book* Homage to Catalonia *records his disillusionment as he discovered that the Communists were interested
more in eliminating their competitors to the Left, especially the anarchists, than in saving the republic and establishing a true social
democracy. Orwell continued to believe that he was fighting on the
right side in Spain, but not because of the original naive enthusiasm
that caused him to enlist.*

Orwell's *Homage to Catalonia*

In the Lenin Barracks in Barcelona, the day before I joined the militia, I saw an Italian militiaman standing in front of the officers' table.

He was a tough-looking youth of twenty-five or six, with reddish-yellow
hair and powerful shoulders. His peaked leather cap was pulled fiercely

Abridged from George Orwell, *Homage to Catalonia* (© 1952 by Sonia Brownell Orwell), (New York: Harcourt Brace Jovanovich, 1952), pp. 3–6, 180–82, 229–32. Reprinted
by permission of Harcourt Brace Jovanovich, Inc., and A. M. Heath & Company Ltd.

over one eye. He was standing in profile to me, his chin on his breast, gazing with a puzzled frown at a map which one of the officers had open on the table. Something in his face deeply moved me. It was the face of a man who would commit murder and throw away his life for a friend — the kind of face you would expect in an Anarchist, though as likely as not he was a Communist. There were both candour and ferocity in it; also the pathetic reverence that illiterate people have for their supposed superiors. Obviously he could not make head or tail of the map; obviously he regarded map-reading as a stupendous intellectual feat. I hardly know why, but I have seldom seen anyone — any man, I mean — to whom I have taken such an immediate liking. While they were talking round the table some remark brought it out that I was a foreigner. The Italian raised his head and said quickly:

"Italiano?"

I answered in my bad Spanish: "No, Ingles. Y tu?"

"Italiano."

As we went out he stepped across the room and gripped my hand very hard. Queer, the affection you can feel for a stranger! It was as though his spirit and mine had momentarily succeeded in bridging the gulf of language and tradition and meeting in utter intimacy. I hoped he liked me as well as I liked him. But I also knew that to retain my first impression of him I must not see him again; and needless to say I never did see him again. One was always making contacts of that kind in Spain.

I mention this Italian militiaman because he has stuck vividly in my memory. With his shabby uniform and fierce pathetic face he typifies for me the special atmosphere of that time. He is bound up with all my memories of that period of the war — the red flags in Barcelona, the gaunt trains full of shabby soldiers creeping to the front, the grey war-stricken towns farther up the line, the muddy, ice-cold trenches in the mountains.

This was in late December, 1936, less than seven months ago as I write, and yet it is a period that has already receded into enormous distance. Later events have obliterated it much more completely than they have obliterated 1935, or 1905, for that matter. I had come to Spain with some notion of writing newspaper articles, but I had joined the militia almost immediately, because at that time and in that atmosphere it seemed the only conceivable thing to do. The Anarchists were still in virtual control of Catalonia and the revolution was still in full swing. To anyone who had been there since the beginning it probably seemed even in December or January that the revolutionary period was ending; but when one came straight from England the aspect of Barcelona was something startling and overwhelming. It was the first time that I had ever been in a town where the working class was in the saddle. Practically every building of any size had been seized by the workers and was draped with red flags or with the red and black flag of the Anarchists; every wall was scrawled with the hammer and sickle and with the initials of the revolutionary parties; almost every church had been gutted and its images burnt. Churches here and there were being systematically demolished by gangs of workmen. Every shop and café had an inscription saying that it had been collectivized; even the bootblacks had been collectivized and their boxes painted red and black. Waiters and shop-walkers looked you in the face and treated you as an equal. Servile and even ceremonial forms of speech had temporarily disappeared. Nobody said 'Señor' or 'Don' or even 'Usted'; everyone called everyone else 'Comrade' and 'Thou,' and said 'Salud!' instead of 'Buenos dias.' Tipping had been forbidden by law since the time of Primo de Rivera; almost my first experience was receiving a lecture from an hotel manager for trying to tip a lift-boy. There were no private motor cars, they had all been commandeered, and all the trams and taxis and much of the other transport were painted red and black. The revolutionary posters were everywhere, flaming from the walls in clean reds and blues that made the few remaining advertisements look like daubs of mud. Down the Ramblas, the wide central artery of the town where crowds of people streamed constantly to and fro, the loud-speakers were bellowing revolutionary songs all day and far into the night. And it was the aspect of the crowds that was the queerest thing of all. In outward appearance it was a town in which the wealthy classes had practically ceased to exist. Except for a small number of women and foreigners there were no 'well-dressed' people at all. Practically everyone wore rough working-class clothes, or blue overalls or some variant of the militia uniform. All this was queer and moving. There was much in it that I did not understand, in some ways I did not even like it, but I recognized it immediately as a state of affairs worth fighting for. Also I believed that things were as they appeared, that this was really a workers' State and that the entire bourgeoisie had either fled, been killed, or voluntarily come over to the workers' side; I did not realize that great numbers of well-to-do bourgeois were simply lying low and disguising themselves as proletarians for the time being.

Together with all this there was something of the evil atmosphere of war. The town had a gaunt untidy look, roads and buildings were in poor repair, the streets at night were dimly lit for fear of air-raids, the shops were mostly shabby and half-empty. Meat was scarce and milk practically unobtainable, there was a shortage of coal, sugar, and petrol, and a really serious shortage of bread. Even at this period the bread-queues were often hundreds of yards long. Yet so far as one could judge the people were contented and hopeful. There was no unemployment, and the price of living was still extremely low; you saw very few conspicuously destitute people, and no beggars except the gipsies. Above all, there was a belief in the revolution and the future, a feeling of having suddenly emerged into an era of equality and freedom. Human beings were trying to behave as human beings and not as cogs in the capitalist machine. In the barbers' shops were Anarchist notices (the barbers were mostly Anarchists) solemnly explaining that barbers were no longer slaves. In the streets were coloured posters appealing to prostitutes to stop being prostitutes. To anyone from the hard-boiled, sneering civilization of the English-speaking races there was something rather pathetic in the literalness with which these idealistic Spaniards took the hackneyed phrases of revolution. At that time revolutionary ballads of the naïvest kind, all about proletarian brotherhood and the wickedness of Mussolini, were being sold on the streets for a few centimes each. I have often seen an illiterate militiaman buy one of these ballads, laboriously spell out the words, and then, when he had got the hang of it, begin singing it to an appropriate tune. . . .

It must have been three days after the Barcelona fighting ended that we returned to the front. After the fighting — more particularly after the slanging-match in the newspapers — it was difficult to think about this war in quite the same naïvely idealistic manner as before. I suppose there is no one who spent more than a few weeks in Spain without being in some degree disillusioned. My mind went back to the newspaper correspondent whom I had met my first day in Barcelona, and who said to me: "This war is a racket the same as any other." The remark had shocked me deeply, and at that time (December) I do not believe it was true; it was not true even now, in May; but it was becoming truer. The fact is that every war suffers a kind of progressive degradation with every month that it continues, because such things as individual liberty and a truthful press are simply not compatible with military efficiency.

One could begin now to make some kind of guess at what was likely to happen. It was easy to see that the Caballero Government would fall and be replaced by a more Right-wing Government with a stronger Communist influence (this happened a week or two later), which would set itself to break the power of the trade unions once and for all. And afterwards, when Franco was beaten — and putting aside the huge problems raised by the reorganization of Spain — the prospect was not rosy. As for the newspaper talk about this being a 'war for democracy,' it was plain eye-wash. No one in his senses supposed that there was any hope of democracy, even as we understand it in England or France, in a country so divided and exhausted as Spain would be when the war was over. It would have to be a dictatorship, and it was clear that the chance of a working-class dictatorship had passed. That meant that the general movement would be in the direction of some kind of Fascism. Fascism called, no doubt, by some politer name, and — because this was Spain — more human and less efficient than the German or Italian varieties. The only alternatives were an infinitely worse dictatorship by Franco, or (always a possibility) that the war would end with Spain divided up, either by actual frontiers or into economic zones.

Whichever way you took it it was a depressing outlook. But it did not follow that the Government was not worth fighting for as against the more naked and developed Fascism of Franco and Hitler. Whatever faults the post-war Government might have, Franco's régime would certainly be worse. To the workers — the town proletariat — it might in the end make very little difference who won, but Spain is primarily an agricultural country and the peasants would almost certainly benefit by a Government victory. Some at least of the seized lands would remain in their possession, in which case there would also be a distribution of land in the territory that had been Franco's, and the virtual serfdom that had existed in some parts of Spain was not likely to be restored. The Government in control at the end of the war would at any rate be anti-clerical and anti-feudal. It would keep the Church in check, at least for the time being, and would modernize the country — build roads, for instance, and promote education and public health; a certain amount had been done in this direction even during the war. Franco, on the other hand, in so far as he was not merely the puppet of Italy and Germany, was tied to the big feudal landlords and stood for a stuffy clerico-military reaction. The Popular Front might be a swindle, but Franco was an anachronism. Only millionaires or romantics could want him to win.

Moreover, there was the question of the international prestige of Fascism, which for a year or two past had been haunting me like a nightmare. Since 1930 the Fascists had won all the victories; it was time they got a beating, it hardly mattered from whom. If we could drive Franco and his foreign mercenaries into the sea it might make an immense improvement in the world situation, even if Spain itself emerged with a stifling dictatorship and all its best men in jail. For that alone the war would have been worth winning.

This was how I saw things at the time. I may say that I now think much more highly of the Negrin Government than I did when it came into office. It has kept up the difficult fight with splendid courage, and it has shown more political tolerance than anyone expected. But I still believe that — unless Spain splits up, with unpredictable consequences — the tendency of the post-war Government is bound to be Fascistic. Once again I let this opinion stand, and take the chance that time will do to me what it does to most prophets. . . .

I think we stayed three days in Banyuls. It was a strangely restless time. In this quiet fishing-town, remote from bombs, machine-guns, food-queues, propaganda, and intrigue, we ought to have felt profoundly relieved and thankful. We felt nothing of the kind. The things we had seen in Spain did not recede and fall into proportion now that we were away from them; instead they rushed back upon us and were far more vivid than before. We thought, talked, dreamed incessantly of Spain. For months past we had been telling ourselves that 'when we get out of

Spain' we would go somewhere beside the Mediterranean and be quiet for a little while and perhaps do a little fishing; but now that we were here it was merely a bore and a disappointment. It was chilly weather, a persistent wind blew off the sea, the water was dull and choppy, round the harbour's edge a scum of ashes, corks, and fish-guts bobbed against the stones. It sounds like lunacy, but the thing that both of us wanted was to be back in Spain. Though it could have done no good to anybody, might indeed have done serious harm, both of us wished that we had stayed to be imprisoned along with the others. I suppose I have failed to convey more than a little of what those months in Spain mean to me. I have recorded some of the outward events, but I cannot record the feeling they have left me with. It is all mixed up with sights, smells, and sounds that cannot be conveyed in writing: the smell of the trenches, the mountain dawns stretching away into inconceivable distances, the frosty crackle of bullets, the roar and glare of bombs; the clear cold light of the Barcelona mornings, and the stamp of boots in the barrack yard, back in December when people still believed in the revolution; and the food-queues and the red and black flags and the faces of Spanish militiamen; above all the faces of militiamen — men whom I knew in the line and who are now scattered Lord knows where, some killed in battle, some maimed, some in prison — most of them, I hope, still safe and sound. Good luck to them all; I hope they win their war and drive all the foreigners out of Spain, Germans, Russians and Italians alike. This war, in which I played so ineffectual a part, has left me with memories that are mostly evil, and yet I do not wish that I had missed it. When you have had a glimpse of such a disaster as this — and however it ends the Spanish war will turn out to have been an appalling disaster, quite apart from the slaughter and physical suffering — the result is not necessarily disillusionment and cynicism. Curiously enough the whole experience has left me with not less but more belief in the decency of human beings. And I hope the account I have given is not too misleading. I believe that on such an issue as this no one is or can be completely truthful. It is difficult to be certain about anything except what you have seen with your own eyes, and consciously or unconsciously everyone writes as a partisan. In case I have not said this somewhere earlier in the book I will say it now: beware of my partisanship, my mistakes of fact and the distortion inevitably caused by my having seen only one corner of events. And beware of exactly the same things when you read any other book on this period of the Spanish war.

Because of the feeling that we ought to be doing something, though actually there was nothing we could do, we left Banyuls earlier than we had intended. With every mile that you went northward France grew greener and softer. Away from the mountain and the vine, back to the meadow and the elm. When I had passed through Paris on my way to

Spain it had seemed to me decayed and gloomy, very different from the Paris I had known eight years earlier, when living was cheap and Hitler was not heard of. Half the cafés I used to know were shut for lack of custom, and everyone was obsessed with the high cost of living and the fear of war. Now, after poor Spain, even Paris seemed gay and prosperous. And the Exhibition was in full swing, though we managed to avoid visiting it.

And then England — southern England, probably the sleekest landscape in the world. It is difficult when you pass that way, especially when you are peacefully recovering from sea-sickness with the plush cushions of a boat-train carriage under your bum, to believe that anything is really happening anywhere. Earthquakes in Japan, famines in China, revolutions in Mexico? Don't worry, the milk will be on the doorstep tomorrow morning, the *New Statesman* will come out on Friday. The industrial towns were far away, a smudge of smoke and misery hidden by the curve of the earth's surface. Down here it was still the England I had known in my childhood: the railway-cuttings smothered in wild flowers, the deep meadows where the great shining horses browse and meditate, the slow-moving streams bordered by willows, the green bosoms of the elms, the larkspurs in the cottage gardens; and then the huge peaceful wilderness of outer London, the barges on the miry river, the familiar streets, the posters telling of cricket matches and Royal weddings, the men in bowler hats, the pigeons in Trafalgar Square, the red buses, the blue policemen — all sleeping the deep, deep sleep of England, from which I sometimes fear that we shall never wake till we are jerked out of it by the roar of bombs.

Aggression and Appeasement

Early works on Hitler's foreign policy often erroneously gave the impression that Hitler had a timetable for his conquest of Lebensraum, *but he was too much a tactician and improviser to adhere to a rigid timetable. During his first two years in office, he continuously emphasized his desire for peace in order to have time to consolidate his power. Only in 1935 did he begin to openly violate the Versailles Treaty. By 1937, however, with his domestic power secure and his four-year plan for the rearmament of Germany launched, Hitler determined to solve the various international problems confronting Germany in a more determined manner. The so-called Hossbach Memorandum was the report of a conference Hitler conducted with his leading military personnel on November 5, 1937, in which he*

128 The Second World War

revealed to them his intention of going to war by 1943 at the latest and discussed various contingencies that might lead to military action earlier.

Hitler's monologue is not important as a statement of a timetable but rather as a statement of intentions. He begins by restating the crude Social Darwinist economy theory, which is scattered throughout his work, with which he justifies the necessity of securing Lebensraum for the German people. As with Hitler's anti-Semitism, once his basic premises are accepted, his logic necessarily follows. Thus Hitler could see no alternative to securing Lebensraum if the German people were to be saved. His 1943 deadline was determined by military considerations and concern over the length of his own life — he was, after all, a unique opportunity for the German people. In any case, the contingencies Hitler discussed did not arise, although the problems were solved and Germany went to war even earlier than he anticipated. Austria was annexed in March, 1938, and the Sudetenland was taken in September. Some of the officers attending the meeting were frightened by Hitler's intentions, which seemed to call for too much too soon, and Hitler purged the army and foreign office following the meeting. The minutes of the meeting were recorded by Hitler's personal adjutant, Colonel Hossbach.

The Hossbach Memorandum is a good background against which to consider Prime Minister Chamberlain's address to his people at the time of the Munich Crisis. It reflects the basic unwillingness of the British government to become engaged in a war over the borders of eastern Europe, an attitude already in evidence at the time of Locarno. Only after the invasion of Prague in March, 1939, did Chamberlain conclude that the borders established by Versailles in the east were vital to British interests.

The Hossbach Memorandum

BERLIN, November 10, 1937

MINUTES OF THE CONFERENCE IN THE REICH CHANCELLERY, BERLIN, NOVEMBER 5, 1937, FROM 4:15 TO 8:30 P.M.

Present: The Führer and Chancellor
    Field Marshal von Blomberg, War Minister
    Colonel General Baron von Fritsch, Commander in Chief, Army

From *Documents on German Foreign Policy, 1918–1945*, series D, vol. 1 (Washington, D.C., 1949), no. 19.

Admiral Dr. h. c. Raeder, Commander in Chief, Navy
Colonel General Göring, Commander in Chief, *Luftwaffe*
Baron von Neurath, Foreign Minister
Colonel Hossbach

The Führer began by stating that the subject of the present conference was of such importance that its discussion would, in other countries, certainly be a matter for a full Cabinet meeting, but he — the Führer — had rejected the idea of making it a subject of discussion before the wider circle of the Reich Cabinet just because of the importance of the matter. His exposition to follow was the fruit of thorough deliberation and the experiences of his 4½ years of power. He wished to explain to the gentlemen present his basic ideas concerning the opportunities for the development of our position in the field of foreign affairs and its requirements, and he asked, in the interests of a long-term German policy, that his exposition be regarded, in the event of his death, as his last will and testament.

The Führer then continued:

The aim of German policy was to make secure and to preserve the racial community [*Volksmasse*] and to enlarge it. It was therefore a question of space.

The German racial community comprised over 85 million people and, because of their number and the narrow limits of habitable space in Europe, constituted a tightly packed racial core such as was not to be met in any other country and such as implied the right to a greater living space than in the case of other peoples. If, territorially speaking, there existed no political result corresponding to this German racial core, that was a consequence of centuries of historical development, and in the continuance of these political conditions lay the greatest danger to the preservation of the German race at its present peak. To arrest the decline of Germanism [*Deutschtum*] in Austria and Czechoslovakia was as little possible as to maintain the present level in Germany itself. Instead of increase, sterility was setting in, and in its train disorders of a social character must arise in course of time, since political and ideological ideas remain effective only so long as they furnish the basis for the realization of the essential vital demands of a people. Germany's future was therefore wholly conditional upon the solving of the need for space, and such a solution could be sought, of course, only for a foreseeable period of about one to three generations.

Before turning to the question of solving the need for space, it had to be considered whether a solution holding promise for the future was to be reached by means of autarchy or by means of an increased participation in world economy.

AUTARCHY

Achievement only possible under strict National Socialist leadership of the State, which is assumed; accepting its achievement as possible, the following could be stated as results:

A. In the field of raw materials only limited, not total, autarchy.

1. In regard to coal, so far as it could be considered as a source of raw materials, autarchy was possible.

2. But even as regards ores, the position was much more difficult. Iron requirements can be met from home resources and similarly with light metals, but with other raw materials — copper, tin — this was not the case.

3. Synthetic textile requirements can be met from home resources to the limit of timber supplies. A permanent solution impossible.

4. Edible fats — possible.

B. In the field of food the question of autarchy was to be answered by a flat "No."

With the general rise in the standard of living compared with that of 30 to 40 years ago, there has gone hand in hand an increased demand and an increased home consumption even on the part of the producers, the farmers. The fruits of the increased agricultural production had all gone to meet the increased demand, and so did not represent an absolute production increase. A further increase in production by making greater demands on the soil, which already, in consequence of the use of artificial fertilizers, was showing signs of exhaustion, was hardly possible, and it was therefore certain that even with the maximum increase in production, participation in world trade was unavoidable. The not inconsiderable expenditure of foreign exchange to insure food supplies by imports, even when harvests were good, grew to catastrophic proportions with bad harvests. The possibility of a disaster grew in proportion to the increase in population, in which, too, the excess of births of 560,000 annually produced, as a consequence, an even further increase in bread consumption, since a child was a greater bread consumer than an adult.

It was not possible over the long run, in a continent enjoying a practically common standard of living, to meet the food supply difficulties by lowering that standard and by rationalization. Since, with the solving of the unemployment problem, the maximum consumption level had been reached, some minor modifications in our home agricultural production might still, no doubt, be possible, but no fundamental alteration was possible in our basic food position. Thus autarchy was untenable in regard both to food and to the economy as a whole.

PARTICIPATION IN WORLD ECONOMY

To this there were limitations which we were unable to remove. The establishment of Germany's position on a secure and sound foundation was obstructed by market fluctuations, and commercial treaties afforded no guarantee for actual execution. In particular it had to be remembered that since the World War, those very countries which had formerly been food exporters had become industrialized. We were living in an age of economic empires in which the primitive urge to colonization was again manifesting itself; in the cases of Japan and Italy economic motives underlay the urge for expansion, and with Germany, too, economic need would supply the stimulus. For countries outside the great economic empires, opportunities for economic expansion were severely impeded.

The boom in world economy caused by the economic effects of rearmament could never form the basis of a sound economy over a long period, and the latter was obstructed above all also by the pronounced military weakness in those states which depended for their existence on foreign trade. As our foreign trade was carried on over the sea routes dominated by Britain, it was more a question of security of transport than one of foreign exchange, which revealed, in time of war, the full weakness of our food situation. The only remedy, and one which might appear to us as visionary, lay in the acquisition of greater living space — a quest which has at all times been the origin of the formation of states and of the migration of peoples. That this quest met with no interest at Geneva or among the satiated nations was understandable. If, then, we accept the security of our food situation as the principal question, the space necessary to insure it can only be sought in Europe, not, as in the liberal-capitalist view, in the exploitation of colonies. It is not a matter of acquiring population but of gaining space for agricultural use. Moreover, areas producing raw materials can be more usefully sought in Europe in immediate proximity to the Reich, than overseas; the solution thus obtained must suffice for one or two generations. Whatever else might prove necessary later must be left to succeeding generations to deal with. The development of great world political constellations progressed but slowly after all, and the German people with its strong racial core would find the most favorable prerequisites for such achievement in the heart of the continent of Europe. The history of all ages — the Roman Empire and the British Empire — had proved that expansion could only be carried out by breaking down resistance and taking risks; setbacks were inevitable. There had never in former times been spaces without a master, and there were none today; the attacker always comes up against a possessor.

The question for Germany ran: where could she achieve the greatest gain at the lowest cost.

German policy had to reckon with two hate-inspired antagonists, Britain and France, to whom a German colossus in the center of Europe was a thorn in the flesh, and both countries were opposed to any further strengthening of Germany's position either in Europe or overseas; in support of this opposition they were able to count on the agreement of all their political parties. Both countries saw in the establishment of German military bases overseas a threat to their own communications, a safeguarding of German commerce, and, as a consequence, a strengthening of Germany's position in Europe.

Because of opposition of the Dominions, Britain could not cede any of her colonial possessions to us. After England's loss of prestige through the passing of Abyssinia into Italian possession, the return of East Africa was not to be expected. British concessions could at best be expressed in an offer to satisfy our colonial demands by the appropriation of colonies which were not British possessions — e.g., Angola. French concessions would probably take a similar line.

Serious discussion of the question of the return of colonies to us could only be considered at a moment when Britain was in difficulties and the German Reich armed and strong. The Führer did not share the view that the Empire was unshakable. Opposition to the Empire was to be found less in the countries conquered than among her competitors. The British Empire and the Roman Empire could not be compared in respect of permanence; the latter was not confronted by any powerful political rival of a serious order after the Punic Wars. It was only the disintegrating effect of Christianity, and the symptoms of age which appear in every country, which caused ancient Rome to succumb to the onslaught of the Germans.

Beside the British Empire there existed today a number of states stronger than she. The British motherland was able to protect her colonial possessions not by her own power, but only in alliance with other states. How, for instance, could Britain alone defend Canada against attack by America, or her Far Eastern interests against attack by Japan!

The emphasis on the British Crown as the symbol of the unity of the Empire was already an admission that, in the long run, the Empire could not maintain its position by power politics. Significant indications of this were:

(*a*) The struggle of Ireland for independence.

(*b*) The constitutional struggles in India where Britain's half measures had given to the Indians the opportunity of using later on as a weapon against Britain, the nonfulfillment of her promises regarding a constitution.

(c) The weakening by Japan of Britain's position in the Far East.

(d) The rivalry in the Mediterranean with Italy who — under the spell of her history, driven by necessity and led by a genius — was expanding her power position, and thus was inevitably coming more and more into conflict with British interests. The outcome of the Abyssinian War was a loss of prestige for Britain which Italy was striving to increase by stirring up trouble in the Mohammedan world.

To sum up, it could be stated that, with 45 million Britons, in spite of its theoretical soundness, the position of the Empire could not in the long run be maintained by power politics. The ratio of the population of the Empire to that of the motherland of 9:1, was a warning to us not, in our territorial expansion, to allow the foundation constituted by the numerical strength of our own people to become too weak.

France's position was more favorable than that of Britain. The French Empire was better placed territorially; the inhabitants of her colonial possessions represented a supplement to her military strength. But France was going to be confronted with internal political difficulties. In a nation's life about 10 percent of its span is taken up by parliamentary forms of government and about 90 percent by authoritarian forms. Today, nonetheless, Britain, France, Russia, and the smaller states adjoining them, must be included as factors [*Machtfaktoren*] in our political calculations.

Germany's problem could only be solved by means of force and this was never without attendant risk. The campaigns of Frederick the Great for Silesia and Bismarck's wars against Austria and France had involved unheard-of risk, and the swiftness of the Prussian action in 1870 had kept Austria from entering the war. If one accepts as the basis of the following exposition the resort to force with its attendant risks, then there remain still to be answered the questions "when" and "how." In this matter there were three cases [*Fälle*] to be dealt with:

CASE 1: PERIOD 1943–1945

After this date only a change for the worse, from our point of view, could be expected.

The equipment of the army, navy, and *Luftwaffe*, as well as the formation of the officer corps, was nearly completed. Equipment and armament were modern; in further delay there lay the danger of their obsolescence. In particular, the secrecy of "special weapons" could not be preserved forever. The recruiting of reserves was limited to current age groups; further drafts from older untrained age groups were no longer available.

Our relative strength would decrease in relation to the rearmament which would by then have been carried out by the rest of the world. If we did not act by 1943–45, any year could, in consequence of a lack of reserves, produce the food crisis, to cope with which the necessary foreign exchange was not available, and this must be regarded as a "waning point of the regime." Besides, the world was expecting our attack and was increasing its countermeasures from year to year. It was while the rest of the world was still preparing its defenses [*sich abriegele*] that we were obliged to take the offensive.

Nobody knew today what the situation would be in the years 1943–45. One thing only was certain, that we could not wait longer.

On the one hand there was the great *Wehrmacht,* and the necessity of maintaining it at its present level, the aging of the movement and of its leaders; and on the other, the prospect of a lowering of the standard of living and of a limitation of the birth rate, which left no choice but to act. If the Führer was still living, it was his unalterable resolve to solve Germany's problem of space at the latest by 1943–45. The necessity for action before 1943–45 would arise in cases 2 and 3.

CASE 2

If internal strife in France should develop into such a domestic crisis as to absorb the French Army completely and render it incapable of use for war against Germany, then the time for action against the Czechs had come.

CASE 3

If France is so embroiled by a war with another state that she cannot "proceed" against Germany.

For the improvement of our politico-military position our first objective, in the event of our being embroiled in war, must be to overthrow Czechoslovakia and Austria simultaneously in order to remove the threat to our flank in any possible operation against the West. In a conflict with France it was hardly to be regarded as likely that the Czechs would declare war on us on the very same day as France. The desire to join in the war would, however, increase among the Czechs in proportion to any weakening on our part and then her participation could clearly take the form of an attack toward Silesia, toward the north or toward the west.

If the Czechs were overthrown and a common German-Hungarian frontier achieved, a neutral attitude on the part of Poland could be the more certainly counted on in the event of a Franco-German conflict. Our agreements with Poland only retained their force as long as Germany's strength remained unshaken. In the event of German setbacks a Polish action against East Prussia, and possibly against Pomerania and Silesia as well, had to be reckoned with.

On the assumption of a development of the situation leading to action on our part as planned, in the years 1943–45, the attitude of France, Britain, Italy, Poland, and Russia could probably be estimated as follows:

Actually, the Führer believed that almost certainly Britain, and probably France as well, had already tacitly written off the Czechs and were reconciled to the fact that this question would be cleared up in due course by Germany. Difficulties connected with the Empire, and the prospect of being once more entangled in a protracted European war, were decisive considerations for Britain against participation in a war against Germany. Britain's attitude would certainly not be without influence on that of France. An attack by France without British support, and with the prospect of the offensive being brought to a standstill on our western fortifications, was hardly probable. Nor was a French march through Belgium and Holland without British support to be expected; this also was a course not to be contemplated by us in the event of a conflict with France, because it would certainly entail the hostility of Britain. It would of course be necessary to maintain a strong defense [*eine Abriegelung*] on our western frontier during the prosecution of our attack on the Czechs and Austria. And in this connection it had to be remembered that the defense measures of the Czechs were growing in strength from year to year, and that the actual worth of the Austrian Army also was increasing in the course of time. Even though the populations concerned, especially of Czechoslovakia, were not sparse, the annexation of Czechoslovakia and Austria would mean an acquisition of foodstuffs for 5 to 6 million people, on the assumption that the compulsory emigration of 2 million people from Czechoslovakia and 1 million people from Austria was practicable. The incorporation of these two States with Germany meant, from the politico-military point of view, a substantial advantage because it would mean shorter and better frontiers, the freeing of forces for other purposes, and the possibility of creating new units up to a level of about 12 divisions, that is, 1 new division per million inhabitants.

Italy was not expected to object to the elimination of the Czechs, but it was impossible at the moment to estimate what her attitude on the Austrian question would be; that depended essentially upon whether the Duce were still alive.

The degree of surprise and the swiftness of our action were decisive factors for Poland's attitude. Poland — with Russia at her rear — will have little inclination to engage in war against a victorious Germany.

Military intervention by Russia must be countered by the swiftness of our operations; however, whether such an intervention was a practical contingency at all was, in view of Japan's attitude, more than doubtful.

Should case 2 arise — the crippling of France by civil war — the situation thus created by the elimination of the most dangerous opponent must be seized upon *whenever it occurs* for the blow against the Czechs.

The Führer saw case 3 coming definitely nearer; it might emerge from the present tensions in the Mediterranean, and he was resolved to take advantage of it whenever it happened, even as early as 1938.

Broadcast Speech by Prime Minister Chamberlain, September 27, 1938

Tomorrow Parliament is going to meet, and I shall be making a full statement of the events which have led up to the present anxious and critical situation. An earlier statement would not have been possible when I was flying backwards and forwards across Europe, and the position was changing from hour to hour. But today there is a lull for a brief time, and I want to say a few words to you, men and women of Britain and the Empire, and perhaps to others as well.

First of all I must say something to those who have written to my wife or myself in these last weeks to tell us of their gratitude for my efforts and to assure us of their prayers for my success. Most of these letters have come from women — mothers or sisters of our own countrymen. But there are countless others besides — from France, from Belgium, from Italy, even from Germany, and it has been heart-breaking to read of the growing anxiety they reveal and their intense relief when they thought, too soon, that the danger of war was past.

If I felt my responsibility heavy before, to read such letters has made it seem almost overwhelming. How horrible, fantastic, incredible it is that we should be digging trenches and trying on gas-masks here because of a quarrel in a far-away country between people of whom we know nothing. It seems still more impossible that a quarrel which has already been settled in principle should be the subject of war.

I can well understand the reasons why the Czech Government have felt unable to accept the terms which have been put before them in the German memorandum. Yet I believe after my talks with Herr Hitler that, if only time were allowed, it ought to be possible for the arrangements for transferring the territory that the Czech Government has agreed to give to Germany to be settled by agreement under conditions which would assure fair treatment to the population concerned.

You know already that I have done all that one man can do to com-

From Neville Chamberlain, *In Search of Peace* (New York: Putnam, 1939), pp. 173–75. Reprinted by permission of G. P. Putnam's Sons.

pose this quarrel. After my visits to Germany I have realized vividly how Herr Hitler feels that he must champion other Germans, and his indignation that grievances have not been met before this. He told me privately, and last night he repeated publicly, that after this Sudeten German question is settled, that is the end of Germany's territorial claims in Europe.

After my first visit to Berchtesgaden I did get the assent of the Czech Government to proposals which gave the substance of what Herr Hitler wanted, and I was taken completely by surprise when I got back to Germany and found that he insisted that the territory should be handed over to him immediately, and immediately occupied by German troops without previous arrangements for safeguarding the people within the territory who were not Germans, or did not want to join the German Reich.

I must say that I find this attitude unreasonable. If it arises out of any doubts that Herr Hitler feels about the intentions of the Czech Government to carry out their promises and hand over the territory, I have offered on the part of the British Government to guarantee their words, and I am sure the value of our promise will not be underrated anywhere. I shall not give up the hope of a peaceful solution, or abandon my efforts for peace, as long as any chance for peace remains. I would not hesitate to pay even a third visit to Germany if I thought it would do any good. But at this moment I see nothing further that I can usefully do in the way of mediation.

Meanwhile there are certain things we can and shall do at home. Volunteers are still wanted for air-raid precautions, for fire brigade and police services, and for the Territorial units. I know that all of you, men and women alike, are ready to play your part in the defence of the country, and I ask you all to offer your services, if you have not already done so, to the local authorities, who will tell you if you are wanted and in what capacity.

Do not be alarmed if you hear of men being called up to man the anti-aircraft defences or ships. These are only precautionary measures such as a Government must take in times like this. But they do not necessarily mean that we have determined on war or that war is imminent.

However much we may sympathize with a small nation confronted by a big and powerful neighbour, we cannot in all circumstances undertake to involve the whole British Empire in war simply on her account. If we have to fight it must be on larger issues than that. I am myself a man of peace to the depths of my soul. Armed conflict between nations is a nightmare to me; but if I were convinced that any nation had made up its mind to dominate the world by fear of its force, I should feel that it must be resisted. Under such a domination life for people who believe in liberty would not be worth living; but war is a fearful thing, and we must be very clear, before we embark on it, that it is really the great issues that are at stake, and that the call to risk everything in their defence, when all the consequences are weighed, is irresistible.

For the present I ask you to await as calmly as you can the events of the next few days. As long as war has not begun, there is always hope that it may be prevented, and you know that I am going to work for peace to the last moment. Good night.

The Extermination
of the Jews

Hitler was a politician who kept at least some of his promises. On January 30, 1939, he announced, "If international-finance Jewry inside and outside of Europe should succeed once more in plunging nations into another world war, the consequence will not be the Bolshevization of the earth and thereby the victory of Jewry, but the annihilation of the Jewish race in Europe." By the end of the war, six million of Europe's Jews were dead. The largest number of these had been either shot in ditches by special units (Einsatzgruppen) or gassed in the chambers constructed at the various concentration camps in eastern Europe. The extermination policy was the logical conclusion of the racial anti-Semitism espoused by the Nazis. If Jews are evil by nature, then their elimination in the manner of rodents and lice could be viewed as a positive contribution to the welfare of the races threatened by them. The Jews, however, were not the only groups the Nazis singled out for genocide. The gypsies were eliminated in a similar manner, and Himmler's S.S. was also contemplating the destruction of large numbers of Slavs in order to free living space for the Germans. There would be considerable work after the elimination of the Jews.

The Nazis did move somewhat slowly in coming to a decision on the "final solution." They gave some thought to sending the Jews to Madagascar. The capture of vast numbers of Jews in Poland and Russia, however, made this unrealistic, and Hitler instructed Reich Field Marshal Hermann Goering to oversee the implementation of the final solution. The actual work was to be done by the S.S. In January, 1942, S.S. General Heydrich discussed the matter with fifteen officials of the various ministries at Wannsee, a lovely lake on the outskirts of

Berlin. One of those present was the infamous Adolf Eichmann, who organized the transportation of the victims. The peculiar achievement of Himmler, Heydrich, Eichmann, and their colleagues was to transform murder into an administrative and bureaucratic affair. This approach to the problems of liquidating large numbers of human beings is typified by Rudolf Hoess, the commandant at the most notorious of the death camps, Auschwitz, in his confession at Nuremberg in 1946.

Extracts from the Minutes of the Wannsee Conference, January 24, 1942

II. At the beginning of the meeting the Chief of the Security Police and the SD, SS Lieutenant General Heydrich, reported his appointment by the Reich Marshal to service as Commissioner for the Preparation of the Final Solution of the European Jewish Problem, and pointed out that the officials had been invited to this conference in order to clear up the fundamental problems. The Reich Marshal's request to have a draft submitted to him on the organizational, factual, and material requirements with respect to the Final Solution of the European Jewish Problem, [organisatorischen, sachlichen und materiellen Belange im Hinblick auf die Endloesung der europaeischen Judenfrage] necessitated this previous general consultation by all the central offices directly concerned, in order that there should be coordination in the policy [Parallelisierung der Linienfuehrung].

The primary responsibility [Federfuehrung] for the administrative handling of the Final Solution of the Jewish Problem will rest centrally with the Reich Leader SS and the Chief of the German Police (Chief of the Security Police and the SD) — regardless of geographic boundaries.

The Chief of the Security Police and the SD thereafter gave a brief review of the battle conducted up to now against these enemies. The most important aspects are —

1. Forcing the Jews out of the various fields of the community life of the German people.
2. Forcing the Jews out of the living space [Lebensraum] of the German people.

In execution of these efforts there was undertaken — as the only possible provisional solution — the acceleration of the emigration of the Jews from Reich territory on an intensified and methodical scale.

From Nuremberg Military Tribunals, *Trials of War Criminals*, vol. 13 (Washington, D.C.: 1947–1949), pp. 211–13.

By decree of the Reich Marshal, a Reich Central Office for Jewish Emigration was set up in January 1939, and the direction of this office was entrusted to the Chief of the Security Police and the SD. It had in particular the task —

1. Of taking all steps for the *preparation* for an intensified emigration of the Jews.
2. Of *steering* the emigration stream.
3. Of expediting the emigration *in individual cases.*

The objective of these tasks [*Aufgabenziel*] was to clear the German living space of Jews in a legal way.

The disadvantages which such a forcing of emigration brought with it were clear to all the authorities. But in view of the lack of alternative solutions, they had to be accepted in the beginning. . . .

Meanwhile, in view of the dangers of an emigration during the war and in view of the possibilities in the East, the Reich Leader SS and Chief of the German Police had forbidden the emigrating of the Jews.

III. The emigration program has now been replaced by the evacuation of the Jews to the East as a further solution possibility, in accordance with previous authorization by the Fuehrer.

These actions are of course to be regarded only as a temporary substitute; nonetheless, here already, the coming Final Solution [*Kommende Endloesung*] of the Jewish Question is of great importance.

In the course of this Final Solution of the European Jewish Problem, approximately 11 million Jews are involved. They are distributed among the individual countries as follows:

Country	Number
A. Original Reich Territory [Altreich]	131,800
Austria	43,700
Eastern Territories	420,000
Government General	2,284,000
Bialystok	400,000
Protectorate Bohemia and Moravia	74,200
Estonia — free of Jews	
Latvia	3,500
Lithuania	34,000
Belgium	43,000
Denmark	5,600
France: Occupied territory	165,000
Unoccupied territory	700,000
Greece	69,600
The Netherlands	160,800
Norway	1,300

Country	Number
B. Bulgaria	48,000
England	330,000
Finland	2,300
Ireland	4,000
Italy, including Sardinia	58,000
Albania	200
Croatia	40,000
Portugal	3,000
Rumania, including Bessarabia	342,000
Sweden	8,000
Switzerland	18,000
Serbia	10,000
Slovakia	88,000
Spain	6,000
Turkey (European part)	55,500
Hungary	742,800
U.S.S.R.	5,000,000
Ukraine	2,994,684
White Russia, excluding Bialystok	446,484
Total	over 11,000,000

In the Jewish population figures given for the various foreign countries however, only those of Jewish faith are included as the stipulations for defining Jews along racial lines still are in part lacking there. . . .

Under proper direction the Jews should now in the course of the Final Solution [*Endloesung*] be brought to the East in a suitable way for use as labor. In big labor gangs, with separation of the sexes, the Jews capable of work are brought to these areas and employed in road building, in which task undoubtedly a great part will fall out through natural diminution [*natuerliche Verminderung*].

The remnant that finally is able to survive all this — since this is undoubtedly the part with the strongest resistance — must be treated accordingly [*entsprechend behandelt werden*] since these people, representing a natural selection, are to be regarded as the germ cell of a new Jewish development. (See the experience of history.)

In the program of the practical execution of the Final Solution [*Endloesung*], Europe is combed through from the West to the East. The Reich area, including the Protectorate of Bohemia and Moravia, will have to be taken in advance, alone, for reasons of the housing problem and other social and political necessities.

The evacuated Jews are brought first group by group into the so-called transit ghettos, in order to be transported from there farther to the East.

Affidavit of Rudolf Hoess, at the Nuremberg Trials

I, Rudolf Franz Ferdinand Hoess, being first duly sworn, depose and say as follows:

1. I am forty-six years old, and have been a member of the NSDAP since 1922; a member of the SS since 1934; a member of the Waffen-SS since 1939. I was a member from 1 December 1934 of the SS Guard Unit, the so-called Deathshead Formation [*Totenkopf Verband*].

2. I have been constantly associated with the administration of concentration camps since 1934, serving at Dachau until 1938; then as Adjutant in Sachsenhausen from 1938 to May 1, 1940, when I was appointed Commandant of Auschwitz. I commanded Auschwitz until 1 December 1943, and estimate that at least 2,500,000 victims were executed and exterminated there by gassing and burning, and at least another half million succumbed to starvation and disease making a total dead of about 3,000,000. This figure represents about 70% or 80% of all persons sent to Auschwitz as prisoners, the remainder having been selected and used for slave labor in the concentration camp industries. Included among the executed and burnt were approximately 20,000 Russian prisoners of war (previously screened out of Prisoner of War cages by the Gestapo) who were delivered at Auschwitz in Wehrmacht transports operated by regular Wehrmacht officers and men. The remainder of the total number of victims included about 100,000 German Jews, and great numbers of citizens, mostly Jewish from Holland, France, Belgium, Poland, Hungary, Czechoslovakia, Greece, or other countries. We executed about 400,000 Hungarian Jews alone at Auschwitz in the summer of 1944.

3. WVHA (SS Main Economic and Administration Office), headed by Obergruppenfuehrer Oswald Pohl, was responsible for all administrative matters such as billeting, feeding and medical care, in the concentration camps. Prior to establishment of the RSHA, Secret State Police Office (Gestapo) and the Reich Office of Criminal Police were responsible for arrests, commitments to concentration camps, punishments and executions therein. After organization of the RSHA, all of these functions were carried on as before, but pursuant to orders signed by Heydrich as Chief of the RSHA. While Kaltenbrunner was Chief of RSHA, orders for protective custody, commitments, punishment, and individual executions were signed by Kaltenbrunner or by Mueller, Chief of the Gestapo, as Kaltenbrunner's deputy.

4. Mass executions by gassing commenced during the summer 1941 and continued until fall 1944. I personally supervised executions at Auschwitz until the first of December 1943 and know by reason of my

From Office of the U.S. Chief of Counsel for Prosecution of Axis Criminality, *Nazi Conspiracy and Aggression*, vol. 6 (Washington, D.C.: 1946), pp. 787–90.

continued duties in the Inspectorated of Concentration Camps WVHA that these mass executions continued as stated above. All mass executions by gassing took place under the direct orders, supervisions, and responsibility of RSHA. I received all orders for carrying out these mass executions directly from RSHA.

5. On 1 December 1943 I became Chief of AMT 1 in AMT Group D of the WVHA and in that office was responsible for coordinating all matters arising between RSHA and concentration camps under the administration of WVHA. I held this position until the end of the war. Pohl, as Chief of WVHA, and Kaltenbrunner, as Chief of RSHA, often conferred personally and frequently communicated orally and in writing concerning concentration camps. On 5 October 1944 I brought a lengthy report regarding Mauthausen Concentration Camp to Kaltenbrunner at his office at RSHA, Berlin. Kaltenbrunner asked me to give him a short oral digest of this report and said he would reserve any decision until he had had an opportunity to study it in complete detail. This report dealt with the assignment to labor of several hundred prisoners who had been condemned to death — so-called "nameless prisoners."

6. The "final solution" of the Jewish question meant the complete extermination of all Jews in Europe. I was ordered to establish extermination facilities at Auschwitz in June 1941. At that time, there were already in the general government three other extermination camps; Belzek, Treblinka, and Wolzek. These camps were under the Einsatzkommando of the Security Police and SD. I visited Treblinka to find out how they carried out their extermination. The Camp Commandant at Treblinka told me that he had liquidated 80,000 in the course of one-half year. He was principally concerned with liquidating all the Jews from the Warsaw ghetto. He used monoxide gas and I did not think that his methods were very efficient. So when I set up the extermination building at Auschwitz, I used Cyclon B, which was a crystallized prussic acid which we dropped into the death chamber from a small opening. It took from 3 to 15 minutes to kill the people in the death chamber depending upon climatic conditions. We knew when the people were dead because their screaming stopped. We usually waited about one-half hour before we opened the doors and removed the bodies. After the bodies were removed our special commandos took off the rings and extracted the gold from the teeth of the corpses.

7. Another improvement we made over Treblinka was that we built our gas chambers to accommodate 2,000 people at one time, whereas at Treblinka their 10 gas chambers only accommodated 200 people each. The way we selected our victims was as follows: we had two SS doctors on duty at Auschwitz to examine the incoming transports of prisoners. The prisoners would be marched by one of the doctors who would make spot decisions as they walked by. Those who were fit for work were sent

into the Camp. Others were sent immediately to the extermination plants. Children of tender years were invariably exterminated since by reason of their youth they were unable to work. Still another improvement we made over Treblinka was that at Treblinka the victims almost always knew that they were to be exterminated and at Auschwitz we endeavored to fool the victims into thinking that they were to go through a delousing process. Of course, frequently they realized our true intentions and we sometimes had riots and difficulties due to that fact. Very frequently women would hide their children under the clothes but of course when we found them we would send the children in to be exterminated. We were required to carry out these exterminations in secrecy but of course the foul and nauseating stench from the continuous burning of bodies permeated the entire area and all of the people living in the surrounding communities knew that exterminations were going on at Auschwitz.

8. We received from time to time special prisoners from the local Gestapo office. The SS doctors killed such prisoners by injections of benzine. Doctors had orders to write ordinary death certificates and could put down any reason at all for the cause of death.

9. From time to time we conducted medical experiments on women inmates, including sterilization and experiments relating to cancer. Most of the people who died under these experiments had been already condemned to death by the Gestapo.

10. Rudolf Mildner was the chief of the Gestapo at Kattowitz and as such was head of the Political Department at Auschwitz which conducted third degree methods of interrogation, from approximately March 1941 until September 1943. As such, he frequently sent prisoners to Auschwitz for incarceration or execution. He visited Auschwitz on several occasions. The Gestapo Court, the SS Standgericht, which tried persons accused of various crimes, such as escaping Prisoners of War, etc., frequently met within Auschwitz, and Mildner often attended the trial of such persons, who usually were executed in Auschwitz following their sentence. I showed Mildner throughout the extermination plant at Auschwitz and he was directly interested in it since he had to send the Jews from his territory for execution at Auschwitz.

I understand English as it is written above. The above statements are true; this declaration is made by me voluntarily and without compulsion; after reading over the statement, I have signed and executed the same at Nuremberg, Germany, on the fifth day of April 1946.

                                        Rudolf Franz Ferdinand Hoess

Subscribed and sworn to before me this 5th day of April 1946,
at Nuremberg, Germany
Smith W. Brookhart Jr., Lt. Colonel, IGD.

The Defeat of France

The great French Jewish historian Marc Bloch (1885–1944) escaped Hitler's gas chambers but was executed as a member of the French Resistance in 1944. Bloch's methodological innovations have not only revolutionized the writing of medieval agrarian history but have also exerted a profound influence on all historical writing. Bloch, however, was more than a scholar. He was an ardent French patriot who had served as an officer in World War I and who volunteered to serve again in 1939. Immediately following the defeat of France, he decided to set down his experiences and an analysis of its causes so that his children and friends might at least have his eyewitness account and reflections upon the disaster. The work is a brilliant criticism of the French military, political, and social conditions responsible for the defeat, just as it is a moving document of French patriotism.

Bloch's *Strange Defeat*

Every conceivable sin is laid at the door of the political regime which governed France in the years before the war. I have only to look about me to feel convinced that the parliamentary system has too often favoured intrigue at the cost of intelligence and true loyalty. The men who govern us to-day were, for the most part, brought up in a land of mental bogs. If now they turn against the methods which made them what they are, that is only because they are sly old foxes who think the trick worth trying. The dishonest clerk who cracks the office safe is not likely to carry a bunch of skeleton keys about with him for all to see. He is far too frightened that someone cleverer than himself will pocket them and scoop the loot.

When the time for real reform at last comes round, when we can once again demand that we be led into the light of day, and that the political sects which have lost the nation's confidence be swept from the stage, we shall have to do better than set our feet in the tracks of the immediate past. The monstrously swollen assemblies which, in recent years, have claimed to rule us were one of the more absurd legacies of history. It mattered little that the States-General, convened to pronounce a simple "Yes" or "No," should have a membership of hundreds. But a chamber whose function is to run the country must become chaotic once it has allowed itself to degenerate into a mob. It is, indeed, a question whether a chamber which was designed merely to sanction and control,

From Marc Bloch, *Strange Defeat: A Statement of Evidence Written in 1940*, trans. Gerard Hopkins (New York: Norton, 1968), pp. 156–62, 174–76. Reprinted by permission of Oxford University Press.

can govern. Our party machinery had already begun to give off the smell of a dry-rot which it had acquired in small cafés and obscure back rooms. It could not even offer the excuse that it was strong, because at the first breath of despotism it collapsed like a house of cards. Imprisoned in doctrines which they knew to be outmoded, of programmes which they had long abandoned as signposts to practical politics, the great parties served as sham rallying-points for men who, on all the major problems of the movement — as was only too obvious after Munich — held utterly opposed views. They declared themselves to be at odds with others whose members thought, in fact, precisely as they did. More often than not they failed even to determine who was to wield the power. They served merely as spring-boards for clever careerists who spent their time knocking one another off the top of the political structure.

It was entirely owing to our ministers and our assemblies that we were so ill prepared for war. Of that there can be not the slightest doubt. Not, it is true, that the High Command did much to help them. But nothing shed a cruder light on the spinelessness of Government than its capitulation to the technicians. In 1915 a succession of Parliamentary Commissions did more to provide us with heavy artillery than did all the artillery-men put together. Why did not their successors do more, and do it quicker, in the matter of aeroplanes and tanks? The history of the Ministry of Munitions reads like a lesson in unreason. It is incredible that we should have had to wait until the war was several months old before it was even set up, and then only as a makeshift organization. It should have been ready to start work, with a staff already picked and prepared, on the very day that mobilization was ordered. Only very exceptionally did Parliament ever refuse credits if the specialists demanded them with sufficient firmness, but it lacked the power to compel their proper use. It could, had it so wished, have put its hand in the elector's pocket, but it was afraid of irritating him. Its dislike of imposing on reservists the necessary period of field-training undermined the whole principle of the nation in arms. True, the routine of the barrack-square — not the best way of utilizing these periods of instruction — did at least set that particular ball rolling, but that is not saying much. More than once the leaders of the Government found themselves driven to ask for extraordinary powers — which was tantamount to admitting that the constitutional machinery was getting rusty. It would have been far better to redesign the machine while there was yet time. Those extraordinary powers were the line of least resistance, though nobody seems to have realized that they merely served to reinforce the existing practices of government and did nothing towards reforming them. Spoiled by a long familiarity with the lobbies, our political leaders imagined that they were gleaning information when all they were doing was to collect gossip from chance acquaintances. All problems, of the world as well as of the nation, appeared to them in the light of personal rivalries.

That the system suffered from weaknesses there can be no denying; but it was not so inherently vicious as has sometimes been argued. Many of the crimes of which it has been accused were, I should say, purely imaginary. It is often said that party, and, in particular, anti-clerical, passions disorganized the armed forces. I can bear witness from my own experience that at Bohain General Blanchard went to Mass every Sunday. To assume that he had waited until war broke out to do so would be to level a gratuitous insult at his civic courage. It was right and proper that he, as a believer, should publicly perform his religious duties. The unbeliever who held such acts against him showed himself to be a fool or a boor. But I see no reason to maintain that those religious convictions, loyally adhered to, stood in the way of his being given an army by a succession of so-called Left-Wing governments, or of his leading it to defeat.

Did those parliaments of ours, if it comes to that, or the ministries born of them, ever really concentrate the government of the country in their own hands? Earlier systems had left a legacy of public corporations which the politicians never really succeeded in controlling. No doubt party considerations did to some extent weigh in the appointment of the heads of these bodies, and, as the winds of the moment blew, so did personalities change — not always with the happiest results. But, fundamentally, these great organizations were self-governing, and the men who formed their rank and file always remained, roughly, of the same type. The École des Sciences Politiques, for instance, was always the spiritual home of scions of rich and powerful families. Its graduates filled the embassies, the Treasury, the Council of State, and the Public Audit Office. The École Polytechnique, with its curious power of leaving an indelible and recognizable imprint on the young men who had passed through it, did far more than supply recruits for the general staffs of industry. It unlocked the door to a career in public engineering, where promotion had almost the automatic precision of a well-oiled machine. The universities, through the medium of a complex arrangement of councils and committees, filled any vacancies there might be in their teaching-staffs by a system of co-option which was not without its dangers when the need for new blood arose, and could offer to their successful students guarantees of permanent employment which the system at present in force has — provisionally, it is said — abolished. The Institute of France, entrenched in its wealth and in that prestige which the glitter of a title can always impose even on those who pass for being philosophically minded, still retains, for good or ill, the full dignity of its intellectual pre-eminence. If the Academy might occasionally be influenced in its elections by political considerations, it can scarcely be maintained that these have been of a Left-Wing kind. 'I know of only three citadels of Conservatism,' said Paul Bourget on one occasion, 'the House of Lords, the German General Staff, and the French Academy.'

Was the regime right or wrong in the consideration it habitually showed to these ancient corporations? The subject might be discussed endlessly. Some will uphold them in the interests of stability and in recognition of an honourable tradition. Others, with whom, I confess, my own sympathies lie, will argue against them on grounds of bureaucratic tendencies, routine mentality, and professional arrogance. But there are certainly two things for which a heavy responsibility lay at their door.

They raised a clamorous outcry when a Popular Front Government, in an effort to break down the monopoly held by the École des Sciences Politiques, presumed to establish a School of Administration. Not that the project was a particularly good one. It would have been very much better to throw open an administrative career to all by means of a system of public scholarships, and to let candidates be prepared by the universities along those cultural lines which have served the English civil service so well. But, for all that, the underlying idea was sound. Whatever the complexion of its government, a country is bound to suffer if the *instruments* of power are hostile to the spirit which obtains in the various branches of its public institutions. A monarchy needs a personnel composed of monarchists. A democracy becomes hopelessly weak, and the general good suffers accordingly, if its higher officials, bred up to despise it, and necessarily drawn from those very classes the dominance of which it is pledged to destroy, serve it only half-heartedly.

The other point which can justly be brought against them is this. The system of co-option which, whether officially or unofficially, was the rule in almost all the great public corporations, tended to give much too prominent a place to age. As in the Army, promotion — with very few exceptions — was, generally speaking, slow, and the old men at the top, even when they did show willingness to help their juniors up the ladder, were inclined to pick their men from among those who had shown themselves to be model pupils — almost excessively model. We judge revolutions to be admirable or hateful according as their principles are or are not our own. All of them, however, have one supreme virtue which is inseparable from the vigour out of which they grow: they do thrust the young into positions of prominence. I detest Nazism, but, like the French Revolution, with which one should blush to compare it, it did put at the head, both of its armed forces and of its Government, men who, because their brains were fresh and had not been formed in the routine of the schools, were capable of understanding 'the surprising and the new.' All we had to set against them was a set of bald-pates and youngish dotards.

But however powerful the resistance offered by a Government's machinery may be, the *system* is the creation of the society which is said to be governed by it. Sometimes the engine may run away with the driver, but, as a rule, it will give good service if it is properly handled. I find it difficult not to laugh when I hear certain business men of my acquaintance inveighing against the venality of the Press just after they have managed to get some article 'planted' (in return for good hard cash) on one of our more respectable dailies, or when they have commissioned a former minister to write a book which will bolster up their own petty interests, fulminating against 'Parliamentary men of straw'! Who most deserves to be hanged, the corrupted or the corrupter? Our rich *bourgeois* like nothing better than to grumble at the teaching profession. In the days when they controlled the money-bags much more completely than they do to-day, they had it in their power to provide in the budget for a reasonable scale of pay for schoolmasters. What, in fact, they did was to give those who were entrusted with the education of their sons far less than they would have dreamed of giving to their servants. The reputation for avarice has done the French people an infinity of harm: and it is this provincial attitude of mind that has been responsible.

But what, more than anything else, has injured our machinery of State, and, literally, stopped it from working, is that major lack of understanding which lies like a blight over the minds of almost all Frenchmen. . . .

We find ourselves to-day in this appalling situation — that the fate of France no longer depends upon the French. Since that moment when the weapons which we held with too indeterminate a grasp fell from our hands, the future of our country and of our civilization has become the stake in a struggle of which we, for the most part, are only the rather humiliated spectators. What will become of us if, by some hideous mischance, Great Britain is in turn defeated? Our recovery as a nation will, it is quite certain, be long retarded. But *only* retarded, of that I am sure. The deep-seated vitality of our people is intact, and, sooner or later, will show signs of recovery. That of nazified Germany, on the contrary, cannot endure indefinitely the increasing strain which its masters see fit to impose upon it. Foreign systems brought into France in the 'baggage wagons of the enemy' have, on more than one occasion, lasted for a limited time. But the destination of a proud nation has always, in the long run, proved too strong, and, sooner or later, sentence has been pronounced. Already we feel the iron of occupation eating more cruelly into our flesh. The seeming good-nature of the early days no longer deceives anybody. We have but to see Hitlerism in its day-to-day manifestations to condemn it. But I would so much rather look forward to an eventual British victory! I cannot tell when the hour will sound when, thanks to our Allies, we can once more control our own destiny. But when it does sound, shall we see scraps and corners of our territory liberate themselves successively from the enemy? Shall we see wave after wave of volunteer armies spring into being all agog to answer to the renewed appeal of 'The Country in Danger'? Maybe some tiny autonomous government will suddenly appear in some remote district and spread like a patch of oil. It may be, on the other hand, that a great surge of national feeling will develop swiftly. An elderly historian likes to arrange patterns with these pictures of a possible future, though imperfect knowledge makes it impossible for him to choose between them. My only hope, and I make no bones about it, is that when the moment comes we shall have enough blood left to shed, even though it be the blood of those who are dear to us (I say nothing of my own, to which I attach no importance). For there can be no salvation where there is not some sacrifice, and no national liberty in the fullest sense unless we have ourselves worked to bring it about.

The duty of reconstructing our country will not fall on the shoulders of my generation. France in defeat will be seen to have had a government of old men. That is but natural. France of the new springtime must be the creation of the young. As compared with their elders of the last war, they will have one sad privilege: they will not have to guard against the lethargy bred of victory. Whatever form the final triumph may take, it will be many years before the stain of 1940 can be effaced. It may be a good thing that these young people will have to work in a white heat of rage. It would be impertinent on my part to outline a programme for them. They will search for the laws of the future in the intimacy of their heads and of their hearts. The map of the future will be drawn as a result of the lessons they have learned. All I beg of them is that they shall avoid the dry inhumanity of systems which, from rancour or from pride, set themselves to rule the mass of their countrymen without providing them with adequate instruction, without being in true communion with them. Our people deserve to be trusted, to be taken into the confidence of their leaders. I hope, too, that though they may do new things, many new things, they will not break the links that bind us to our authentic heritage, which is not at all, or, at least, not wholly, what some self-styled apostles of tradition have imagined it to be. On one occasion Hitler said to Rauschning: 'It is very much better to bank on the vices of men than on their virtues. The French Revolution appealed to virtue. We shall be better advised to do the contrary.' A Frenchman, that is to say, a civilized man — for the two are identical — will be forgiven if he substitute for this teaching that of the Revolution and of Montesquieu: "A State founded on the People needs a mainspring: and that mainspring is virtue." What matter if the task is thereby made more difficult — as it will be? A free people in pursuit of noble ends runs a double risk. But are soldiers on the field of battle to be warned against the spirit of adventure?

GUÉRET-FOUGÈRES (CREUSE)
July–September 1940

THE AFTERMATH OF WAR
Chapter 6

One of the illusions that may have helped to make the destructiveness of the two world wars bearable was the belief that a better world would emerge from the holocausts. Although the two wars certainly prevented German hegemony in Europe and World War II prevented the triumph of a regime unrivaled in its inhumanity, both wars demonstrated that war is a poor foundation for social and international reconstruction, for once the emergency of combat is past, the sense of urgency, the willingness to experiment, and the acceptance of the novel pass with it. War leaves exposed in a manner more brutal than normal the role that force and power play in international affairs. The conclusion of a war, therefore, may serve to point the way only to new rivalries and suspicions. This is not to say that there was a precise parallel between the post-1918 return to "normalcy" and the developments after 1945. Real attempts were made on the national and international levels to avoid the mistakes of the past and correct the conditions that had brought on the disaster. Nevertheless, the most constructive and significant measures of reconstruction after World War II developed not out of the conclusion of peace but out of the threats and problems presented by the development of the cold war. As a consequence, even where economic reconstruction made headway, political practice tended to fall back on prewar patterns, and basic structural reforms such as those desperately needed in higher education were evaded or neglected.

It is striking, for example, how quickly Italy and France returned to the divisive multiparty parliamentary politics that had characterized the former before Mussolini's advent to power and the latter before 1940, even though both countries recognized the need for new constitutions and styles of partisan politics. The French elected a constituent assembly to frame a new constitution on October 21, 1945, and the Italians took the same step on June 2, 1946. In both countries important new Christian Democratic parties developed, and popular front governments of Christian Democrats, Socialists, and Communists were created. Yet, the new constitutions contained few significant innovations, and the popular front governments proved casualties of their internal tensions and increasing international tension. By 1947 all that remained of reform efforts were some experiments with nationalization and welfare state practices. In Great Britain, the political framework for reconstruction was more helpful. In June, 1945, the electorate turned out Winston Churchill and the Conservatives and installed a Labour government under Clement Attlee. Attlee's nationalization and social welfare measures fulfilled many of his campaign promises, but they did not solve the basic economic problems of the country, and Labour's austerity program soon lost the party its popularity. By 1951 the Conservatives were back in power.

The Second World War really drove home the lesson that the First World War had begun to teach: Europe could not recover on its own. Furthermore, the second defeat of Germany marked the final passing of the European political and military predominance of past centuries to the great continental powers of Russia and America. Wartime coalitions have never been known for their stability, and the rivalry between Russia and America was inevitable and, indeed, was predicted by Alexis de Tocqueville in the middle of the nineteenth century. The origins of the cold war, however, remain in dispute and probably will continue to be disputed until historians can examine all the relevant documents and discover the true intentions of the leaders on both sides. Suspicion existed from the beginning because of ideological differences and the prehistory of the war. The Russians neither forgot nor forgave the Munich agreement, which confirmed their suspicions that the West was prepared to isolate them and would not have been sorry if Russia and Nazi Germany had fought each other to mutual exhaustion. The West could not forget the Nazi-Soviet Pact and the joint aggression against Poland. During the war, differences were bridged over, but the Russians continuously complained about the failure of the Western powers to open a second front, while the latter tried to reassure the Russians with Lend Lease and the policy of unconditional surrender. As the war drew to a close, the sources of friction increased, and vague understandings at Yalta in February, 1945, and Potsdam in July, 1945, papered over differences and laid the groundwork for the misunderstandings of the future.

From the perspective of the present it is clear that the fate of Eastern Europe was determined by Russian occupation and Russian power in the area rather than by decisions made at Yalta or Potsdam. Russia had been devastated by the war, and it is reasonable to estimate that it lost twenty million people between 1941 and 1945. It bore the brunt of the struggle, and security and recovery were bound to be of paramount importance after the war. Stalin naturally viewed Eastern Europe as a Russian sphere of influence, just as he naturally tried to exploit the occupied territories of Germany, Austria, and Hungary. Furthermore, both Churchill and Roosevelt seemed willing to accept the idea of Russian predominance in Eastern Europe and substantial reparations to the Soviet Union. What is unclear is the extent to which Stalin was prepared to impose ideological uniformity in Eastern Europe and to extend Soviet power beyond that area. Similarly, it is difficult to measure the extent to which the hardening American attitude following Roosevelt's death ruined the possibilities of better relations with the Russians. By 1947 America had assumed responsibility for the military protection and economic recovery of Western Europe with the Truman Doctrine and Marshall Plan. The Communist coup in Czechoslovakia in February, 1948, and the Berlin Blockade of 1948–1949 completed the polarization of Europe and much of the world into two hostile camps.

The Fourth French Republic

Although Charles de Gaulle will always remain controversial, his devotion to the greatness and grandeur of France is unquestionable as is his understanding of some of the vital needs and problems of his nation. Before the war, he vainly argued for new strategic conceptions that would employ armor in precisely the way in which the Germans, who had read De Gaulle's works, employed their tanks when they invaded France. After France's defeat, he kept the spirit of resistance alive by setting up a Free French regime to oppose Vichy. Despite Roosevelt's suspicions that De Gaulle was a fascist, the Allies finally were compelled to work with him, and the Free French forces made significant contributions to the war effort. De Gaulle returned to France with the Allies and hoped that the new Fourth Republic would correct the mistakes of the Third by giving more power to the executive. His disappointment led to his resignation as president in January, 1946. In 1958, De Gaulle came forth to serve his country in another crisis, and, as first president of the Fifth Republic, established a constitution that mitigated many of the worst aspects of the previous domination of the executive by the legislature.

De Gaulle's Memoirs

Now it was November. The war had been over for two months, the nation's attention was flagging and great actions no longer held the stage. Everything pointed to the reappearance of yesterday's regime, less adapted than ever to the nation's needs. If I was still in power, it could only be provisionally. But to France and the French, I owed something further — to take my leave as a man morally intact.

The Constituent Assembly convened on November 6. Cuttoli, a Radical deputy and the senior member, presided. Although this first session was a purely formal one, I had insisted on being present. Some may have felt that the transmission of public powers from De Gaulle to the national representation should be made with some formality. But the notion that my visit to the Palais Bourbon might involve a degree of ceremony antagonized the provisional committee and even the men of protocol. So everything was accomplished without a show of state and, on the whole, in a mediocre manner.

Cuttoli made a speech paying homage to Charles de Gaulle but lavishing criticisms on his policy. The praises found few echoes among those present but the disparagements received strong applause from the Left, while the Right abstained from any manifestation whatever. Then the presiding officer read aloud my letter announcing that the government would resign once the Constituent Assembly had elected its committee. There was no particular reaction. As for myself, sitting in a lower row of the arena, I sensed converging upon me the ponderous stares of six hundred parliamentarians and I felt, almost physically, the weight of the general uneasiness.

After the Assembly had elected Félix Gouin as its president, its next task was to elect the President of the Government. Naturally I abstained from submitting my candidacy or making any reference to my eventual platform. They would take me as I was or not take me at all. During an entire week, there were many trying conferences among the various groups. Meanwhile, on November 11, I presided over the ceremony in the Place de l'Étoile. Fifteen coffins, brought from every battlefield, were arranged around the Tomb of the Unknown Soldier, as if the combatants had come to pay the final homage of their own sacrifice before being transferred to a casemate of the Mont Valérien military cemetery. Speaking a few words at the foot of the Arc de Triomphe, I appealed for unity and fraternity in order to cure wounded France. "Let us walk together," I said, "on the same road, at the same pace, singing the same song! Let us

From Charles de Gaulle, *The War Memoirs of Charles de Gaulle. Volume 3: Salvation, 1944–1946* (© 1959 by Simon and Schuster, Inc.; © 1956 by Libraire Plons), trans. Richard Howard (New York: Simon and Schuster, 1960), pp. 310–19. Reprinted by permission of Simon and Schuster, Inc.

look toward the future with the eyes of a great united people!" Around the circumference of the Place de l'Étoile, the crowd was as enthusiastic as ever; but at my side the official faces indicated that the government was about to change its nature.

Nevertheless, two days later, the National Assembly unanimously elected me President of the Government of the French Republic and proclaimed that "Charles de Gaulle had deserved well of his country." Although this demonstration occurred only after eight days of disagreeable palavers, it might be interpreted as expressing a conscious intention of assembling around me in order to support my policy. This was what Mr. Winston Churchill, for example, appeared to believe after passing through Paris on November 13, dining at my table and subsequently hearing the election results, Churchill expressed his enthusiasm in a generous letter. Recalling Plutarch's remark, "Ingratitude toward men is the sign of a strong people," which had recently been taken as an epigraph for a celebrated book, he wrote, in his turn, "Plutarch lied!" But I knew that the vote was a form of homage addressed to my past action, not a promise that engaged the future.

This was immediately brought home to me. On November 15, undertaking to constitute the government, I was to step in one wasp's nest of intrigue after another. The leftist groups, who formed a considerable majority in the Assembly, raised many objections. The Radicals informed me that they would not participate in any government of mine. If any of their members accepted a portfolio nevertheless, it would be against the explicit will of the entire party. The Socialists, suspicious and anxious, made inquiries as to my platform, multiplied their conditions and declared that in any case they would grant their votes only to a Cabinet that had the support and the participation of the Communists. The latter were playing for high stakes; for them Maurice Thorez demanded at least one of the three ministries they regarded as most important: National Defense, Interior, or Foreign Affairs. This was indeed the question. If I should yield to their demands, the Communists would hold one of the state's essential powers and thereby have means of taking control in a moment of confusion. If I should refuse, I ran the risk of finding myself powerless to form a government. But then the "party," having demonstrated that it was stronger than De Gaulle, would become the master of the hour.

I decided to take a decisive step; I would oblige the Communists either to enter the government under my conditions or to leave it altogether. I informed Thorez that neither the Ministry of Foreign Affairs, nor that of National Defense, nor that of the Interior would be assigned to any member of his party. To the latter I offered only "economic" ministries. As a result of this move, the Communists published furious diatribes, declaring that by refusing to give them what they asked I was "insulting the memory of the war dead," and invoking their "75,000 assassinated men," an entirely arbitrary figure, moreover, for happily the total number of their adherents who had fallen before the firing squads did not amount to a fifth of this number, and furthermore those Frenchmen who had sacrificed their lives had done so — Communists included — for France, not for a party.

Thereupon I was flooded by the alarmed reproofs of various men of the Left who urged me to yield in order to avoid a fatal crisis, while the other factions remained silent and withdrawn. But my resolution was firm. I intended to oblige the National Assembly to support me against the Marxist Left, and on November 17 I therefore wrote to the President of the Constituent Assembly that since I was unable to create a unified government, I was restoring to the national representation the mandate it had entrusted to me. The following day, speaking on the radio, I called the people to witness the abusive demands which partisan groups claimed to impose upon me. I announced that for obvious national and international reasons, I refused to put the Communists in a position to dominate our policy by surrendering to them "the diplomacy which expresses it, the Army which sustains it or the police which protects it." This being so, I would form a government with the support of those who chose to follow me. Otherwise, I would resign from office immediately and without bitterness.

Moreover, however threatening the atmosphere, every intangible factor, the expression of every apprehension, led me to believe that I would succeed in my design. And indeed, after a debate I did not attend, the Assembly re-elected me President of the Government by every vote save those of the Communists. It is true that André Philip, spokesman for the Socialists, had tried to explain his party's reluctant adherence by proclaiming that the Chamber was conveying to me the "imperative charge" of setting up a Ministry in which the extreme Left would be represented. This formulation deceived no one. It was clear that the Communists had not been able to impose their will. Not a single deputy, outside their own group, had supported them, and in the decisive vote, they were isolated against all others, without exception. Thus was broken, from the start, a spell which had indeed threatened to become calamitous.

The Communists drew the appropriate conclusions at once. The next day, their delegation called to inform me they were willing to enter my government without stipulating conditions, and asserted I would find no support firmer than theirs. Without deluding myself as to the sincerity of this sudden reversal, I accepted their support, considering that for a while at least their rallying to my cause could further the social harmony of which the nation stood in such need.

On November 21 the government was constituted. Four portfolios went to Communist deputies — Billoux, Croizat, Paul and Tillon; four to

Socialists — Moch, Tanguy-Prigent, Thomas and Tixier; four to Popular Republicans — Bidault, Michelet, Prigent and Teitgen; two to resistance leaders of the Democratic Union — Pleven and Soustelle; one to Giacobbi, a Radical; one to Dautry and one to Malraux, neither of whom was a parliamentarian or had any party affiliation whatever; the entire structure was surmounted by four Ministers of State — a Socialist, Auriol; a Popular Republican, Gay; a Moderate, Jacquinot; a Communist, Thorez. As expected and announced, the Marxist Left received only economic ministries — National Economy, Labor, Production and Armament Manufacture.

On November 23 I made a speech before the Assembly in which I emphasized the gravity of the nation's present circumstances, the necessity of adopting as soon as possible institutions assuring "the responsibility, the stability, the authority of the executive power," and lastly the duty of the French and their representatives to unite in order to re-create France. Once again, the national representation supported me unanimously. In the crisis which had been prolonged for seventeen days without any valid reason, only the political parties had found their sustenance and their satisfaction.

Despite the record achieved, I could not doubt that my power hung by a thread. Nevertheless, during the month of December I had the government adopt and the Assembly pass a law nationalizing the Bank of France and four credit establishments, and instituted a National Credit Council serving under the Minister of Finance. Shortly after, another law settled the terms of transferring the production and distribution of gas and electricity to the state. In both these issues all demogogic amendments had been successfully discarded. Furthermore, on December 15 I had the satisfaction of inaugurating the National School of Administration, an important institution which would co-ordinate and standardize the recruiting and training of the principal public servants, who had hitherto come to office from various disciplines. The school, springing full-fledged from the brain and the labors of my adviser Michel Debré, saw the light of day, it was true, in an atmosphere of skepticism on the part of the major bodies of public service and the parliamentary milieus. Yet it was to see their prejudices dissolve as it gradually became, from the point of view of administrative training, attitude and action, the foundation of the new state. Nevertheless, and by a sort of ironic coincidence, at the very moment when this nursery of the future servants of the Republic was being created, the threat of a general strike of civil servants sorely tried the cohesion of the government and my own authority.

It was only too true, of course, that the standard of living of these public servants had suffered greatly from the inflation. Their wage increases were not sufficient to meet the rise of prices. But what the trade unions demanded for them could not be granted without unbalancing the budget and depleting the treasury. Although this was acknowledged by the Council of Ministers, although I had indicated my determination not to allocate more than the reasonable increase proposed by René Pleven and my resolve to forbid the strike under threat of penalties to be imposed on the offenders, I noticed violent agitation rising within the government itself. Several Socialist members, following their party's instructions, gave me to understand that they would retire rather than send a refusal to the trade union and penalize the functionaries and employees who abstained from work. At the same time, the civil servants were convened by their federations on December 15 at the Vélodrome d'Hiver in order to stigmatize "the absurd inadequacy of the measures contemplated by the government" and to call for a general strike.

By a curious complication, at the moment when a major crisis seemed inevitable, it was Communist support that permitted me to avert it. Within the Council, which was holding another session, Maurice Thorez suddenly declared that there must be no yielding to such intolerable pressures provided a few minor modifications were made; the arrangements proposed by the Finance Minister and approved by the President should be applied. Immediately the possibility of a Cabinet checkmate vanished from sight. That afternoon, at the Vélodrome d'Hiver, when the speakers mandated by the trade unions and in conjunction with the Socialist party had requested the audience to stop work and take action against the government, the Communist representative, to the general astonishment, violently opposed the agitators. "If the civil servants go on strike," he declared, "they will be committing a crime against their country!" Then, taking advantage of the confusion produced by this unexpected outburst from the "workers' party," he caused the decision to strike to be postponed. Thereafter, in order to settle the question, there remained only the parliamentary procedures to be executed.

On December 18, at the end of the debate the National Assembly had opened on the subject, I made it clear that the government could not go beyond the measures it had adopted, whatever its regret at being unable to do more for the state workers. "We have come," I said, "to the moment when, economically and financially speaking, we may lose everything or save nothing." I added, "We must know if the present government, confronting a serious difficulty and offering its solution, has or has not your confidence. We must know too if the National Assembly will or will not be able to devote itself to the nation's general interest beyond party concerns." The order of the day ultimately voted was as confused and ineffectual as I could wish.

But this success was a temporary one. A few days later, it was shown still more clearly how precarious General de Gaulle's power had become in relation to the parties and to the Assembly.

The 1946 budget was under discussion. For form's sake the government insisted that the final vote be taken on January first. But on that day, as the discussion seemed to draw to a close, the Socialists suddenly demanded a 20 per cent reduction of the credits assigned to National Defense. It was obvious that so sudden and summary a proposition, directed against an order of expenditures which evidently could not be reduced to such proportions from one day to the next, was inspired by both electoral demagogy and hostility toward me.

Since I was detained in the Rue St.-Dominique on New Year's Day by the visits of the diplomatic corps and the authorities, the Palais Bourbon debate dragged on without reaching an outcome. Though Minister of Finance Pleven, Minister of the Armies Michelet, Minister of Armament Tillon and Minister of State Auriol followed my instructions and declared that the government rejected the proposition, the Left — Socialists, Communists and the majority of the Radicals — which together comprised the majority, was prepared to vote it through. However, and as if to prove that the real issue was De Gaulle, the Assembly postponed any conclusion until I came in person to take part in the discussion.

I did so during the afternoon. In my presence, Messrs. Philip and Gazier led the attack with passion, supported by the applause of their Socialist colleagues, the Radicals counting the blows. Actually, the challengers protested their intention was not to destroy the government; they were taking action, they said, only to oblige it to yield before the parliamentary will. The Popular Republicans made it clear that they did not approve the aggression launched against me on such grounds, while the Right voiced its anxiety, but these fractions of the Assembly were careful not to condemn the opposition in explicit terms. As for the Communists, hesitating between the immediate imperative of demagogy and their tactics of the moment, they informed me that the assault had not been made with their agreement, but that if the Socialists were to bring the matter to vote, they themselves would be obliged to deny me their support.

That evening, probing hearts and hopes, I realized that the matter was already decided, that it would be vain and even unworthy to presume to govern when the parties, their power restored, had resumed their old tricks; in short, that I must now prepare my own departure from the scene.

In two brief interventions, I indicated to the Assembly the absurdity of the constraint they hoped to impose upon me and the frivolity with which the representatives of the people were preparing to cut into the national defense in order to give themselves the advantage of a partisan maneuver. Then, proceeding to the heart of the matter, I declared that this debate posed the entire problem of tomorrow's institutions. Once the government, acting in full knowledge of the case, had assumed its responsibility in so serious a matter, was it acceptable that the parliament should now wish to oblige it to contradict and humiliate itself? Were we imitating the regime of the Assembly? For my part, I refused to do so. If the credits requested were not voted that same evening, the government would not remain in office another hour.

"I should like to add a word," I said, "which is not for the present but, even now, for the future. The point that divides us is a general conception of the government and its relations with the national representation. We have begun to reconstruct the Republic. After me, you will continue to do so. I must tell you in all conscience — and doubtless this is the last time I shall be speaking to you from this place — that if you do not take into account the absolute necessities of governmental authority, dignity and responsibility, you will find yourselves in a situation which I predict will cause you bitter regret for having taken the way you have chosen."

As if the opposition wished to emphasize the fact that its attitude had been nothing but ruse and palinode, it suddenly fell silent. The order of the day, adopted virtually unanimously by the Assembly, imposed no conditions upon me. After which, the budget was passed without difficulty. But although my defeat had not been accomplished, the mere fact that it had appeared possible produced a profound effect. My government had been breached by the majority during a threat-crammed debate. Henceforth, perhaps, the same effect could be accomplished apropos of virtually any issue. It was apparent that if De Gaulle tolerated this situation to remain in office, his prestige would decline, until one day the parties would either no longer tolerate him or else relegate him to some harmless and decorative function. But I had neither the right nor the inclination to lend myself to such calculations. As I left the Palais Bourbon on the evening of January 1, I had determined upon my departure from office. All that remained was to select the date, without making any concessions whatever.

Negotiations with Stalin

Winston Churchill's brilliant memoirs record his career as the wartime leader of Great Britain. Though he was a staunch supporter of the alliance with Russia, he never lost his suspicion of Stalin and the Soviet regime. Nevertheless, as a conservative and a believer in Realpolitik, Churchill was much more willing to divide up spheres of influence with the Russians than Roosevelt was. At the same time, he was particularly fearful of the withdrawal of American power from Europe. He was much less optimistic than Roosevelt about believing that the Russians would be reasonable if the West did not have force behind its diplomacy. The selection that follows records Churchill and Stalin's proposal for the division of the Balkans into spheres of influence made during Churchill's visit to Moscow in October, 1944, and Churchill's account of the Yalta Conference in February, 1945. As Churchill points out, the future organization of Germany was left vague, whereas the discussions of a future world organization begun at Dumbarton Oaks in September, 1944, were followed up with the important decision to establish a veto by the great powers in the Security Council, which Russia employed time and again after the creation of the United Nations. The most difficult problem, however, was that of Poland. Russia had no intention of surrendering the areas occupied in September, 1939, and the Allies were prepared to agree on the Curzon Line, first proposed by Lord Curzon at the end of the First World War, as a boundary. Poland was to be compensated with German territory. The Oder-Neisse Line, however, was left unclear and later became the subject of considerable dispute. Finally, there was the problem of Poland's future government and the rivalry between the non-Communist London government-in-exile and the Russian-supported Lublin Poles.

Churchill: On the Division of the Balkans and the Yalta Conference

We alighted at Moscow on the afternoon of October 9, and were received very heartily and with full ceremonial by Molotov and many high Russian personages. This time we were lodged in Moscow itself, with every care and comfort. I had one small, perfectly appointed house, and Anthony another near by. We were glad to dine alone together and rest. At ten o'clock that night we held our first important meeting in the Kremlin. There were only Stalin, Molotov, Eden, Harriman, and I, with Major Birse and Pavlov as interpreters. . . .

The moment was apt for business, so I said, "Let us settle about our affairs in the Balkans. Your armies are in Rumania and Bulgaria. We have interests, missions, and agents there. Don't let us get at cross-purposes in small ways. So far as Britain and Russia are concerned, how would it do for you to have ninety per cent predominance in Rumania,

From Winston S. Churchill, *The Second World War, Volume 6: Triumph and Tragedy* (© 1953 by Houghton Mifflin Company) (Boston: Houghton Mifflin, 1953), pp. 226–28, 349–54, 357, 365–69, 385–87. Reprinted by permission of Houghton Mifflin Company and Cassell and Company Ltd.

for us to have ninety per cent of the say in Greece, and go fifty-fifty about Yugoslavia?" While this was being translated I wrote out on a half-sheet of paper:

Rumania	
Russia	90%
The others	10%
Greece	
Great Britain (in accord with U.S.A.)	90%
Russia	10%
Yugoslavia	50–50%
Hungary	50–50%
Bulgaria	
Russia	75%
The others	25%

I pushed this across to Stalin, who had by then heard the translation. There was a slight pause. Then he took his blue pencil and made a large tick upon it, and passed it back to us. It was all settled in no more time than it takes to set down.

Of course we had long and anxiously considered our point, and were only dealing with immediate war-time arrangements. All larger questions were reserved on both sides for what we then hoped would be a peace table when the war was won.

After this there was a long silence. The pencilled paper lay in the centre of the table. At length I said, "Might it not be thought rather cynical if it seemed we had disposed of these issues, so fateful to millions of people, in such an offhand manner? Let us burn the paper." "No, you keep it," said Stalin. . . .

The first plenary meeting of the [Yalta] Conference started at a quarter past four on the afternoon of February 5. We met in the Livadia Palace, and took our seats at a round table. With the three interpreters we were twenty-three. With Stalin and Molotov were Vyshinsky, Maisky, Gousev, the Russian Ambassador in London, and Gromyko, the Russian Ambassador at Washington. Pavlov acted as interpreter. The American delegation was headed by President Roosevelt and Mr. Stettinius, and included Admiral Leahy, Byrnes, Harriman, Hopkins, Matthews, Director of European Affairs in the State Department, and Bohlen, special assistant from the State Department, who also interpreted. Eden sat beside me, and my own party included Sir Alexander Cadogan, Sir Edward Bridges, and Sir Archibald Clark Kerr, our Ambassador in Moscow. Major Birse interpreted for us, as he had always done since my first meeting with Stalin at Moscow in 1942.

The discussion opened on the future of Germany. . . .

Stalin now asked how Germany was to be dismembered. Were we to have one Government or several, or merely some form of administration? If Hitler surrendered unconditionally should we preserve his Government or refuse to treat with it? At Teheran Mr. Roosevelt had suggested dividing Germany into five parts, and he had agreed with him. I, on the other hand, had hesitated and had only wanted her to be split into two, namely, Prussia and Austria-Bavaria, with the Ruhr and Westphalia under international control. The time had now come, he said, to take a definite decision.

I said that we all agreed that Germany should be dismembered, but the actual method was much too complicated to be settled in five or six days. It would require a very searching examination of the historical, ethnographical, and economic facts, and prolonged examination by a special committee, which would go into the different proposals and advise on them. There was so much to consider. What to do with Prussia? What territory should be given to Poland and the U.S.S.R.? Who was to control the Rhine valley and the great industrial zones of the Ruhr and the Saar? These were questions which needed profound study, and His Majesty's Government would want to consider carefully the attitude of their two great Allies. A body should be set up at once to examine these matters, and we ought to have its report before reaching any final decision.

I then speculated on the future. If Hitler or Himmler were to come forward and offer unconditional surrender it was clear that our answer should be that we would not negotiate with any of the war criminals. If they were the only people the Germans could produce we should have to go on with the war. It was more probable that Hitler and his associates would be killed or would disappear, and that another set of people would offer unconditional surrender. If this happened the three Great Powers must immediately consult and decide whether they were worth dealing with or not. If they were, the terms of surrender which had been worked out would be laid before them; if not, the war would be continued and the whole country put under strict military government.

Mr. Roosevelt suggested asking our Foreign Secretaries to produce a plan for studying the question within twenty-four hours and a definite plan for dismemberment within a month. Here, for a time, the matter was left.

Other questions were discussed, but not settled. The President asked whether the French should be given a zone of occupation in Germany. We agreed that this should certainly be done by allocating to them part of the British and American zones, and that the Foreign Secretaries should consider how this area was to be controlled.

At Stalin's request M. Maisky then expounded a Russian scheme for making Germany pay reparations and for dismantling her munitions industries. I said that the experience of the last war had been very disappointing, and I did not believe it would be possible to extract from Germany anything like the amount which M. Maisky had suggested should be paid to Russia alone. Britain too had suffered greatly. Many buildings had been destroyed. We had parted with much of our foreign investments and were faced with the problem of how to raise our exports sufficiently to pay for the imports of food on which we depended. I doubted whether these burdens could be substantially lightened by German reparations. Other countries had also suffered and would have to be considered. What would happen if Germany were reduced to starvation? Did we intend to stand by and do nothing and say it served her right? Or did we propose to feed the Germans, and, if so, who would pay? Stalin said that these questions would arise anyway, and I answered that if you wanted a horse to pull your wagon you had to give him some hay. We eventually agreed that the Russian proposal should be examined by a special commission, which would sit in secret at Moscow.

We then arranged to meet next day and consider two topics which were to dominate our future discussions, namely, the Dumbarton Oaks scheme for world security and Poland.

At this first meeting Mr. Roosevelt had made a momentous statement. He had said that the United States would take all reasonable steps to preserve peace, but not at the expense of keeping a large army in Europe, three thousand miles away from home. The American occupation would therefore be limited to two years. Formidable questions rose in my mind. If the Americans left Europe Britain would have to occupy single-handed the entire western portion of Germany. Such a task would be far beyond our strength.

At the opening of our second meeting on February 6 I accordingly pressed for French help in carrying such a burden. To give France a zone of occupation was by no means the end of the matter. Germany would surely rise again, and while the Americans could always go home the French had to live next door to her. A strong France was vital not only to Europe but to Great Britain. She alone could deny the rocket sites on her Channel coast and build up an army to contain the Germans.

We then turned to the World Instrument for Peace. The President said that in the United States public opinion was decisive. If it was possible to agree on the Dumbarton Oaks proposals or something like them his country would be more likely to take a full part in organising peace throughout the world, because there was a large measure of support in the United States for such a World Organisation. But . . . the conference at Dumbarton Oaks had ended without reaching any agreement about the all-important question of voting rights in the Security Council.

On December 5, 1944, the President had made new suggestions to

Stalin and myself. They were as follows: Each member of the Council should have one vote. Before any decision could be carried out seven members must vote in favour of it. This would suffice for details of procedure. All large matters, such as admitting or expelling States from the organisation, suppressing and settling disputes, regulating armaments and providing armed forces, would need the concurring votes of all the permanent members. In other words, unless the "Big Four" were unanimous the Security Council was virtually powerless. If the United States, the U.S.S.R., Great Britain, or China disagreed, then the country disagreeing could refuse its assent and stop the Council doing anything. Here was the Veto.

Mr. Roosevelt's proposals had contained one other refinement. The dispute might be settled by peaceful methods. If so, this also would need seven votes, and the permanent members — that is to say, the "Big Four" — would all have to agree. But if any member of the Council (including the "Big Four") were involved in the dispute it could discuss the decision but could not vote on it. Such was the plan which Mr. Stettinius unfolded at this second meeting on February 6. . . .

When we met again on the following afternoon Molotov accepted the new scheme. At Dumbarton Oaks, he explained, the Russians had done all they could to preserve the unity of the three Powers after the war, and they thought that the plans which had emerged from the Conference would secure collaboration between all nations, great and small. They were now satisfied with the new voting procedure, and with the provision that the three Great Powers must be unanimous. . . .

Poland was discussed at no fewer than seven out of the eight plenary meetings of the Yalta Conference, and the British record contains an interchange on this topic of nearly eighteen thousand words between Stalin, Roosevelt, and myself. Aided by our Foreign Ministers and their subordinates, who also held tense and detailed debate at separate meetings among themselves, we finally produced a declaration which represented both a promise to the world and agreement between ourselves on our future actions. The painful tale is still unfinished and the true facts are as yet imperfectly known, but what is here set down may perhaps contribute to a just appreciation of our efforts at the last but one of the war-time Conferences. The difficulties and the problems were ancient, multitudinous, and imperative. The Soviet-sponsored Lublin Government of Poland, or the "Warsaw" Government as the Russians of all names preferred to call it, viewed the London Polish Government with bitter animosity. Feeling between them had got worse, not better, since our October meeting in Moscow. Soviet troops were flooding across Poland, and the Polish Underground Army was freely charged with the murder of Russian soldiers and with sabotage and attacks on their rear areas and their lines of communication. Both access and information were denied to the Western Powers. In Italy and on the Western Front nearly half a million Poles were fighting valiantly for the final destruction of the Nazi armies. They and many others elsewhere in Europe were eagerly looking forward to the liberation of their country and a return to their homeland from voluntary and honourable exile. The large community of Poles in the United States anxiously awaited a settlement between the three Great Powers.

The questions which we discussed may be summarised as follows:

How to form a single Provisional Government for Poland.

How and when to hold free elections.

How to settle the Polish frontiers, both in the east and the west.

How to safeguard the rear areas and lines of communication of the advancing Soviet armies.

. . . Poland had indeed been the most urgent reason for the Yalta Conference, and was to prove the first of the great causes which led to the breakdown of the Grand Alliance.

When we met on February 6 President Roosevelt opened the discussion by saying that, coming from America, he had a distant view on the Polish question. There were five or six million Poles in the United States, mostly of the second generation, and most of them were generally in favour of the Curzon Line. They knew they would have to give up East Poland. They would like East Prussia and part of Germany, or at any rate something with which to be compensated. As he had said at Teheran, it would make it easier for him if the Soviet Government would make some concession such as Lvov, and some of the oil-bearing lands, to counterbalance the loss of Königsberg. But the most important point was a permanent Government for Poland. General opinion in the United States was against recognising the Lublin Government, because it represented only a small section of Poland and of the Polish nation. There was a demand for a Government of national unity, drawn perhaps from the five main political parties.

He knew none of the members of either the London or Lublin Governments. He had been greatly impressed by Mikolajczyk when he had come to Washington, and felt he was an honest man. He therefore hoped to see the creation of a Government of Poland which would be representative, and which the great majority of Poles would support even if it was only an interim one. There were many ways in which it might be formed, such as creating a small Presidential Council to take temporary control and set up a more permanent institution.

I then said it was my duty to state the position of His Majesty's Government. I had repeatedly declared in Parliament and in public my resolution to support the claim of the U.S.S.R. to the Curzon Line as interpreted by the Soviet Government. That meant including Lvov in the U.S.S.R. I had been considerably criticised in Parliament (as had the Foreign Secretary) and by the Conservative Party for this. But I had always thought that, after the agonies Russia had suffered in defending herself against the Germans, and her great deeds in driving them back and liberating Poland, her claim was founded not on force but on right. If however she made a gesture of magnanimity to a much weaker Power, and some territorial concession, such as the President had suggested, we should both admire and acclaim the Soviet action.

But a strong, free, and independent Poland was much more important than particular territorial boundaries. I wanted the Poles to be able to live freely and live their own lives in their own way. That was the object which I had always heard Marshal Stalin proclaim with the utmost firmness, and it was because I trusted his declarations about the sovereignty, independence, and freedom of Poland that I rated the frontier question as less important. This was dear to the hearts of the British nation and the Commonwealth. It was for this that we had gone to war against Germany — that Poland should be free and sovereign. Everyone knew what a terrible risk we had taken when we had gone to war in 1939 although so ill-armed. It had nearly cost us our life, not only as an Empire but as a nation. Great Britain had no material interest of any kind in Poland. Honour was the sole reason why we had drawn the sword to help Poland against Hitler's brutal onslaught, and we could never accept any settlement which did not leave her free, independent, and sovereign. Poland must be mistress in her own house and captain of her own soul. Such freedom must not cover any hostile design by Poland or by any Polish group, possibly in intrigue with Germany, against Russia; but the World Organisation that was being set up would surely never tolerate such action or leave Soviet Russia to deal with it alone.

At present there were two Governments of Poland, about which we differed. I had not seen any of the present London Government of Poland. We recognised them, but had not sought their company. On the other hand, Mikolajczyk, Romer, and Grabski were men of good sense and honesty, and with them we had remained in informal but friendly and close relations. The three Great Powers would be criticised if they allowed these rival Governments to cause an apparent division between them, when there were such great tasks in hand and they had such hopes in common. Could we not create a Government or governmental instrument for Poland, pending full and free elections, which could be recognised by all? Such a Government could prepare for a free vote of the Polish people on their future constitution and administration. If this could be done we should have taken one great step forward towards the future peace and prosperity of Central Europe. I said I was sure that the communications of the Russian Army, now driving forward in victorious pursuit of the Germans, could be protected and guaranteed.

After a brief adjournment Stalin spoke. He said that he understood the British Government's feeling that Poland was a question of honour, but for Russia it was a question both of honour and security; of honour because the Russians had had many conflicts with the Poles and the Soviet Government wished to eliminate the causes of such conflicts; of security, not only because Poland was on the frontiers of Russia, but because throughout history Poland had been a corridor through which Russia's enemies had passed to attack her. During the last thirty years the Germans had twice passed through Poland. They passed through because Poland had been weak. Russia wanted to see a strong and powerful Poland, so that she would be able to shut this corridor of her own strength. Russia could not keep it shut from the outside. It could only be shut from the inside by Poland herself, and it was for this reason that Poland must be free, independent, and powerful. This was a matter of life and death for the Soviet State. Their policy differed greatly from that of the Czarist Government. The Czars had wanted to suppress and assimilate Poland. Soviet Russia had started a policy of friendship, and friendship moreover with an independent Poland. That was the whole basis of the Soviet attitude, namely, that they wanted to see Poland independent, free, and strong. . . .

When the Conference reassembled at a quarter to five Mr. Eden read out a statement to which the three Foreign Secretaries had agreed. I was concerned to note that it said nothing about frontiers, and I said that the whole world would want to know why. We were all agreed in principle about the western frontier, and the only question was where exactly the line should be drawn and how much we should say about it. The Poles should have part of East Prussia and be free to go up to the line of the Oder if they wished, but we were very doubtful about going any farther or saying anything on the question at this stage, and I told the Conference that we had had a telegram from the War Cabinet which strongly deprecated any reference to a frontier as far west as the Western Neisse because the problem of moving the population was too big to manage.

Mr. Roosevelt said he would prefer to hear what the new Polish Government of National Unity said about it, and suggested omitting all reference to the line in the west.

"We should certainly mention the eastern frontier," said Stalin.

I supported him in this, although I knew there would be much criticism.

As for the western frontier, I said that the wishes of the new Polish Government should first be ascertained, and that the frontier itself should be determined as part of the peace settlements. After some further discussion, which was complicated by the President's inability under the United States Constitution to settle matters of this kind without the approval of the Senate, we eventually agreed what to do. The communiqué issued at the end of the Conference accordingly included a joint declaration about Poland, and ran as follows:

11 Feb. 45

We came to the Crimea Conference to settle our differences about Poland. We discussed fully all aspects of the question. We reaffirm our common desire to see established a strong, free, independent, and democratic Poland. As a result of our discussions we have agreed on the conditions in which a new Polish Provisional Government of National Unity may be formed in such a manner as to command recognition by the three major Powers.

The agreement reached is as follows:

A new situation has been created in Poland as a result of her complete liberation by the Red Army. This calls for the establishment of a Polish Provisional Government which can be more broadly based than was possible before the recent liberation of Western Poland. The Provisional Government which is now functioning in Poland should therefore be reorganized on a broader democratic basis, with the inclusion of democratic leaders from Poland itself and from Poles abroad. This new Government should then be called the Polish Provisional Government of National Unity.

M. Molotov, Mr. Harriman, and Sir A. Clark Kerr are authorised as a commission to consult in the first instance in Moscow with members of the present Provisional Government and with other Polish democratic leaders from within Poland and from abroad with a view to the reorganisation of the present Government along the above lines. This Polish Provisional Government of National Unity shall be pledged to the holding of free and unfettered elections as soon as possible on the basis of universal suffrage and secret ballot. In these elections all democratic and anti-Nazi parties shall have the right to take part and to put forward candidates.

When a Polish Provisional Government of National Unity has been properly formed in conformity with the above, the Government of the Union of Soviet Socialist Republics, which now maintains diplomatic relations with the present Provisional Government of Poland, and the Government of the United Kingdom and the Government of the United States will establish diplomatic relations with the new Polish Government of National Unity, and will exchange Ambassadors, by whose reports the respective Governments will be kept informed about the situation in Poland.

The three heads of Governments consider that the eastern frontier of Poland should follow the Curzon Line, with digressions from it in some regions of five to eight kilometres in favour of Poland. They recognise that Poland must receive substantial accessions of territory in the north and west. They feel that the opinion of the new Polish Provisional Government of National Unity should be sought in due course on the extent of these accessions, and that the final delimitation of the western frontier of Poland should thereafter await the Peace Conference.

The Policy
of Containment

*George F. Kennan, a distinguished career diplomat, was a key member
of the American Embassy in Moscow in the early 1930's and during
the crucial period from 1944 to 1946. He was critical of the American
policy of concessions to the Soviet Union beyond those necessary for
collaboration in the war effort, and he was convinced that firmness was
necessary to contain Soviet ambitions and deal with the ruthless dictatorship of Stalin. In January, 1947, he anonymously published his
famous article "The Sources of Soviet Conduct" in Foreign Affairs.
The identity of "Mr. X" was quickly revealed, and the article has
often been viewed as the earliest expression and rationale of the
policy of "containment" pursued by the United States. After Stalin's
death and the development of the Sino-Soviet dispute, Kennan concluded that containment had outlived its usefulness. Furthermore, he
argued that his ideas had been misinterpreted and too rigidly applied
and that the goal of his policy was to bring the Russians to reason by
making them understand the limits of what the West would tolerate
and by making them feel the internal costs of continued expansionism.
The object was not to permanently divide Europe into two armed
camps or to institutionalize Soviet-American conflict.*

Kennan's "The Sources of Soviet Conduct"

. . . So much for the historical background. What does it spell in
terms of the political personality of Soviet power as we know it today?

Of the original ideology, nothing has been officially junked. Belief is
maintained in the basic badness of capitalism, in the inevitability of its
destruction, in the obligation of the proletariat to assist in that destruction and to take power into its own hands. But stress has come to be laid
primarily on those concepts which relate most specifically to the Soviet
regime itself: to its position as the sole truly Socialist regime in a dark
and misguided world, and to the relationships of power within it.

The first of these concepts is that of the innate antagonism between
capitalism and Socialism. We have seen how deeply that concept has
become imbedded in foundations of Soviet power. It has profound implications for Russia's conduct as a member of international society. It

From Mr. X (George F. Kennan), "The Sources of Soviet Conduct," *Foreign Affairs*, vol.
25, no. 4 (July, 1947), pp. 571–82. Copyright held by the Council on Foreign Relations,
Inc., New York, N.Y. Reprinted by permission.

means that there can never be on Moscow's side any sincere assumption of a community of aims between the Soviet Union and powers which are regarded as capitalism. It must invariably be assumed in Moscow that the aims of the capitalist world are antagonistic to the Soviet regime and, therefore, to the interests of the peoples it controls. If the Soviet government occasionally sets its signature to documents which would indicate the contrary, this is to be regarded as a tactical maneuver permissible in dealing with the enemy (who is without honor) and should be taken in the spirit of *caveat emptor*. Basically, the antagonism remains. It is postulated. And from it flow many of the phenomena which we find disturbing in the Kremlin's conduct of foreign policy: the secretiveness, the lack of frankness, the duplicity, the war suspiciousness, and the basic unfriendliness of purpose. These phenomena are there to stay, for the foreseeable future. There can be variations of degree and of emphasis. When there is something the Russians want from us, one or the other of these features of their policy may be thrust temporarily into the background; and when that happens there will always be Americans who will leap forward with gleeful announcements that "the Russians have changed," and some who will even try to take credit for having brought about such "changes." But we should not be misled by tactical maneuvers. These characteristics of Soviet policy, like the postulate from which they flow, are basic to the internal nature of Soviet power, and will be with us, whether in the foreground or the background, until the internal nature of Soviet power is changed.

This means that we are going to continue for a long time to find the Russians difficult to deal with. It does not mean that they should be considered as embarked upon a do-or-die program to overthrow our society by a given date. The theory of the inevitability of the eventual fall of capitalism has the fortunate connotation that there is no hurry about it. The forces of progress can take their time in preparing the final *coup de grâce*. Meanwhile, what is vital is that the "Socialist fatherland" — that oasis of power which has been already won for Socialism in the person of the Soviet Union — should be cherished and defended by all good Communists at home and abroad, its fortunes promoted, its enemies badgered and confounded. The promotion of premature, "adventuristic" revolutionary projects abroad which might embarrass Soviet power in any way would be an inexcusable, even a counter-revolutionary act. The cause of Socialism is the support and promotion of Soviet power, as defined in Moscow.

This brings us to the second of the concepts important to contemporary Soviet outlook. That is the infallibility of the Kremlin. The Soviet concept of power, which permits no focal points of organization outside the Party itself, requires that the Party leadership remain in theory the sole repository of truth. For if truth were to be found elsewhere, there would be justification for its expression in organized activity. But it is precisely that which the Kremlin cannot and will not permit. . . .

But we have seen that the Kremlin is under no ideological compulsion to accomplish its 'purposes in a hurry. Like the Church, it is dealing in ideological concepts which are of long-term validity, and it can afford to be patient. It has no right to risk the existing achievements of the revolution for the sake of vain baubles of the future. The very teachings of Lenin himself require great caution and flexibility in the pursuit of Communist purposes. Again, these precepts are fortified by the lessons of Russian history: of centuries of obscure battles between nomadic forces over the stretches of a vast unfortified plain. Here caution, circumspection, flexibility and deception are the valuable qualities; and their value finds natural appreciation in the Russian or the oriental mind. Thus the Kremlin has no compunction about retreating in the face of superior force. And being under the compulsion of no timetable, it does not get panicky under the necessity for such retreat. Its political action is a fluid stream which moves constantly, wherever it is permitted to move, toward a given goal. Its main concern is to make sure that it has filled every nook and cranny available to it in the basin of world power. But if it finds unassailable barriers in its path, it accepts these philosophically and accommodates itself to them. The main thing is that there should always be pressure, increasing constant pressure, toward the desired goal. There is no trace of any feeling in Soviet psychology that that goal must be reached at any given time.

These considerations make Soviet diplomacy at once easier and more difficult to deal with than the diplomacy of individual aggressive leaders like Napoleon and Hitler. On the one hand it is more sensitive to contrary force, more ready to yield on individual sectors of the diplomatic front when that force is felt to be too strong, and thus more rational in the logic and rhetoric of power. On the other hand it cannot be easily defeated or discouraged by a single victory on the part of its opponents. And the patient persistence by which it is animated means that it can be effectively countered not by sporadic acts which represent the momentary whims of democratic opinion but only by intelligent long-range policies on the part of Russia's adversaries — policies no less steady in their purpose, and no less variegated and resourceful in their application, than those of the Soviet Union itself.

In these circumstances it is clear that the main element of any United States policy toward the Soviet Union must be that of a long-term, patient but firm and vigilant containment of Russian expansive tendencies. It is important to note, however, that such a policy has nothing to do with outward histrionics: with threats or blustering or superfluous gestures of outward "toughness." While the Kremlin is basically flexible in its reaction to political realities, it is by no means unamenable to considerations of prestige. Like almost any other government, it can be placed by tactless and threatening gestures in a position where it cannot afford to yield even though this might be dictated by its sense of realism. The Russian leaders are keen judges of human psychology, and as such they are highly conscious that loss of temper and of self-control is never a source of strength in political affairs. They are quick to exploit such evidences of weakness. For these reasons, it is a *sine qua non* of successful dealing with Russia that the foreign government in question should remain at all times cool and collected and that its demands on Russian policy should be put forward in such a manner as to leave the way open for a compliance not too detrimental to Russian prestige. . . .

In the light of the above, it will be clearly seen that the Soviet pressure against the free institutions of the Western world is something that can be contained by the adroit and vigilant application of counter-force at a series of constantly shifting geographical and political points, corresponding to the shifts and maneuvers of Soviet policy, but which cannot be charmed or talked out of existence. The Russians look forward to a duel of infinite duration, and they see that already they have scored great successes. It must be borne in mind that there was a time when the Communist Party represented far more of a minority in the sphere of Russian national life than Soviet power today represents in the world community.

But if ideology convinces the rulers of Russia that truth is on their side and that they can therefore afford to wait, those of us on whom that ideology has no claim are free to examine objectively the validity of that premise. The Soviet thesis not only implies complete lack of control by the West over its own economic destiny, it likewise assumes Russian unity, discipline and patience over an infinite period. Let us bring this apocalyptic vision down to earth, and suppose that the Western world finds the strength and resourcefulness to contain Soviet power over a period of ten to fifteen years. What does that spell for Russia itself?

The Soviet leaders, taking advantage of the contributions of modern technique to the arts of despotism, have solved the question of obedience within the confines of their power. Few challenge their authority; and even those who do are unable to make that challenge valid as against the organs of suppression of the state.

The Kremlin has also proved able to accomplish its purpose of building up in Russia, regardless of the interests of the inhabitants, an industrial foundation of heavy metallurgy, which is, to be sure, not yet complete but which is nevertheless continuing to grow and is approaching those of the other major industrial countries. All of this, however, both the maintenance of internal political security and the building of heavy industry, has been carried out at a terrible cost in human life and in human hopes and energies. It has necessitated the use of forced labor on a scale unprecedented in modern times under conditions of peace. It has involved the neglect or abuse of other phases of Soviet economic life, particularly agriculture, consumers' goods production, housing and transportation.

To all that, the war has added its tremendous toll of destruction, death and human exhaustion. In consequence of this, we have in Russia today a population which is physically and spiritually tired. The mass of the people are disillusioned, skeptical and no longer as accessible as they once were to the magical attraction which Soviet power still radiates to its followers abroad. The avidity with which people seized upon the slightest respite accorded to the Church for tactical reasons during the war was eloquent testimony to the fact that their capacity for faith and devotion found little expression in the purposes of the regime.

In these circumstances, there are limits to the physical and nervous strength of people themselves. These limits are absolute ones, and are binding even for the cruelest dictatorship, because beyond them people cannot be driven. The forced labor camps and the other agencies of constraint provide temporary means of compelling people to work longer hours than their own volition or mere economic pressure would dictate; but if people survive them at all they become old before their time and must be considered as human casualties to the demands of dictatorship. In either case their best powers are no longer available to society and can no longer be enlisted in the service of the state.

Here only the younger generation can help. The younger generation, despite all vicissitudes and sufferings, is numerous and vigorous; and the Russians are a talented people. But it still remains to be seen what will be the effects on mature performance of the abnormal emotional strains of childhood which Soviet dictatorship created and which were enormously increased by the war. Such things as normal security and placidity of home environment have practically ceased to exist in the Soviet Union outside of the most remote farms and villages. And observers are not yet sure whether that is not going to leave its mark on the over-all capacity of the generation now coming into maturity. . . .

Meanwhile, a great uncertainty hangs over the political life of the Soviet Union. That is the uncertainty involved in the transfer of power from one individual or group of individuals to others.

This is, of course, outstandingly the problem of the personal position of Stalin. We must remember that his succession to Lenin's pinnacle of preeminence in the Communist movement was the only such transfer of individual authority which the Soviet Union has experienced. That transfer took twelve years to consolidate. It cost the lives of millions of people and shook the state to its foundations, the attendant tremors were felt all through the international revolutionary movement, to the disadvantage of the Kremlin itself.

It is always possible that another transfer of preeminent power may take place quietly and inconspicuously, with no repercussions anywhere. But again, it is possible that the questions involved may unleash, to use some of Lenin's words, one of those "incredibly swift transitions" from "delicate deceit" to "wild violence" which characterize Russian history, and may shake Soviet power to its foundations. . . .

Thus the future of Soviet power may not be by any means as secure as Russian capacity for self-delusion would make it appear to the men in the Kremlin. That they can keep power themselves, they have demonstrated. That they can quietly and easily turn it over to others remains to be proved. Meanwhile, the hardships of their rule and the vicissitudes of international life have taken a heavy toll of the strength and hopes of the great people on whom their power rests. . . .

It is clear that the United States cannot expect in the foreseeable future to enjoy political intimacy with the Soviet regime. It must continue to regard the Soviet Union as a rival, not a partner, in the political arena. It must continue to expect that Soviet policies will reflect no abstract love of peace and stability, no real faith in the possibility of a permanent happy coexistence of the Socialist and capitalist worlds, but rather a cautious, persistent pressure toward the disruption and weakening of all rival influence and rival power.

Balanced against this are the facts that Russia, as opposed to the Western world in general, is still by far the weaker party, that Soviet policy is highly flexible, and that Soviet society may well contain deficiencies which will eventually weaken its own total potential. This would of itself warrant the United States entering with reasonable confidence upon a policy of firm containment, designed to confront the Russians with unalterable counter-force at every point where they show signs of encroaching upon the interests of a peaceful and stable world.

But in actuality the possibilities for American policy are by no means limited to holding the line and hoping for the best. It is entirely possible for the United States to influence by its actions the internal developments, both within Russia and throughout the international Communist movement, by which Russian policy is largely determined. This is not only a question of the modest measure of informational activity which this government can conduct in the Soviet Union and elsewhere, although that, too, is important. It is rather a question of the degree to which the United States can create among the peoples of the world generally the impression of a country which knows what it wants, which is coping successfully with the problems of its internal life and with the responsibilities of a World Power, and which has a spiritual vitality capable of holding its own among the major ideological currents of the time. To the extent that such an impression can be created and maintained, the aims of Russian Communism must appear sterile and quixotic, the hopes and enthusiasm of Moscow's supporters must wane, and added strain must be imposed on the Kremlin's foreign policies. For the palsied decrepitude of the capitalist world is the keystone of Communist philosophy. Even the failure of the United States to experience the early economic depression which the ravens of the Red Square have been predicting with such complacent confidence since hostilities ceased would have deep and important repercussions throughout the Communist world.

By the same token, exhibitions of indecision, disunity and internal disintegration within this country have an exhilarating effect on the whole Communist movement. At each evidence of these tendencies, a thrill of hope and excitement goes through the Communist world; a new jauntiness can be noted in the Moscow tread; new groups of foreign supporters climb on to what they can only view as the band wagon of international politics; and Russian pressure increases all along the line in international affairs.

It would be an exaggeration to say that American behavior unassisted and alone could exercise a power of life and death over the Communist movement and bring about the early fall of Soviet power in Russia. But the United States has it in its power to increase enormously the strains under which Soviet policy must operate, to force upon the Kremlin a far greater degree of moderation and circumspection than it has had to observe in recent years, and in this way to promote tendencies which must eventually find their outlet in either the break-up or the gradual mellowing of Soviet power. For no mystical, Messianic movement — and particularly not that of the Kremlin — can face frustration indefinitely without eventually adjusting itself in one way or another to the logic of that state of affairs.

Thus the decision will really fall in large measure in this country itself. The issue of Soviet-American relations is in essence a test of the over-all worth of the United States as a nation among nations. To avoid destruction the United States need only measure up to its own best traditions and prove itself worthy of preservation as a great nation.

Surely, there was never a fairer test of national quality than this. In the light of these circumstances, the thoughtful observer of Russian-American relations will find no cause for complaint in the Kremlin's challenge to American society. He will rather experience a certain gratitude to a Providence which, by providing the American people with this implacable challenge, has made their entire security as a nation dependent on their pulling themselves together and accepting the responsibilities of moral and political leadership that history plainly intended them to bear.

The Truman Doctrine and the Marshall Plan

The two most important expressions of the containment policy and the opening of the cold war were the Truman Doctrine and the Marshall Plan. In February, 1947, Britain informed the United States that it could no longer afford to support Greece and Turkey. The situation in Greece was particularly critical because of Communist guerrilla warfare against the regime, and both countries were vital from the standpoint of maintaining American interests in the eastern Mediterranean. Truman's decision to step in and replace Britain in the effort to prevent further Communist inroads, first announced in a message to Congress on March 12, 1947, began the active policy of opposing further Communist expansion. At the same time, the United States recognized that Europe's capacity to resist internal subversion depended upon economic reconstruction and that this was impossible without American help. On June 5, 1947, Secretary of State George C. Marshall gave his famous Harvard commencement speech outlining what was to become known as the Marshall Plan. Although the plan did not preclude economic assistance to Eastern European countries, countries within the Soviet orbit refused American assistance and denounced the plan as an instrument of Western imperialism.

Truman's Message to Congress, March 12, 1947

Mr. President, Mr. Speaker, Members of the Congress of the United States:

The gravity of the situation which confronts the world today necessitates my appearance before a joint session of the Congress.

The foreign policy and the national security of this country are involved.

One aspect of the present situation, which I present to you at this time for your consideration and decision, concerns Greece and Turkey.

The United States has received from the Greek Government an urgent appeal for financial and economic assistance. Preliminary reports from the American Economic Mission now in Greece and reports from the American Ambassador in Greece corroborate the statement of the Greek Government that assistance is imperative if Greece is to survive as a free nation.

From the *Congressional Record*, 1947, pp. 1980–81.

I do not believe that the American people and the Congress wish to turn a deaf ear to the appeal of the Greek Government.

Greece is not a rich country. Lack of sufficient natural resources has always forced the Greek people to work hard to make both ends meet. Since 1940, this industrious, peace loving country has suffered invasion, four years of cruel enemy occupation, and bitter internal strife.

When forces of liberation entered Greece they found the retreating Germans had destroyed virtually all the railways, roads, port facilities, communications, and merchant marine. More than a thousand villages had been burned. Eighty-five percent of the children were tubercular. Livestock, poultry, and draft animals had almost disappeared. Inflation had wiped out practically all savings.

As a result of these tragic conditions, a militant minority, exploiting human want and misery, was able to create political chaos which, until now, has made economic recovery impossible.

Greece is today without funds to finance the importation of those goods which are essential to bare subsistence. Under these circumstances the people of Greece cannot make progress in solving their problems of reconstruction. Greece is in desperate need of financial and economic assistance to enable it to resume purchases of food, clothing, fuel and seeds. These are indispensable for the subsistence of its people and are obtainable only from abroad. Greece must have help to import the goods necessary to restore internal order and security so essential for economic and political recovery.

The Greek Government has also asked for the assistance of experienced American administrators, economists and technicians to insure that the financial and other aid given to Greece shall be used effectively in creating a stable and self-sustaining economy and in improving its public administration.

The very existence of the Greek state is today threatened by the terrorist activities of several thousand armed men, led by Communists, who defy the government's authority at a number of points, particularly along the northern boundaries. A Commission appointed by the United Nations Security Council is at present investigating disturbed conditions in northern Greece and alleged border violations along the frontier between Greece on the one hand and Albania, Bulgaria, and Yugoslavia on the other.

Meanwhile, the Greek Government is unable to cope with the situation. The Greek army is small and poorly equipped. It needs supplies and equipment if it is to restore authority to the government throughout Greek territory.

Greece must have assistance if it is to become a self-supporting and self-respecting democracy.

The United States must supply this assistance. We have already extended to Greece certain types of relief and economic aid but these are inadequate.

There is no other country to which democratic Greece can turn.

No other nation is willing and able to provide the necessary support for a democratic Greek government.

The British Government, which has been helping Greece, can give no further financial or economic aid after March 31. Great Britain finds itself under the necessity of reducing or liquidating its commitments in several parts of the world, including Greece.

We have considered how the United Nations might assist in this crisis. But the situation is an urgent one requiring immediate action, and the United Nations and its related organizations are not in a position to extend help of the kind that is required.

It is important to note that the Greek Government has asked for our aid in utilizing effectively the financial and other assistance we may give to Greece, and in improving its public administration. It is of the utmost importance that we supervise the use of any funds made available to Greece, in such a manner that each dollar spent will count toward making Greece self-supporting, and will help to build an economy in which a healthy democracy can flourish.

No government is perfect. One of the chief virtues of a democracy, however, is that its defects are always visible and under democratic processes can be pointed out and corrected. The government of Greece is not perfect. Nevertheless it represents 85 percent of the members of the Greek Parliament who were chosen in an election last year. Foreign observers, including 692 Americans, considered this election to be a fair expression of the views of the Greek people.

The Greek Government has been operating in an atmosphere of chaos and extremism. It has made mistakes. The extension of aid by this country does not mean that the United States condones everything that the Greek Government has done or will do. We have condemned in the past, and we condemn now, extremist measures of the right or the left. We have in the past advised tolerance, and we advise tolerance now.

Greece's neighbor, Turkey, also deserves our attention.

The future of Turkey as an independent and economically sound state is clearly no less important to the freedom loving peoples of the world than the future of Greece. The circumstances in which Turkey finds itself today are considerably different from those of Greece. Turkey has been spared the disasters that have beset Greece. And during the war, the United States and Great Britain furnished Turkey with material aid.

Nevertheless, Turkey now needs our support.

Since the war Turkey has sought additional financial assistance from Great Britain and the United States for the purpose of effecting that modernization necessary for the maintenance of its national integrity.

That integrity is essential to the preservation of order in the Middle East.

The British Government has informed us that, owing to its own difficulties, it can no longer extend financial or economic aid to Turkey.

As in the case of Greece, if Turkey is to have the assistance it needs, the United States must supply it. We are the only country able to provide that help.

I am fully aware of the broad implications involved if the United States extends assistance to Greece and Turkey, and I shall discuss these implications with you at this time.

One of the primary objectives of the foreign policy of the United States is the creation of conditions in which we and other nations will be able to work out a way of life free from coercion. This was a fundamental issue in the war with Germany and Japan. Our victory was won over countries which sought to impose their will, and their way of life, upon other nations.

To ensure the peaceful development of nations, free from coercion, the United States has taken a leading part in establishing the United Nations. The United Nations is designed to make possible lasting freedom and independence for all its members. We shall not realize our objectives, however, unless we are willing to help free peoples to maintain their free institutions and their national integrity against aggressive movements that seek to impose upon them totalitarian regimes. This is no more than a frank recognition that totalitarian regimes imposed upon free peoples, by direct or indirect aggression, undermine the foundations of international peace and hence the security of the United States.

The peoples of a number of countries of the world have recently had totalitarian regimes forced upon them against their will. The Government of the United States has made frequent protests against coercion and intimidation, in violation of the Yalta agreement, in Poland, Rumania, and Bulgaria. I must also state that in a number of other countries there have been similar developments.

At the present moment in world history nearly every nation must choose between alternative ways of life. The choice is too often not a free one.

One way of life is based upon the will of the majority, and is distinguished by free institutions, representative government, free elections, guarantees of individual liberty, freedom of speech and religion, and freedom from political oppression.

The second way of life is based upon the will of a minority forcibly imposed upon the majority. It relies upon terror and oppression, a controlled press and radio, fixed elections, and the suppression of personal freedoms.

I believe that it must be the policy of the United States to support free peoples who are resisting attempted subjugation by armed minorities or by outside pressures.

I believe that we must assist free peoples to work out their own destinies in their own way.

I believe that our help should be primarily through economic and financial aid which is essential to economic stability and orderly political processes.

The world is not static, and the *status quo* is not sacred. But we cannot allow changes in the *status quo* in violation of the Charter of the United Nations by such methods as coercion, or by such subterfuges as political infiltration. In helping free and independent nations to maintain their freedom, the United States will be giving effect to the principles of the Charter of the United Nations.

It is necessary only to glance at a map to realize that the survival and integrity of the Greek nation are of grave importance in a much wider situation. If Greece should fall under the control of an armed minority, the effect upon its neighbor, Turkey, would be immediate and serious. Confusion and disorder might well spread throughout the entire Middle East.

Moreover, the disappearance of Greece as an independent state would have a profound effect upon those countries in Europe whose peoples are struggling against great difficulties to maintain their freedoms and their independence while they repair the damages of war.

It would be an unspeakable tragedy if these countries, which have struggled so long against overwhelming odds, should lose that victory for which they sacrificed so much. Collapse of free institutions and loss of independence would be disastrous not only for them but for the world. Discouragement and possibly failure would quickly be the lot of neighboring peoples striving to maintain their freedom and independence.

Should we fail to aid Greece and Turkey in this fateful hour, the effect will be far reaching to the West as well as to the East.

We must take immediate and resolute action.

I therefore ask the Congress to provide authority for assistance to Greece and Turkey in the amount of $400,000,000 for the period ending June 30, 1948. In requesting these funds, I have taken into consideration the maximum amount of relief assistance which would be furnished to Greece out of the $350,000,000 which I recently requested that the Congress authorize for the prevention of starvation and suffering in countries devastated by the war.

In addition to funds, I ask the Congress to authorize the detail of American civilization and military personnel to Greece and Turkey, at the request of those countries, to assist in the tasks of reconstruction, and for the purpose of supervising the use of such financial and material assistance as may be furnished. I recommend that authority also be provided for the instruction and training of selected Greek and Turkish personnel.

Finally, I ask that the Congress provide authority which will permit the speediest and most effective use, in terms of needed commodities, supplies, and equipment, of such funds as may be authorized.

If further funds, or further authority, should be needed for the purposes indicated in this message, I shall not hesitate to bring the situation before the Congress. On this subject the Executive and Legislative branches of the Government must work together.

This is a serious course upon which we embark.

I would not recommend it except that the alternative is much more serious.

The United States contributed $341,000,000,000 toward winning World War II. This is an investment in world freedom and world peace.

The assistance that I am recommending for Greece and Turkey amounts to little more than $\frac{1}{10}$ of 1 percent of this investment. It is only common sense that we should safeguard this investment and make sure that it was not in vain.

The seeds of totalitarian regimes are nurtured by misery and want. They spread and grow in the evil soil of poverty and strife. They reach their full growth when the hope of a people for a better life has died.

We must keep that hope alive.

The free peoples of the world look to us for support in maintaining their freedoms.

If we falter in our leadership, we may endanger the peace of the world — and we shall surely endanger the welfare of this Nation.

Great responsibilities have been placed upon us by the swift movement of events.

I am confident that the Congress will face these responsibilities squarely.

Marshall's Harvard Speech, June 5, 1947

In considering the requirements for the rehabilitation of Europe the physical loss of life, the visible destruction of cities, factories, mines, and railroads was correctly estimated, but it has become obvious during recent months that this visible destruction was probably less serious than the dislocation of the entire fabric of European economy. For the past 10 years conditions have been highly abnormal. The feverish preparation

From the *New York Times*, June 6, 1947.

for war and the more feverish maintenance of the war effort engulfed all aspects of national economies. Machinery has fallen into disrepair or is entirely obsolete. Under the arbitrary and destructive Nazi rule, virtually every possible enterprise was geared into the German war machine. Long-standing commercial ties, private institutions, banks, insurance companies and shipping companies disappeared through loss of capital, absorption through nationalization or by simple destruction. In many countries, confidence in the local currency has been severely shaken. The breakdown of the business structure of Europe during the war was complete. Recovery has been seriously retarded by the fact that 2 years after the close of hostilities a peace settlement with Germany and Austria has not been agreed upon. But even given a more prompt solution of these difficult problems, the rehabilitation of the economic structure of Europe quite evidently will require a much longer time and greater effort than had been foreseen.

There is a phase of this matter which is both interesting and serious. The farmer has always produced the foodstuffs to exchange with the city dweller for the other necessities of life. This division of labor is the basis of modern civilization. At the present time it is threatened with breakdown. The town and city industries are not producing adequate goods to exchange with the food-producing farmer. Raw materials and fuel are in short supply. Machinery is lacking or worn out. The farmer or the peasant cannot find the goods for sale which he desires to purchase. So the sale of his farm produce for money which he cannot use seems to him an unprofitable transaction. He, therefore, has withdrawn many fields from crop cultivation and is using them for grazing. He feeds more grain to stock and finds for himself and his family an ample supply of food, however short he may be on clothing and the other ordinary gadgets of civilization. Meanwhile people in the cities are short of food and fuel. So the governments are forced to use their foreign money and credits to procure these necessities abroad. This process exhausts funds which are urgently needed for reconstruction. Thus a very serious situation is rapidly developing which bodes no good for the world. The modern system of the division of labor upon which the exchange of products is based is in danger of breaking down.

The truth of the matter is that Europe's requirements for the next 3 or 4 years of foreign food and other essential products — principally from America — are so much greater than her present ability to pay that she must have substantial additional help, or face economic, social, and political deterioration of a very grave character.

The remedy lies in breaking the vicious circle and restoring the confidence of the European people in the economic future of their own countries and of Europe as a whole. The manufacturer and the farmer throughout wide areas must be able and willing to exchange their products for currencies the continuing value of which is not open to question.

Aside from the demoralizing effect on the world at large and the possibilities of disturbances arising as a result of the desperation of the people concerned, the consequences to the economy of the United States should be apparent to all. It is logical that the United States should do whatever it is able to do to assist in the return of normal economic health in the world, without which there can be no political stability and no assured peace. Our policy is directed not against any country or doctrine but against hunger, poverty, desperation, and chaos. Its purpose should be the revival of a working economy in the world so as to permit the emergence of political and social conditions in which free institutions can exist. Such assistance, I am convinced, must not be on a piecemeal basis as various crises develop. Any assistance that this Government may render in the future should provide a cure rather than a mere palliative. Any government that is willing to assist in the task of recovery will find full cooperation, I am sure, on the part of the United States Government. Any government which maneuvers to block the recovery of other countries cannot expect help from us. Furthermore, governments, political parties, or groups which seek to perpetuate human misery in order to profit therefrom politically or otherwise will encounter the opposition of the United States.

It is already evident that, before the United States Government can proceed much further in its efforts to alleviate the situation and help start the European world on its way to recovery, there must be some agreement among the countries of Europe as to the requirements of the situation and the part those countries themselves will take in order to give proper effect to whatever action might be undertaken by this Government. It would be neither fitting nor efficacious for this Government to undertake to draw up unilaterally a program designed to place Europe on its feet economically. This is the business of the Europeans. The initiative, I think, must come from Europe. The role of this country should consist of friendly aid in the drafting of a European program and of later support of such a program so far as it may be practical for us to do so. The program should be a joint one, agreed to by a number, if not all European nations.

An essential part of any successful action on the part of the United States is an understanding on the part of the people of America of the character of the problem and the remedies to be applied. Political passion and prejudice should have no part. With foresight, and a willingness on the part of our people to face up to the vast responsibility which history has clearly placed upon our country, the difficulties I have outlined can and will be overcome.

THE END OF
WESTERN HEGEMONY
Chapter 7

Just as the two world wars ended Europe's role as the center of international affairs by placing the fate of the world in the hands of the
superpowers, so the long-run effect of these wars undermined Western
imperialism and paved the way for the liberation of colonial peoples
throughout the world. Although Western imperialism remained quite
strong between the two world wars, the system of mandates established
under the League of Nations constituted a modification of the purpose
and nature of control exercised by European powers, while the Leninist conception of national self-determination went beyond Wilsonian
liberalism in calling for the liberation of colonial peoples from imperialist domination. The two strands of Western European thought,
nationalism and Marxism, merged in a significant way in the colonial
liberation movements. At the same time, they have often been combined with supranationalist conceptions based on religion or race —
for example, Pan-Islamism and Pan-Africanism.

Although the Western powers often had to be forced out of colonial
territories, as with the French in Indochina and Algeria, they frequently left of their own accord in the hope that they could continue
to exercise a measure of control and influence by means of military,
technical, and economic aid. Indeed, the Communists have always
argued that Western assistance to underdeveloped countries is merely
another and more subtle form of imperialism, an argument to which
the Western powers have responded in kind in their own analyses of
Communist support and assistance to underdeveloped countries. In
reality, both sides in the cold war have exploited the needs of the
new nations to exercise influence when it has suited their purposes.
Thus Colonel Gamal Abdel Nasser forced out the English and nation-
alized the Suez Canal in 1956 but then became increasingly dependent
on Russia for economic and military assistance in his struggle with
Israel. The Russians have exploited the situation, which fits in well
with their policy of breaking the Western monopoly in the Mediter-

ranean, while the Americans have supported Israel for domestic as well as for diplomatic reasons. The danger in such situations is that the great powers may become more involved than they wish to be because of the intense hatreds and rivalries of their clients. In contrast, however, situations have also arisen in which cold war politics have victimized the people of the new nations. Rivalry between the United States and Russia exacerbated violent internal conflicts in the former Belgian Congo, for example.

The leaders of the new nations have frequently tried to steer a path of neutrality and autonomy between the great powers and have attempted to act as a third force in international affairs. They have stressed the need for regional agreements to overcome political divisions on the continents of Asia and Africa and to secure the collective strength necessary for the pursuit of an independent role. The African leader Kwame Nkrumah has urged a Pan-African policy, and for a long time India was one of the foremost proponents of a policy of neutrality and collaboration among the peoples of the third world. India seemed particularly well suited for such a role because of the philosophy of nonviolence of the inspiring founder of modern India, Mahatma Gandhi. Yet India's efforts to steer a nonviolent course have suffered some tragic setbacks. Gandhi himself died at the hands of an assassin, and the independence of India was begun with a violent dispute between the Hindus and Moslems over Kashmir. The greatest threat to India's efforts to show the way toward economic development within a democratic and neutral framework, however, has come from Communist China. China's annexation of Tibet in 1951 and the constant border disputes with India reflect the larger conflict between the two countries that is implicit in the fact that they exemplify alternative paths for the new nations.

The rivalry for the leadership of the new nations has become incredibly complicated because of the Chinese Communists. The break between the Chinese and the Russians has created a competition between the two in which the Chinese have distinct advantages. They are a people of the third world, and they share the nationalism and anti-imperialist ideology of the new nations. The immense poverty and overpopulation of these regions and their need for rapid economic development make them natural breeding grounds for revolutionaries, who are bound to be less than enthralled by the Russian policy of peaceful coexistence and to be much more enthusiastic about Chinese militance and such achievements as the Chinese explosion of an atomic bomb in 1964. The future path of the new and underdeveloped nations, then, is unclear. In Latin America, for example, will they choose the path of Fidel Castro in Cuba, or will they settle for military dictatorships of a more social character than those that have been typical of that continent? If they choose Communism, will it be the Russian or the Chinese variety? Will the Chinese gain complete ascendancy in Southeast Asia because of Russia's detente with the United States, despite the Vietnam War? To what extent can Africa pursue a neutral course? The future of the underdeveloped areas is a great unresolved question, but certainly the future of Western civilization will be affected by the answer.

Gamal Abdel Nasser

Colonel Gamal Abdel Nasser (1916–1971) was a member of the military junta led by General Mohammed Naguib that overthrew King Farouk in 1952 and proclaimed Egypt a republic a year later. Nasser quickly replaced Naguib as leader of the new regime. He was a powerful and charismatic leader deeply committed to the cause of Arab nationalism. He also proved himself to be a skilled political leader, able to maintain his power despite Israeli victories and the suspicion of the guerrilla organizations of the Palestinian refugees. Although he was not able to escape dependence upon the support of the Soviet Union, he was the most important contemporary Arab leader. Throughout his career, he linked Egyptian and Arab nationalism and was keenly aware of the religious foundations of both.

The Philosophy of the Revolution

THE THREE CIRCLES

We should first of all agree upon one thing before we proceed further with this discourse, and that is to define the boundaries of place as far as we are concerned. If I were told that our place is the capital we live in I beg to differ. If I were told that our place is limited by the political boundaries of our country I also do not agree. If our problem, as a whole, is confined within our capital or inside our political boundaries, it will be easy. We would lock ourselves in, close all the doors, and live in an ivory tower away as much as possible from the world, its compli-

From Gamal Abdel Nasser, "The Philosophy of the Revolution," in *Arab Nationalism,* ed. Sylvia G. Haim (Berkeley: University of California Press, 1964), pp. 229–32. Reprinted by permission of The University of California Press.

cations, its wars and crises. All these crash through the gates of our country and leave their effects upon us, though we have nothing to do with them.

But the era of isolation is now gone. Gone also are the days when barbed wires marked the frontiers separating and isolating countries, and every country must look beyond its frontiers to find out where the currents that affected it spring, how it should live with others. . . . It has become imperative that every country should look around itself to find out its position and its environment and decide what it can do, what its vital sphere is, and where the scene of its activity and what its positive role could be in this troubled world.

As I often sit in my study and think quietly of this subject I ask myself, "What is our positive role in this troubled world and where is the scene in which we can play that role?"

I survey our conditions and find out we are in a group of circles which should be the theater of our activity and in which we try to move as much as we can.

Fate does not play jokes. Events are not produced haphazardly. Existence cannot come out of nothing.

We cannot look stupidly at a map of the world, not realizing our place therein and the role determined to us by that place. Neither can we ignore that there is an Arab circle surrounding us and that this circle is as much a part of us as we are a part of it, that our history has been mixed with it and that its interests are linked with ours. These are actual facts and not mere words.

Can we ignore that there is a continent of Africa in which fate has placed us and which is destined today to witness a terrible struggle on its future? This struggle will affect us whether we want or not.

Can we ignore that there is a Muslim world in which we are tied by bonds which are not only forged by religious faith but also tightened by the facts of history? I said once that fate plays no jokes. It is not in vain that our country lies to the southwest of Asia, close to the Arab world, whose life is intermingled with ours. It is not in vain that our country lies to the northeast of Africa, a position from which it gives upon the dark continent wherein rages today the most violent struggle between white colonizers and black natives for the possession of its inexhaustible resources. It is not in vain that Islamic civilization and Islamic heritage, which the Mongols ravaged in their conquest of the old Islamic capitals, retreated, and sought refuge in Egypt, where they found shelter and safety as a result of the counterattack with which Egypt repelled the invasion of these Tartars at Ein Galout.

All these are fundamental facts, whose roots lie deeply in our life; whatever we do, we cannot forget them or run away from them.

I see no reason why, as I sit alone in my study with my thoughts wandering away, I should recall, at this stage of my thinking, a well-known story by the Italian poet Luigi Pirandelli [*sic*] which he called, "Six Personalities in Search of Actors" [*sic*].

The annals of history are full of heroes who carved for themselves great and heroic roles and played them on momentous occasions on the stage. History is also charged with great heroic roles which do not find actors to play them on the stage. I do not know why I always imagine that in this region in which we live there is a role wandering aimlessly about seeking an actor to play it. I do not know why this role, tired of roaming about in this vast region which extends to every place around us, should at last settle down, weary and worn out, on our frontiers beckoning us to move, to dress up for it, and to perform it, since there is nobody else who can do so.

Here I hasten to point out that this role is not a leading role. It is one of interplay of reactions and experiments with all these factors aiming at exploding this terrific energy latent in every sphere around us and at the creation, in this region, of a tremendous power capable of lifting this region up and making it play its positive role in the construction of the future of humanity.

There is no doubt that the Arab circle is the most important and the most widely connected with us. Its history merges with ours. We have suffered the same hardships and lived the same crises, and when we fell prostrate under the spikes of the horses of conquerors they lay with us.

THE ISLAMIC CIRCLE

The third circle now remains, the circle that goes beyond continents and oceans and to which I referred as the circle of our brethren in faith who turn with us, whatever part of the world they are in, toward the same kibla in Mecca and whose pious lips whisper reverently the same prayers.

My faith in the positive efficacy which can be the outcome of further strengthening the Islamic bonds with all other Muslims became deeper when I went to the Saudi Kingdom with the Egyptian mission who went there to offer condolences on the occasion of its late King.

As I stood in front of the Kaaba and felt my sentiments wandering with every part of the world where Islam had extended I found myself exclaiming, "Our idea of the pilgrimage should change. Going to the Kaaba should never be a passport to heaven, after a lengthy life. Neither should it be a simple effort to buy indulgences after an eventful life. The pilgrimage should be a great political power. The press of the world should resort to and follow its news, not as a series of rituals and traditions which are done to amuse and entertain readers, but as a regular political congress wherein the leaders of Muslim states, their public men, their pioneers in every field of knowledge, their writers, their leading industrialists, merchants, and youth draw up in this universal Islamic parliament the main lines of policy for their countries and their coöperation together until they meet again. They should meet reverently, strong, free from greed but active, submissive to the Lord, but powerful against their difficulties and their enemies, dreaming of a new life, firm believers that they have a place under the sun which they should occupy for life."

I recall I expressed some of these sentiments to His Majesty King Saoud. He said to me, "This is the real wisdom of the pilgrimage." Verily I cannot visualize a higher wisdom.

When my mind traveled to the 80 million Muslims in Indonesia, the 50 million in China, and the several other millions in Malaya, Siam, Burma, and the 100 million in Pakistan, the 100 million or more in the Middle East, and the 40 million in Russia as well as the other millions in the distant parts of the world, when I visualize these millions united in one faith I have a great consciousness of the tremendous potentialities that cooperation amongst them all can achieve: a coöperation that does not deprive them of their loyalty to their countries but which guarantees for them and their brethren a limitless power.

I now revert to the wandering role that seeks an actor to perform it. Such is the role, such are its features, and such is its stage.

We, and only we, are impelled by our environment and are capable of performing this role.

Kwame Nkrumah

Kwame Nkrumah has been one of the most eloquent and sincere spokesmen of African nationalism. He refused to accept the partial self-determination offered the Gold Coast by the British in 1951 and continued to fight for total independence even after being imprisoned. By 1957, Nkrumah was victorious, and Ghana became the first black nation of the British Commonwealth. Since that time, Nkrumah has struggled for the end of colonial domination and the end of racism in Africa as a whole, and he has urged the new states of Africa to bury tribal and other differences and join together in the assertion of a common African identity and thereby play a more independent and important role in world affairs. His program of African nationalism was expressed in a speech he delivered at the opening session of the conference of independent African states in Accra on April 13, 1958.

The African Personality

It is my pleasant duty, on behalf of the Government and people of Ghana, to welcome you, our distinguished guests, to our country.

This is a memorable gathering. It is the first time in history that representatives of independent sovereign states in Africa are meeting together with the aim of forging closer links of friendship, brotherhood, co-operation and solidarity between them.

As we look back into the history of our continent, we cannot escape the fact that we have for too long been the victims of foreign domination.

For too long we have had no say in the management of our own affairs or in deciding our own destinies.

Now times have changed, and today we are the masters of our own fate.

This fact is evidenced in our meeting together here as independent sovereign states out of our own free will to speak our minds openly, to argue and discuss, to share our experiences, our aspirations, our dreams and our hopes in the interests of mother Africa.

What is the purpose of this historic conference? We are here to know ourselves and to exchange views on matters of common interest; to explore ways and means of consolidating and safe-guarding our hard-won independence; to strengthen the economic and cultural ties between our countries; to find workable arrangements for helping our brothers still languishing under colonial rule; to examine the central problem which dominates the world today, namely, the problem of how to secure peace.

And, finally, to send out an appeal to the Great Powers of the world to do whatever they can to save the world from destruction and humanity from annihilation.

As we watch the efforts being made to convene a summit conference, we would ask the Great Powers to make a supreme effort to resolve their differences.

In any case, we appeal to them to live in tolerant and peaceful co-existence, and to leave us to live our own lives. These objectives constitute the main purpose of our conference.

But I must inevitably make some reference to the past in order to illustrate the present dangers of two problems which still beset large parts of this great continent of ours — colonialism and racialism.

There have been two decisive factors in the shaping of the history of our continent down to the present time — the slave trade and the rape of Africa by the then great European powers.

Between the 16th and the early 19th centuries when the slave trade was abolished, millions of African men and women were transported to provide slave labour to enrich other continents.

Had the miseries of our continent ended with the slave trade, we might

From *Daily Graphic*, Accra, April 16, 1958.

perhaps have found the means of recovering from the wounds which this system inflicted upon us.

But, alas! a new misfortune — colonialism — befell us. While the slave trade took away from Africa shiploads of our people, colonialism enslaved them in their own territories.

We are all aware of the "Scramble for Africa" in the nineteenth and early twentieth centuries.

For fifty years, from 1830 onwards, France was engaged in a war of conquest in Algeria; then Tunisia became a French protectorate in 1881; Italy occupied Libya after the Turco-Italian war of 1911–12.

Italy made a similar attempt upon Ethiopia in 1896, but was defeated at the battle of Adowa.

Thirty-nine years later, Ethiopia was again invaded and suffered a temporary loss of her independence.

The British occupied Egypt in 1882, and the Sudan was brought into their orbit in 1898. Germany declared her first protectorates in Africa in 1884–85.

Liberia, the oldest republic in Africa, was robbed of much of her original territory and, but for the grace of God and the timely intervention of the United States of America, she might have lost her independence in the nineteen-thirties.

We have learnt much about the old forms of colonialism. Some of them still exist, but I am confident they will all disappear from the face of our continent.

It is not only the old forms of colonialism that we are determined to see abolished, but we are equally determined that the new forms of colonialism which are now appearing in the world, with their potential threat to our precious independence, will not succeed.

Similarly with racialism. Many of the advocates of colonialism claimed in the past — as some of them do now — that they were racially superior and had a special mission to colonise and rule other peoples. This we reject.

We repudiate and condemn all forms of racialism for racialism not only injures those against whom it is used but warps and perverts the very people who preach and protect it; and when it becomes a guiding principle in the life of any nation, as it has become in some other parts of Africa, then that nation digs its own grave.

Within our own countries we must try to practice goodwill towards individuals and minorities, and we must also endeavour to demonstrate the same attitude in our relations with other nations.

Africa is the last remaining stronghold of colonialism. Unlike Asia, there are on the continent of Africa more dependent territories than independent sovereign nations.

Therefore we, the free independent states of Africa, have a responsibility to hasten the total liberation of Africa.

I believe that there are lessons from the past which will help us in discharging this sacred duty.

If I have spoken of racialism and colonialism, it is not, as I have said, because I want to indulge in recrimination with any country by listing a catalogue of wrongs which have been perpetrated upon our continent in the past.

My only purpose in doing so is to illustrate the different forms which colonialism and imperialism — old and new — can take, so that we can be on our guard in adopting measures to safeguard our hard-won independence and national sovereignty.

The imperialists of today endeavour to achieve their ends not merely by military means, but by economic penetration, cultural assimilation, ideological domination, psychological infiltration, and subversive activities to the point of inspiring and promoting, assassination and civil strife.

Very often these methods are adopted in order to influence the foreign policies of small and uncommitted countries in a particular direction. Therefore, we, the leaders of resurgent Africa, must be alert and vigilant.

We, the delegates of this conference, in promoting our foreign relations, must endeavour to seek the friendship of all and the enmity of none.

We stand for international peace and security in conformity with the United Nations charter.

This will enable us to assert our own African personality and to develop according to our own ways of life, our own customs, traditions and cultures.

In the past, the economic pattern of our countries was linked with the metropolitan powers of Europe and we have been accustomed to look to them for the maintenance of our markets and sources of supply.

As independent states, it is in our mutual interest to explore trade possibilities between our respective countries while at the same time enlarging our trade with the rest of the world.

In this connection we should exchange our own efforts to develop our economies, and so strengthen our political independence, we should at the same time welcome economic assistance offered through the organisations of the United Nations, such as the proposed regional economic commission for Africa.

We shall also welcome other forms of economic aid from outside the United Nations, provided it does not compromise our independence.

I believe that the economic and social field offers real opportunities for constructive and co-operative action.

We need to know much about the real resources of our great continent, and to develop them so that the standard of living of our peoples can be raised.

We know the great problems which face every African government today in trying to provide better opportunities by way of education and good social services; in particular those health and sanitary operations which can do so much to remove the scourge of disease from our countries.

Several great schemes have been proposed for various parts of Africa, all of them would require great capital expenditure.

Here, it seems to me, is a special opportunity for co-operative action between the independent African states themselves and also between these states and other peace-loving nations to outside Africa.

Addressing ourselves to the cultural aspects of our relationship, we must also examine ways and means to broaden and strengthen our association with one another through such means as the exchange of students and the visits of cultural, scientific and technical missions both governmental and non-governmental, and the establishment of libraries specialising in various aspects of African history and culture which may become centres of research.

There are no limits to which we on this African continent can enrich our knowledge of our past civilisations and cultural heritage through our co-operative efforts and the pooling of our scientific and technical resources.

The goals which we have set before us require a world of order and security in which we can live and work in tranquillity towards their realisation.

That is why we have a vested interest in world peace. Our foreign policies must therefore be such as to contribute towards the realisation of that fundamental objective.

As free and independent nations we must also endeavour to follow the policy of positive non-alignment so as to enable us at any time to adopt measures which will best suit our national interests and promote the cause of peace.

It is only by avoiding entanglement in quarrels of the Great Powers that we shall be able to assert our African personality on the side of peace in conformity with the charter of the United Nations.

But there can be no lasting peace and security as long as colonialism exists in any form. For let us face facts.

Today in this continent the dynamic forces of African nationalism can only be resisted by resorting to armed force, such as we are now witnessing in Algeria.

The sovereignty and independence of Tunisia and Morocco are already involved in this catastrophic war, and if it is not brought to a speedy termination, it may well lead to a greater conflagration with tragic results for us all.

We have already stated our belief in the inalienable right of all peoples to choose the form of government under which they wish to live, and we therefore abhor and vehemently denounce any attempt by one group of people to impose their own form of government or political ideology upon other people against their will.

At the present time the Great Powers are spending astronomical sums of money on piling up stocks of the most destructive weapons that have ever been contrived; weapons which, if employed, will wipe out mankind and leave this earth barren and desolate.

If these Great Powers can be persuaded to divert a small fraction of this precious capital, which they are now using for destructive ends, to finance the economic and social programmes of the under-developed countries of the world, it will not only raise the standard of living in these countries, but will also contribute greatly to the general cause of humanity and the attainment of world peace.

Like hundreds of millions of people all over the world we appeal to all the powers concerned to cease the testing of nuclear weapons.

Radio-active winds know no international frontiers and it is these tests — in a period of so called peace — which can do more than anything else to threaten our very existence.

But what do we hear? At the very moment when a summit conference is being contemplated it is reputed that plans are being made to use the Sahara as a testing ground for nuclear weapons.

We vehemently condemn this proposal and protest against the use of our continent for such purposes. We appeal to the United Nations to call a halt to this threat to our safety.

I am confident that our conference will be able to send out a message of light to the world which may help to lift from above the head of mankind the clouds of war and fear.

If we are able to do this, then our conference will have made a vital contribution to the overriding problem of the survival of our human civilisation, which has been built up so painfully over long centuries, while at the same time opening up the way to the further advance of our own countries and peoples.

If we can as independent African states show by our own efforts that we can settle our own problems in Africa, then we shall be setting an example to others.

We must be in a position to offer our "good offices" in trying to bring about a settlement of existing disputes, at least those on our continent.

For this reason it may be necessary for this conference to examine the possibility of setting up some sort of machinery to maintain the links we shall forge here and to implement the decisions we shall reach.

For we must leave no stone unturned in our endeavours to lessen tensions in Africa no less than elsewhere, as every success which we are able to achieve in resolving issues like frontier disputes, tribal quarrels and racial and religious antagonisms, will be a step forward in the bringing about of world peace.

To the extent that we are able by our own exertions and examples, to maintain peace and friendship without our own states and on our continent, will we be in a position to exert moral pressures elsewhere and help to quench the flames of war which could destroy us all.

Today we are one. If in the past the Sahara divided us, now it unites us. And an injury to one is an injury to all of us. From this conference must go out a new message: "Hands off Africa! Africa must be free!"

Jawaharlal Nehru

Jawaharlal Nehru (1889–1964) served as India's first prime minister between the founding of the independent state in 1947 and his death in 1964. Nehru, who was a follower of Gandhi, was one of the founders of the nationalist Congress party, which continues to dominate the country. Much of his life was devoted to the cause of Indian independence. The death of both his parents was a consequence of British mistreatment, and he spent ten years in prison because of his insistence on total independence for his country. A believer in democratic socialism, Nehru rejected all forms of totalitarianism and struggled to maintain a neutral position in the cold war. His 1948 speech at Ootacamund, Madras, reflects his sentiments at an early and particularly optimistic stage of his career as prime minister. They demonstrate the merging of his Indian and Asian nationalism. The practical problems of running India made Nehru and his successors more dependent upon outside assistance and much less sanguine about the population problem.

Asia, India, and the World

. . . "There has been talk in the past of One World. Apart from the political aspect of One World, it is even more important to consider the economic aspect and consider it in the economic sense. You are meeting here to deal with Asia and Asia's problems. But you have to look at these problems inevitably in the context of the larger world. We cannot escape looking almost at any problem in the global context to-day.

"Asia is big enough and the subjects you have to deal with are vast and of tremendous importance. The Governor of Madras referred to the numerous papers and memoranda that you have before you. I feel

From *The Hindu*, Madras, June 2, 1948.

rather overwhelmed when I look at these piles of papers and see the experts on this business. But I can only speak as a layman. While experts are quite inevitable in the modern world, sometimes I have a feeling that they become very impersonal and look at problems as if they were mathematical or algebraic formulae. We have to deal with human beings and the future of human beings. In the area under survey in Asia, I suppose there are at least 1,000 million human beings. In India, including Pakistan, there are 40 per cent of this 1,000 millions, i.e., about 400 millions. We have to deal with this vast number, practically half the world's population. If you look at the human aspect of it, i.e., a thousand million human beings, with their families, their sufferings, their needs and wants, their joys, sorrows and troubles, the problem becomes something much more than a dry mathematical problem which is solved on paper. And, the problem assumes a tremendous urgency."

Stressing the neglect in the past of Asia, Pandit Nehru said, "In the past many years, when most of these problems have been considered in the world context, I have had a feeling — I still have that feeling — that the continent of Asia is somewhat neglected, somewhat overlooked. It is not considered important enough for as much attention to be given to it as is given to certain other parts of the world. Possibly, that was so because most of the people who were considering these problems were themselves intimately connected with other parts of the world. And naturally, they thought of them in the first instance. Naturally also if I had to consider the problem, I would, perhaps, attach more importance to Asia, because it affects me more intimately.

"But that kind of reaction apart, it seems to me obvious that if you want to consider the problem of Asia or of Europe or of America or of Africa isolated from the other problems, it just cannot be done. And if some country or countries which are fortunate enough to-day — more fortunate than others — think that they can live their lives apart, whatever happens in the rest of the world, it is obvious that they are under a misapprehension. To-day, if one part of the world goes down economically or otherwise, it has a tendency to drag others with it, just as, if unfortunately war breaks out, other people are involved who do not want war at all. So, it is not a question of the prosperous merely out of generosity of their heart helping those that are not prosperous, though generosity is a good thing. It is a question of an enlightened self-interest, of realising that if some parts of the world did not progress and remained backward, they have an adverse effect on the whole economy of the world and tend to break down those other parts, too, which may be at present prosperous. Therefore, it becomes inevitable to consider these problems in the global way and to pay even more attention to those parts which are relatively backward.

"Asia," Pandit Nehru continued, "has been for many generations past in the same static and backward condition from this point of view. But during the last few years, mighty forces have been at work in Asia. Those forces inevitably thought in terms of political change to begin with, because without political change it was not possible to have any far-reaching or enduring economic change.

"Large parts of Asia were colonial territories dominated by other countries. While by that connection they had got certain advantages and sometimes it did them good, at the same time the domination tended to preserve itself. The political trouble of Asia is, however, largely over, but not entirely. There are parts of Asia where some kind of struggle for political freedom is still going on. And it is obvious that so long as there is that kind of trouble on the political plane, other activities will be ignored and will be thwarted. The sooner it is realised that politically every country in Asia should be completely free and be in a position to follow its own genius within the larger world polity that world organisations may work out, the better it will be. But, one thing is certain and it is this: There will be no peace in any part of Asia where an attempt is made to dominate by force.

"I regret that some such attempts continue to be made in some parts of Asia. They seem to me not only undesirable in themselves, but singularly lacking in foresight, because there can be but one end to that attempt, and that is the complete elimination of any kind of foreign control.

"Now generally speaking," Pandit Nehru said, "this political aspect of Asia's struggle is drawing towards its natural and inevitable culmination. But at the same time, the economic aspect continues and it is bound to affect all manner of other economic problems of the world. From Asia's point of view, it has become essential and a matter of extreme urgency to deal with these problems. From the world point of view, it is equally urgent, because unless these problems are dealt with expeditiously, they would affect other parts of the world."

Exhorting the delegates to pay urgent attention to Asia's problems lest the ends of the United Nations be defeated, Pandit Jawaharlal Nehru observed: "You, who are members of this Commission and who realise the importance of what I have said, will make it clear to the United Nations as a whole that any attempt not to pay enough attention to Asia's problems, economic and other, is likely to defeat the end which the United Nations have in view. In Asia, great historic forces have been at play during the last many years and many things have happened here which are good and many things have happened which are not so good — as it always happens when historic, impersonal forces are in action. These are still in action. We try to mould them a little, to divert them a little here and there, but essentially they will carry on till they fulfil their purpose and their historic destiny. That historic destiny can only be one of complete political and economic freedom within, certainly, some kind of world framework. In Asia and the rest of the world, there are various systems at work, political and economic in different countries. Obviously, it will not be possible to co-operate easily unless we proceed on the basis of not interfering with any system, political or economic, in any country and of leaving that country to develop as it chooses within the larger sphere of world co-operation.

"You can," Pandit Nehru said, "look upon the problems of Asia from the long term point of view and from the short term point of view. The short term view probably demands immediate attention because of the urgency of solving some great difficulty. There is for instance the food aspect."

Pandit Nehru referred in this connection to India's food problem and said, "It is an extraordinary state of affairs that in a country like India or a similar predominantly agricultural country, we should lack food, or we should not have sufficiency of food. There is something obviously wrong when that kind of thing happens. I have no doubt in my mind that India can and will produce enough food for herself but it may not be immediately, I am afraid — it might take a few years for us to come up to the mark in that respect. At the present moment, we have to face this problem of food and it shall no doubt come up before you. Other similar urgent problems will also come up before you. But looking at it from a long term point of view, various deficiencies have to be made good. We have to increase — all our countries have to increase — our production capacity, agricultural and industrial."

Pandit Nehru continued: "It is admitted now all round that industrialisation should proceed ahead in these countries of Asia. In the past, this has rather been frowned upon by various people and various interests. But to-day the need is admitted. But how is it to proceed? No doubt, it can proceed; and even without much help from outside it will proceed, but it will take a much longer time. The real limiting factor in industrialisation is lack of capital equipment. The easiest way, of course, of getting capital equipment and special technical experience is from those countries which happen to possess it and where there is a surplus of it. How far that can be obtained it is for you to calculate and for those countries to decide. If it is not obtained quickly, the process is somewhat delayed.

"But, the process will go on, nevertheless, and the delay in solving the particular problem may create other problems." Stressing the need for giving Asian countries assistance "free from all savour of economic domination," Pandit Jawaharlal Nehru said: "Now, if it is considered right in the larger interests of the world that countries like India and other countries in the East should get industrialised and increase their agricultural production, modernise it and have more industries, then it is to the interests of those countries that can help this process to help the Asian countries with capital equipment and their special experience. But in doing so, it has to be borne in mind that no Asian country will welcome any such assistance if there are conditions attached to it which lead to any kind of economic domination.

"We would rather delay our development, industrial or otherwise," Pandit Nehru declared, "than submit to any kind of economic domination of any country. That is an axiom which is accepted by everyone in India and I should be surprised if other countries in Asia do not accept it also. We want to co-operate in the fullest measure with any policy or programme laid down for the world's good, even though it might involve a surrender in common with other countries of any particular attribute of sovereignty, provided it is for the common good all round. But a long age of foreign domination has made the countries of Asia very sensitive about anything happening which leads to some visible or invisible form of domination. And, therefore, I beg of you to remember this and to fashion your own programmes and policies so as to avoid any savouring of economic domination of one country by another. When visible or invisible economic domination creeps in, it will lead immediately to ill-will and not to that atmosphere of goodwill and co-operation which is so essential in this matter.

"In a long-term view in regard to India, the most essential thing is to develop our power resources. From that will flow the industrialisation of the country, the addition to our food production, agricultural resources, etc. As it is, perhaps you know that India has probably more in the shape of irrigation than any other country in the world. We hope to increase the resources very greatly. We have in view at least a score of various river valley schemes, some very big, some bigger even than the Tennessee Valley in size at least, and some smaller. We hope to push these schemes through by constructing huge dams and reservoirs and thereby adding to the irrigated parts of India and bringing under cultivation large tracts which are not at present probably cultivable."

Pandit Jawaharlal Nehru next referred to the population of India and expressed his view that India was underpopulated. "A great deal," Mr. Nehru said, "has been said and written about the tremendous population of India and how it overwhelms us and how we cannot solve any problem at all unless this growth in Indian population is checked. While I have no desire for the population of India to go on increasing — I am all in favour of the population being checked — I think there is a grave misapprehension. When so much stress is laid on the population of India and every evil that India has to contend against, I entirely disagree with that. I think India is an underpopulated country. "I do not want India to be much more populated, but it is underpopulated because large tracts of India are still unpopulated. It is true that if you go to the

Gangetic plain, you find it is heavily populated. Parts of India are heavily populated, no doubt. But many parts are not populated at all. A delegate to this Conference told me last evening that coming from Karachi to Delhi and to Madras on to Ooty, it was amazing to see the scarcity of population. Of course, the delegate was travelling by plane! (Laughter.) Nevertheless, the whole countryside appeared to him to be largely of desert tract. After all one can judge whether a country is heavily populated or not, and that was a correct impression the delegate got, because it is true that large tracts in India are not populated. We are overpopulated, if you like, because our production capacity is low; but that is a different matter. If we increase our production, agricultural and other, if this population is put to work in production and if each man produces not only enough for himself, but something more, then we will not be overpopulated. So that, the problem is not one of reducing population but of producing more."

Reverting to the development projects, Pandit Nehru said: "We have thus scores of big river valley schemes which, in addition to irrigating land and preventing floods, soil erosion and malaria, will produce a great deal of hydro-electric power and at the same time lead to industrial development. If you look at the map of India — which I hope you will look at — you will see the noble range of the Himalayas to the north and north-east. I do not think there is any part of the world similar in area, which has so much concentrated power — latent and potential power. If only all that can be tapped and used! Well, we intend tapping and using it. To some extent, we have done so and we intend to do so further, and speedily. These Himalayas are also full of a variety of minerals. Of course, there are many other parts of India too, rich in themselves. But my point is that India — I mention India because I happen to know a little more about India — as well as the whole of the Asian region, is full of vast resources, human and material, and the question before us is how to yoke them together and produce results."

Pandit Nehru continued: "It is not that material, human and other, is lacking. You have got these. In order to yoke them together at the moment, the easiest way is, of course, to have certain assistance in capital equipment, experience and technical personnel from those countries which may have a surplus of them. From the world point of view this inevitably knits the world closer. If that cannot be done wholly, then naturally we have to function in a more limited way, but we have to go in that direction anyhow. While increasing production in this way, I think it is important for us to utilise our existing resources better. I do not think they are being utilised to the best advantage. We can get more out of what we have got than we have been doing so far. That involves in India, as in the rest of Asia, many other problems, the economic system, relation between capital and labour, satisfaction of labour and so on.

"There is no doubt at all," Pandit Nehru continued, "that in all or in most — at any rate in most of those Asian countries — there are long-standing social injustices and naturally, where there are these social injustices, you will not get satisfactory work, especially now when there is an acute sense of social wrong and social injustice. In India I have no doubt that our production has suffered because of this acute feeling of social injustice. The individual or a community may undertake to shoulder almost any burden. We have seen during the last war how nations have put up with enormous burdens in the shape of sacrifices. But, always, when there is an attempt to share the burden and there is a sense of injustice of the burden being greater on some than on others, of some being privileged and others being under-privileged, then the stress becomes greater, and you cannot, and you do not, have that harmonious working and co-operation which is quite essential to-day more than in the past. Therefore, this problem has to be viewed from the human point of view, and quite apart from the purely economic theory. If one does view it from that human point of view and tries to co-operate in sizing it without entering into long arguments about pure economic theories, I think we can go far in solving it and in getting that measure of co-operation even among people who may hold different theories."

Concluding, India's Prime Minister exhorted the member nations to have in view this approach in their deliberations and said: "So, I would beg of this Commission to consider this problem from the human point of view of removing social injustices. The Commission of course, is not going to dictate to each individual country about its economic structure. But any advice from the Commission will no doubt go a long way and most countries would probably follow it in the largest measure they can."

Mao Tse-tung

Mao Tse-tung, who has ruled China since the Communist takeover in 1949, was born in 1893 of peasant parents. Throughout his career as leader of the Chinese Communists he has remained convinced that the conditions of the Chinese countryside provided the stuff of revolution. He fought integration with the nationalist Kuomintang of General Chiang Kai-shek as he resisted less openly Russian Communist efforts to direct the Chinese Communist movement in a manner that paid little heed to Chinese conditions or interests. Although Mao has con-sistently sought to apply Marxist-Leninist thought to China, he has also tried to maintain a direct line between his movement and the nationalist movement of Sun Yat-sen, who founded the Chinese Republic in 1911. The effort to combine the two strains of contemporary Chinese history, as well as the desire to tie them to older Chinese traditions, is evident from Mao's speech on the occasion of the twenty-eighth anniversary of the Chinese Communist party. It is one of the clues to the continuing vitality and appeal of his movement and person as well as to many of the peculiarities and vagaries of his regime.

On the People's Democratic Dictatorship (1949)

Imperialist aggression shattered the Chinese dream of learning from the West. They wondered why the teachers always practised aggression against their pupils. The Chinese learned much from the West, but what they learned could not be put into effect. Their ideals could not be realized. [Many struggles, including the Revolution of 1911, had all failed.] Meanwhile, conditions in the country worsened day by day, and the environment was such that the people could not live. Doubt sprang up, it grew and developed. The First World War shook the whole world. The Russians carried out the October Revolution, creating the first socialist country in the world. Under the leadership of Lenin and Stalin the revolutionary energy of the great Russian proletariat and labouring people, which had lain hidden and could not be seen by foreigners, suddenly erupted like a volcano. The Chinese and all mankind then began to look differently at the Russians. Then, and only then, did there appear for the Chinese an entirely new era both in ideology and in living. The Chinese found the universal truth of Marxism-Leninism which holds good everywhere, and the face of China was changed.

It was through the introduction of the Russians that the Chinese found Marxism. Before the October Revolution the Chinese not only did not know Lenin and Stalin, but also did not know Marx and Engels. The gunfire of the October Revolution sent us Marxism-Leninism. The October Revolution helped the progressive elements of the world and of China to use the world outlook of the proletariat as the instrument for perceiving the destiny of the country, and for reconsidering their own problems. Travel the road of the Russians — this was the conclusion. In 1919, the May Fourth movement took place in China, and the CCP was formed in 1921. In his moment of despair Sun Yat-sen came across the October Revolution and the CCP. He welcomed the October Revolution,

From *A Documentary History of Chinese Communism*, ed. Conrad Brandt, Benjamin Schwartz, and John K. Fairbank (Cambridge, Mass.: Harvard University Press, 1952), pp. 451–60. Reprinted by permission of Harvard University Press and George Allen and Unwin Ltd.

welcomed Russian help to China, and welcomed the co-operation of the CCP. Sun Yat-sen died [March 1925] and Chiang Kai-shek came into power. During the long period of twenty-two years [since 1927] Chiang Kai-shek has dragged China into hopeless straits.

During this period the anti-fascist Second World War, with the Soviet Union as its main force, defeated three big imperialist powers, weakened two other big imperialist powers, leaving only one imperialist country in the world — the United States of America, which suffered no loss. However, the domestic crisis in America is very grave. She wants to enslave the entire world and she aided Chiang Kai-shek with arms to slaughter several millions of Chinese. Under the leadership of the CCP, the Chinese people, after having driven away Japanese imperialism, fought the people's war of liberation for three years and gained a basic victory. Thus the civilization of the Western bourgeoisie, the bourgeois democracy, and the pattern of the bourgeois republic all went bankrupt in the minds of the Chinese people. Bourgeois democracy has given way to the people's democracy under the leadership of the proletariat, and the bourgeois republic has given way to the people's republic. A possibility has thus been created of reaching socialism and Communism through the people's republic, of attaining the elimination of classes and universal fraternity. K'ang Yu-wei wrote the book *On Universal Fraternity* [*Ta-t'ung shu*], but he did not, and could not, find the road to it. The bourgeois republic has existed in foreign countries but cannot exist in China, because China is a country oppressed by imperialism. The only (way for us) is to travel the road of the people's republic under the leadership of the proletariat and attain the elimination of classes and universal fraternity.

All other things had been tried and had failed. Of those who yearned for other things, some had fallen, some had awakened to their mistake, and others are in the process of changing their minds. Events developed so swiftly that many people felt surprised and the need to learn anew. This state of mind is understandable, and we welcome such a well-intentioned attitude, that asks to learn things anew.

Having learnt Marxism-Leninism after the October Revolution, the vanguard of the Chinese proletariat established the CCP. Following this, it entered into the political struggle and had to travel a zigzag path for twenty-eight years before it could gain a basic victory. From the experiences of twenty-eight years, just as from the "experiences of forty years" as Sun Yat-sen said in his will, a common conclusion has been reached, namely: "The firm belief that to attain victory we must awaken the masses of the people and unite ourselves in a common struggle with those peoples of the world who treat us on the basis of equality" [quoted from Sun's famous testament]. Sun Yat-sen had a different world outlook from us, and started out from a different class standpoint in observing and dealing with problems, but in the twenties of the twentieth century, on the problem of how to struggle against imperialism, he arrived at a conclusion which was fundamentally in agreement with ours.

Twenty-four years have elapsed since Sun Yat-sen's death, and under the leadership of the CCP, Chinese revolutionary theory and practice have made big forward strides, fundamentally changing the realities of China. Up to the present, the Chinese people have gained the following two major and basic [lessons of] experiences: (1) (We must) awaken the masses in the country. This is to unite the working class, the peasant class, the petty bourgeoisie, and national bourgeoisie into a national united front under the leadership of the working class, and develop it into a state of the people's democratic dictatorship led by the working class with the alliance of workers and peasants as its basis. (2) (We must) unite in a common struggle with those nations of the world who treat us on the basis of equality and with the people of all countries. This is to ally ourselves with the Soviet Union, to ally ourselves with all the New Democratic countries, and to ally ourselves with the proletariat and the broad masses of the people in other countries, to form an international united front.

"You lean to one side." Precisely so. The forty years' experience of Sun Yat-sen and the twenty-eight years' experience of the CCP have taught us to believe that in order to win and to consolidate the victory we must lean to one side. The experiences of forty years and twenty-eight years, respectively, show that, without exception, the Chinese people either lean to the side of imperialism or to the side of socialism. To sit on the fence is impossible; a third road does not exist. We oppose the Chiang Kai-shek reactionary clique who lean to the side of imperialism; we also oppose the illusion of a third road. Not only in China but also in the world, without exception, one either leans to the side of imperialism or to the side of socialism. Neutrality is mere camouflage and a third road does not exist.

"You are too provocative." We are talking of dealing with domestic and foreign reactionaries; that is, imperialists and their running dogs, and not of any other people. With regard to these people [foreign and domestic reactionaries], the question of provocation does not arise, for whether (we are) provocative or not makes no difference to their being reactionaries. Only by drawing a clear line between reactionaries and revolutionaries, only by exposing the designs and plots of the reactionaries, arousing vigilance and attention within the revolutionary ranks, and only by raising our own morale while subjugating the arrogance of the enemy — can the reactionaries be isolated, conquered, or replaced. In front of a wild beast you cannot show the slightest cowardice. We must learn from Wu Sung [one of the 108 heroes in the famous Chinese novel *All Men Are Brothers*, who killed a tiger with bare hands] on the

Ching-yang ridge. To Wu Sung, the tiger on the Ching-yang ridge would eat people all the same whether they were provocative or not. You either kill the tiger or are eaten by it; there is no third choice.

"We want to do business." Entirely correct. Business has to be done. We only oppose domestic and foreign reactionaries who hamper us from doing business, and do not oppose any other people. It should be known that it is no other than imperialists and their lackeys — the Chiang Kai-shek reactionary clique — who hinder our doing business with foreign countries and even hinder our establishing diplomatic relations with foreign countries. Unite all forces at home and abroad to smash the domestic and foreign reactionaries and then there will be business, and the possibility of establishing diplomatic relations with all foreign countries on the basis of equality, mutual benefits, and mutual respect of territorial sovereignty.

"Victory is also possible without international assistance" — this is an erroneous conception. In the era when imperialism exists, it is impossible for the true people's revolution of any country to win its own victory without assistance in various forms from the international revolutionary forces, and it is also impossible to consolidate the victory even when it is won. The great October Revolution was thus won and consolidated, as Stalin has told us long ago. It was also in this way that the three imperialist countries were defeated and the new democratic countries established. This is and will be the case with the People's China at present and in the future. Let us think it over; if the Soviet Union did not exist, or there had been no victory in the anti-fascist Second World War, [no defeat of German, Italian, and Japanese imperialism] and especially for us, no defeat of Japanese imperialism, if the various new democratic countries had not come into being, and no rising struggles of the oppressed nations in the East, if there had been no struggles of the masses of people in the United States, Britain, France, Germany, Italy, Japan, and other capitalist countries against the reactionary cliques ruling over them, and if there were no sum-total of these things, then the reactionary forces bearing down on us would surely be many times greater than they are at present. Could we have won victory under such circumstances? Obviously not; it would also be impossible to consolidate the victory (even) when it was won. The Chinese people have had much experience in this matter. The remark made by Sun Yat-sen before his death, that alliance must be made with the international revolutionary forces, reflected this experience long ago.

"We need the assistance of the British and American governments." This is also a childish idea at the moment. At present the rulers in Britain and the United States are still imperialists. Would they extend aid to a people's state? If we do business with these countries or suppose these countries would be willing in the future to lend us money on terms of mutual benefit, what would be the reason for it? It would be because the capitalists of these countries want to make money and the bankers want to earn interest to relieve their own crisis; that would be no aid to the Chinese people. The Communist Parties and progressive parties and groups in these countries are now working to bring about business (relations), and even to establish diplomatic relations with us. This is well meant; it means to help us, and it cannot be regarded in the same light as the acts of the bourgeoisie in these countries. During his lifetime Sun Yat-sen repeatedly appealed to the imperialist countries for aid. The outcome was futile, and instead he met with merciless attacks. In his lifetime Sun Yat-sen received international aid only once, and that was from the U.S.S.R. The reader can refer to the will of Dr. Sun Yat-sen, in which he did not ask the people to look and hope for aid from imperialist countries, but earnestly bade them "to unite with those peoples of the world who treat us on the basis of equality." Dr. Sun had had the experience; he had been duped. We must remember his words and not be duped again. Internationally we belong to the anti-imperialist front headed by the U.S.S.R., and we can look for genuine friendly aid only from that front, and not from the imperialist front.

"You are dictatorial." Dear sirs, you are right; that is exactly what we are. The experience of several decades, amassed by the Chinese people, tells us to carry out the people's democratic dictatorship. That is, the right of reactionaries to voice their opinions must be abolished and only the people are allowed to have the right of voicing their opinions.

Who are the "people"? At the present stage in China, they are the working class, the peasant class, the petty bourgeoisie, and national bourgeoisie. Under the leadership of the working class and the CP, these classes unite together to form their own state and elect their own government (so as to) carry out a dictatorship over the lackeys of imperialism — the landlord class, the bureaucratic capitalist class, and the KMT reactionaries and their henchmen representing these classes — to suppress them, allowing them only to behave properly and not to talk and act wildly. If they talk and act wildly their (action) will be prohibited and punished immediately. The democratic system is to be carried out within the ranks of the people, giving them freedom of speech, assembly, and association. The right to vote is given only to the people and not to the reactionaries. These two aspects, namely, democracy among the people and dictatorship over the reactionaries, combine to form the people's democratic dictatorship.

Why should it be done this way? Everybody clearly knows that otherwise the revolution would fail, and the people would meet with woe and the State would perish.

"Don't you want to eliminate state authority?" Yes, but we do not want it at present, we cannot want it at present. Why? Because imperialism still exists, the domestic reactionaries still exist, and classes in the country still exist. Our present task is to strengthen the apparatus of the people's state, which refers mainly to the people's army, people's police, and people's courts, for the defence of the country, and the protection of the people's interests; and with this as a condition, to enable China to advance steadily, under the leadership of the working class and the CP, from an agricultural to an industrial country, and from a New Democratic to a Socialist and Communist society, to eliminate classes and to realize the state of universal fraternity. The army, police, and courts of the state are instruments by which classes oppress classes. To the hostile classes the state apparatus is the instrument of oppression. It is violent, and not "benevolent." "You are not benevolent." Just so. We decidedly will not exercise benevolence towards the reactionary acts of the reactionaries and reactionary classes. Our benevolence applies only to the people, and not to the reactionary acts of the reactionaries and reactionary classes outside the people.

The (function of the) people's state is to protect the people. Only when there is the people's state, is it possible for the people to use democratic methods on a nationwide and all-round scale to educate and reform themselves, to free themselves from the influence of reactionaries at home and abroad (this influence is at present still very great and will exist for a long time and cannot be eliminated quickly), to unlearn the bad habits and ideas acquired from the old society and not to let themselves travel on the erroneous path pointed out by the reactionaries, but to continue to advance and develop towards a Socialist and Communist society accomplishing the historic mission of completely eliminating classes and advancing towards a universal fraternity.

The methods we use in this field are democratic; that is, methods of persuasion and not coercion. When people break the law they will be punished, imprisoned, or even sentenced to death. But these are individual cases and are different in principle from the dictatorship over the reactionary class as a class.

After their political régime is overthrown the reactionary classes and the reactionary clique will also be given land and work and a means of living; they will be allowed to re-educate themselves into new persons through work, provided they do not rebel, disrupt, or sabotage. If they are unwilling to work, the people's state will compel them to work. Propaganda and educational work will also be carried out among them, and, moreover, with care and adequacy, as we did among captured officers. This can also be called "benevolent administration," but we shall never forgive their reactionary acts and will never let their reactionary activity have the possibility of a free development.

Such re-education of the reactionary classes can only be carried out in the state of the people's democratic dictatorship. If this work is well done the main exploiting classes of China — the landlord and bureaucratic capitalist classes — will be finally eliminated. (Of the exploiting classes) there remain the national bourgeoisie among many of whom appropriate educational work can be carried out at the present stage. When socialism is realized, that is, when the nationalization of private enterprises has been carried out, they can be further educated and reformed. The people have in their hands a powerful state apparatus and are not afraid of the rebellion of the national bourgeois class.

The grave problem is that of educating the peasants. The peasants' economy is scattered. Judging by the experience of the Soviet Union, it requires a very long time and careful work to attain the socialization of agriculture. Without the socialization of agriculture, there will be no complete and consolidated socialism. And to carry out the socialization of agriculture a powerful industry with state-owned enterprises as the main component must be developed. The state of the people's democratic dictatorship must step by step solve this problem (of the industrialization of the country). The present article does not intend to deal with the economic problem, so I shall not discuss it in detail.

In 1924 a well-known manifesto was passed by the KMT First National Congress, which was directed personally by Sun Yat-sen and participated in by Communists. The manifesto stated: "The so-called democratic system in countries of modern times is often monopolized by the bourgeois class and turned into an instrument for oppressing the common people. But the democracy of the KMT belongs to the people in general and is not the private possession of a few." Except for the question of who is to lead whom, the democracy mentioned here, when viewed as a general political programme, is consistent with the people's democratic dictatorship practised at present by us. [If to the state system, which is only allowed to be the common possession of the common people and not the private possession of the bourgeoisie, is added the leadership of the working class, this state system is that of the people's democratic dictatorship.]

Chiang Kai-shek betrayed Sun Yat-sen and used the dictatorship of the bureaucratic capitalist class and the landlord class as an instrument for oppressing the common people of China. This counter-revolutionary dictatorship remained in force for twenty-two years, and not until now has it been overthrown by the Chinese common people under our leadership.

The foreign reactionaries who vilify us for carrying out "dictatorship" and "totalitarianism" are in fact the very people who are carrying out dictatorship and totalitarianism of one class, the bourgeoisie, over the proletariat and other people. They are the very people referred to by Sun Yat-sen as the bourgeois class in countries of modern times who oppress the common people. Chiang Kai-shek's counter-revolutionary dictatorship was learnt from these reactionary fellows.

Chu Hsi, a philosopher of the Sung dynasty [A.D. 960–1260], wrote many books and said many things which we have forgotten, but there is one sentence we have not forgotten and this is "Apply to anyone the method he has first used on others." This is what we are doing. That is, to apply to imperialism and its lackeys, the Chiang Kai-shek reactionary clique, the same method with which they treated others. Simply this and nothing else!

The revolutionary dictatorship and the counter-revolutionary dictatorship are opposite in nature. The former learns from the latter. This process of learning is very important, for if the revolutionary people do not learn the methods of ruling over counter-revolutionaries, they will not be able to maintain their régime, which will be overthrown by the reactionary cliques at home and abroad. The reactionary cliques at home and abroad will then restore their rule in China and bring woe to the revolutionary people.

The basis of the people's democratic dictatorship is the alliance of the working class, peasant class, and the urban petty-bourgeois class, and is mainly the alliance of the working class and the peasant class because they constitute eighty to ninety per cent of the Chinese population. It is mainly through the strength of these two classes that imperialism and the KMT reactionary clique were overthrown. The passing from New Democracy to Socialism mainly depends on the alliance of these two classes.

The people's democratic dictatorship needs the leadership of the working class, because only the working class is most far-sighted, just and unselfish and endowed with revolutionary thoroughness. The history of the entire revolution proves that without the leadership of the working class, the revolution is bound to fail, and with the leadership of the working class, the revolution is victorious. In the era of imperialism no other class in any country can lead any genuine revolution to victory. This is clearly proved by the fact that the Chinese national bourgeoisie had led the revolution many times and each time had failed.

The national bourgeoisie is of great importance at the present stage. Imperialism is still standing near us and this enemy is very fierce. A long time is required for China to realize true economic independence and become free from reliance on imperialist nations. Only when China's industries are developed, and she no longer depends economically on powerful nations, can there be real independence. The proportion of China's modern industry in the entire national economy is still very small. There are still no reliable figures at present, but according to certain data it is estimated that modern industry only occupies about ten per cent of the total productive output in the national economy of the whole country. To cope with imperialist oppression, and to raise our backward economic status one step higher, China must utilize all urban and rural factors of capitalism which are beneficial and not detrimental to the national economy and the people's livelihood, and unite with the national bourgeoisie in a common struggle. Our present policy is to restrict capitalism and not to eliminate it. But the national bourgeoisie cannot be the leader of the revolutionary united front and should not occupy the main position of state power. This is because the social and economic status of the national bourgeoisie has determined its feebleness; it lacks foresight, lacks courage, and in large part fears the masses.

Sun Yat-sen advocated "awakening the masses" or "helping the peasants and workers." Who is to awaken and help them? Sun Yat-sen meant the petty bourgeoisie and the national bourgeoisie. But this is in fact not feasible. Sun Yat-sen's forty years of revolutionary work was a failure. Why? The reason lies precisely here, in that in the era of imperialism it is impossible for the bourgeoisie to lead any true revolution towards success.

Our twenty-eight years are entirely different. We have plenty of invaluable experience. A party with discipline, armed with the theories of Marx, Engels, Lenin, and Stalin, employing the method of self-criticism, and linked up closely with the masses; an army led by such a party; a united front of various revolutionary strata and groups led by such a party; these three are our main (lessons of) experience. They all mark us off from our predecessors. Relying on these three things, we have won a basic victory. We have traversed tortuous paths and struggled against rightist and leftist opportunistic tendencies within the Party. Whenever serious mistakes were committed in these three matters, the revolution suffered set-backs. The mistakes and set-backs taught us and made us wiser. Thus we were able to do better work. Mistakes are unavoidable for any party or person, but we ask that fewer mistakes be committed. When a mistake is committed, correction must be made, the quicker and the more thoroughly the better.

THE STRUGGLE FOR
A NEW WORLD ORDER
Chapter 8

The cold war was a tragedy, but it did have clarity and neatness. The iron curtain that smashed down in the late 1940's and the wall between the two Germanys that went up in August, 1961, marked a clear division between two worlds and two powerful alliances. American economic and military presence in Europe backed up Western European efforts for greater economic and political unity. The North Atlantic Treaty Organization (1949) and the European Coal and Steel Community (1951) were new departures in European collaboration. The admission of the Federal Republic of Germany to sovereignty and membership in NATO in 1955 and the creation of the Common Market and EURATOM in 1957 were further steps in this direction. The vitality of the Western European revival and the relative absence of constraint in the relations between the United States and its European allies contrasted sharply with the economic exploitation practiced by the Soviet Union in COMECON (1949) and Russian domination of the Warsaw Pact (1955). The East Berlin uprising in June, 1953, the Hungarian Revolution of 1956, and the Czechoslovak "spring" of 1968 — all of which were put down by Russian arms — encouraged and continue to encourage statesmen to think along sharp lines of division and opposition characteristic of the cold war.

Nevertheless, there is clear evidence that neither the cold war nor the alliance systems upon which it is based are quite what they used to be. One reason is that the American policy of containment worked in Europe; the Russians did not cross over their line, nor did the Americans. Whatever the talk and fantasies about "liberating captive peoples," the West did nothing to help the East Germans, Hungarians, or Czechs. While West German politicians continue to talk from time to time about the "provisional" nature of the Oder-Neisse Line and the future reunification of Germany, the borders between West and East would present no practical problems were it not for the thorny problem of Berlin. There are other important reasons for the reduction of tensions between the two blocs in Europe, however. Both the Soviet Union and the United States have found the costs of the arms race difficult to bear, and, as the central interests of their diplomatic and military activity have shifted away from Europe, their interest in an agreement on European affairs has increased. Russian anxiety over a possible war with China seems to have been particularly important in increasing its desires for better relations with Western Europe, while American involvement in Southeast Asia and financial difficulties at home have distracted American attention from Europe and increased congressional reluctance to support continued substantial American military presence on the European continent. Although Russia's naval breakthrough into the Mediterranean in the late 1960's and commitment to the Arab cause in the Middle East may revive the sharp tension between the Soviet Union and the United States and may revive conflict in Europe, the basic tendency during the 1960's has been toward a detente and a loosening of the military confrontation in Europe.

These tendencies have been complemented by developments within Europe itself. The brilliant economic and political recovery of Western Europe and the diminution of the external threat have given Europeans a chance to think more about their own problems and their own role in world affairs. The most extreme expression of this was provided by Charles de Gaulle when he took France out of NATO and embarked upon an independent atomic policy. Since his departure from the presidency of the Fifth Republic, French foreign policy has been less flamboyant, but the interest in a more independent and European-oriented economic and foreign policy persists and has even been intensified by the American economic penetration of Europe. Tendencies toward expansion of the Common Market to include Great Britain and the Scandinavian countries point further in the direction of European consolidation. Perhaps the most important shift in foreign policy, however, has been that of the German Federal Republic. The establishment of a Social Democratic government under Willy Brandt in 1969 broke the uninterrupted reign of the Christian Democrats and the cold war psychology and rigid formulas that characterized their approach to foreign affairs. Brandt remains committed to the American alliance and has acted with American blessings in his effort to reach accords with the Soviet Union and other members of the Eastern bloc, but his policy is predicated on the eventual withdrawal of American military presence and the need for a more autonomous European policy. Underlying the rapprochement between Germany and the Eastern bloc are also strong interests in developing and expanding trade relations.

The Soviet Union has been much less willing than the United States

to permit allies to go their own way. It is clear that the Czechs went
too far for their own good. The Rumanians, on the other hand,
have been more skillful and have achieved a good measure of autonomy. It is difficult to say how much more the Soviet Union will relax
totalitarian controls at home and within Eastern Europe than it has
since Stalin's death in 1953. The startling denunciation of Stalinism
by Khrushchev in 1956 and the development of "collective leadership"
has mitigated some of the harshness of the Russian regime. Though it
continues to be ruled by an authoritarian bureaucracy, its ruling elite
seems determined to avoid the ruthless purges of which they were so
often the victims. In its concern with Russia's economic development
and in its relatively undogmatic approach to international relations,
the bureaucrats running the Soviet Union today are not so dissimilar
to the technocrats, managers, and politicians in the West. Although
the range of freedoms now available in the East can scarcely be compared to those of the West, the gulf that once made communication
virtually impossible seems to have narrowed considerably.

Konrad Adenauer and
the Western Alliance

*Konrad Adenauer served as first chancellor of the German Federal
Republic from 1949, when he was seventy-three, until 1963, when he
was eighty-seven. This remarkable man had already had a distinguished career as lord mayor of Cologne and had been one of the
leading lights of the Catholic Center party in the Weimar Republic.
He ruled the Christian Democratic Union, which succeeded the Center party, with an iron hand, and he dominated the country much as
De Gaulle dominated the Fifth Republic. Adenauer was a particularly
strong proponent of the alliance with the West as well as of Western
European unity, and he brought the Federal Republic into the European Defense Community over the objections of the Social Democrats
and their leader Kurt Schumacher, who thought that a total commitment to the West was an error because it would seal the disunity of
Germany. Adenauer, while insisting on the principle of German unity,
thought that the Federal Republic had no option and that "unity in
freedom" could not be achieved in any other way. The Adenauer policy did bring solid results in the economic and political revival of
Germany, but his policy of combining alliance with the West with an*

insistence on the provisional character of the Oder-Neisse Line and of the division of Germany introduced elements of inflexibility into West German diplomacy that were maintained until Socialist Willy Brandt's government took office in 1969.

Adenauer's Memoirs

It had been clear to me for many years that a policy of Franco-German reconciliation would encounter great difficulties. One had to accept the the likelihood of these difficulties reasserting themselves again and again. Psychological obstacles such as existed between our peoples cannot be overcome from one day to the next. The debate on the defence contribution in the French parliament in February 1952 told this tale with particular clarity.

And yet there are political necessities so compelling that in the long run they must prevail. By the two wars, by revolutions and insurrections subsequent upon them, and especially by the tremendous expansion of the Soviet Union — notably in Europe — the unification of the free peoples of Europe had become a political necessity of the first order. The optimism which I preserved in all my endeavours despite all our difficulties was nothing but faith in the force of this necessity, to which the oscillations of daily politics could make no essential difference. At the heart of European unification, however, lay the problem of Franco-German understanding.

In my opinion the European nation states had a past but no future. This applied in the political and economic as well as in the social sphere. No single European country could guarantee a secure future to its people by its own strength. I regarded the Schuman Plan and the European Defence Community as preliminary steps to a political unification of Europe. In the EDC treaty there was a specific provision for a controlling body, the so-called Parliamentary Assembly — incidentally the same assembly that exercised the parliamentary controlling function in the Coal and Steel Community — to examine the questions arising from the parallelism of diverse existing or future organizations of European cooperation, with a view to securing their coordination in the framework of a federal or confederate structure.

The military aspect was only one dimension of a nascent Europe, or, more rightly at first, Western Europe. If a perfect partnership was to be achieved within Western Europe, one could not stop with defence.

I could not understand the *Ohne-mich* attitude; it was irresponsible

From Konrad Adenauer, *Memoirs, 1945–53*, trans. Beate Ruhm von Oppen (Chicago: Regnery, 1966), pp. 415–19, 426–27. Reprinted by permission of Henry Regnery Company and George Weidenfeld & Nicolson Ltd.

and in the last resort hopeless, yet it was widespread in the Federal Republic. I was well aware that there would be no simple and easy decisions for a German politician. I never forgot that the fate of many millions of people was at stake, including the millions in the Soviet zone. But there is one thing a responsible politician cannot do: he cannot simply escape into inactivity only because every action available to him has its drawbacks. For then others will act over the head of this politician and his country, and then the country is certain to be the loser. After twelve years of National Socialism there simply were no perfect solutions for Germany and certainly none for a divided Germany. There was very often only the policy of the lesser evil.

We were a small and very exposed country. By our own strength we could achieve nothing. We must not be a no-man's-land between East and West, for then we would have friends nowhere and a dangerous neighbour in the East. Any refusal by the Federal Republic to make common cause with Europe would have been German isolationism, a dangerous escape into inactivity. There was a cherished political illusion in the Federal Republic in those years: many people believed that America was in any case tied to Europe or even to the Elbe. American patience, however, had its limits. My motto was 'Help yourself and the United States will help you.'

The deeply offensive statements by Dr. Schumacher . . . displayed a shocking ignorance of the entire political situation. It was even more shocking that the representatives of the SPD stayed away from the solemn act of signature of the Convention on 26 May in Bonn. What were the Western powers to think of us? Was it worth their trouble to continue to negotiate with Germany? Or were they to share the German spoils with the fourth victorious power, Soviet Russia?

There were those in Germany who thought that for us the choice was either a policy for Europe or a policy for German unity. I considered this 'either/or' a fatal error. Nobody could explain how German unity in freedom was to be achieved without a strong and united Europe. When I say 'in freedom' I mean freedom before, during and above all after all-German elections. No policy is made with wishes alone and even less from weakness. Only when the West was strong might there be a genuine point of departure for peace negotiations to free not only the Soviet zone but all of enslaved Europe east of the iron curtain, and free it peacefully. To take the road that led into the European Community appeared to me the best service we could render the Germans in the Soviet zone.

With the signing of the treaties the Federal Republic was to enter into the community of free peoples. To my mind the process by which the Federal Republic was to be firmly placed in a treaty system created by the free nations for the pursuit of their common goals had a significance for the future of Germany that could not be overestimated. Every German had experienced in his own life, and most of them even on their own bodies, the way in which Germany's relations with the rest of the world and with her neighbours determined the weal or woe of every German citizen.

The signature under the Convention and under the treaty on the EDC meant the turning of a new leaf after the terrible war and post-war period. We Germans would enter a political community in which we shared all rights but also all duties with our partners. The series of agreements that had taken about a year to achieve, which involved four countries in the case of the Convention and six in the case of the treaty on the EDC, probably gave no country the chance to say: it is all as we hoped it would be. The process of give and take is the only way to come to an understanding, to achieve cooperation, and above all to grow together into a community. It had been the guiding idea in our work.

I had negotiated on the Convention with the High Commissioners in more than thirty sessions, often lasting days on end. The hours spent by the experts in negotiations were almost impossible to count. The same applied to the treaty on the EDC. The result represented a tremendous amount of work. Naturally every country concerned had wanted to make its own point of view prevail and to pursue its own interests. At the same time however a readiness to compromise had been alive on all sides. Without this readiness the Agreements could never have been concluded. Everyone had had to yield somewhere. Everyone had renounced this or that desire. The Federal Republic was no exception. It was unthinkable that the system of Agreements could look perfect in the eyes of any single country. The underlying principles were what mattered most.

The representatives of the governments of France, Great Britain, the United States of America and the Federal Republic had signed the Convention in Bonn on 26 May. On 27 May representatives of the governments of France, Italy, the Netherlands, Belgium, Luxembourg and Germany signed the treaty on the European Defence Community in the French Ministry of the Exterior in Paris. The contracting parties were not the same for both sets of Agreements. Nevertheless the Agreements formed an invisible whole. By the Convention with the three powers the Federal Republic regained its freedom of action in all fields. It was thus put in a position under international law to conclude the treaty on the EDC. It was enabled to enter agreements and alliances.

With the formation of the European Defence Community the Federal Republic achieved a firm link with the Atlantic pact. By joining the EDC the Federal Government would realize one of its aims, the inclusion of Germany in the European community, which in turn had its place in the worldwide structure of treaties the free world had created for the preservation of peace. We were no longer alone. We had ceased being the mere object of the foreign policy of other powers. The full weight of this fact must have struck everyone who, during those May days of historic change, cast his mind back to those days of May 1945 when the extent of the catastrophe became clear to us all. Three years after the signing of the Basic Law of the Federal Republic of Germany in the Bundesrat hall we had regained our freedom of action under international law in the same hall on 26 May 1952. We first used it to sign the treaty on the EDC to help found an enterprise that could in the long run turn the course of German and European history for the better.

At the time of the signing of the Agreements I was perfectly aware that many problems were still unsolved. Germany was still divided, the European communities were confined to Western Europe. I was convinced that the league of the European peoples would attract and appeal to other European countries and would thus become a magnetic field for the reunification of Germany and for the emergence of European unity.

Undoubtedly the treaty on the EDC was the more important of the Agreements signed. It was to give a new shape to the future. The Convention created the necessary preconditions by settling the past. On the way from being an enemy to being a partner of the free world the Convention restored to Germany many freedoms that had been denied us in the period of occupation. They were freedoms we needed in order to become partners in anything, and so to be able to conclude a European treaty.

It was not without significance that Bonn and Paris were the two sites of signature; more was to be concluded than the post-war phase of the last seven years. A whole epoch was ended, the epoch of enmities and wars between the peoples of the West. France and Germany had been the chief agents and sufferers of this tragic estrangement. The signatures in Bonn and Paris were a symbol of the final turning away from this past.

It was impossible for us whole-heartedly to enjoy a political event as long as Germany was divided. The signature of the Agreements gave us no cause for jubilation let alone for triumph, but we must not allow our political judgment to be confused. The Agreements did not constitute an obstacle to the reunification of Germany. On the contrary I saw in them the only means to bring us closer to German unity in freedom. In the hard world of facts there were only two ways open to the Federal Republic, to go with the West or to go with the Soviets. Anything that lay between was not politics but illusion; for everything that lay between would inflict on us the impotence of isolation and make us a plaything of contending forces. Powerless between the powers we would be booty that was still to be distributed, a magnet for a war.

There was no possibility of going with the Soviets. In league with them one could only become a satellite, a will-less and exploited tool of

Moscow's power politics. We saw this everywhere east of the iron curtain, we saw it closest and most clearly in the German Soviet zone. This demonstration sufficed. Germany belongs to the West by tradition and by conviction. The whole of Germany belongs to the West. In this partnership alone lies our future.

There were those who did not regard the way I had indicated as the road to German unity. Nevertheless for the time being there was no other way for us. Sooner or later the Soviets would see that they had come to terms with the West, that they could not impose their will on it. In such a peaceful understanding lay my hope and in it I saw our chance. It would, however, only be a chance for us if, at the moment of such a general settlement between West and East, we had already proved ourselves the reliable partners of the West. Only then would the West make our interests its own. . . .

It was sometimes urged in public discussion that ratification of the two treaties would make reunification with the Soviet zone impossible. I held, on the contrary, that by concluding these treaties we had taken an important step toward the goal expressed almost unanimously by the Bundestag in one of its first sessions in the formula "reunification of Germany in peace and freedom and in a free Europe."

It was and is true that reunification in freedom can be brought about only with the consent of the four Allies, that is with Russia's consent as well. To this end I thought it wise to secure the help of at least three of the four great powers as we did in the Convention. Once we had the help of these three powers, I hoped that it would be possible at the right moment to get to the negotiating table with the Russians. No one can have honestly believed that the Soviet Union would spontaneously surrender the Soviet zone. I could therefore not see at all how we were lessening the chances of reunification in freedom by concluding these treaties. A united Germany as the Russians were demanding in their Notes, a neutralized Germany based on the Potsdam Agreement, was impossible for us. We would have to try with the help of the three Western Allies to get Russia to give up this demand. I felt that once she had been convinced that the conclusion of the EDC precluded the success of further attempts to gain control of the Federal Republic by way of the cold war — and first by neutralization — she would respect the new political situation and adjust her policy accordingly. One thing was sure: if we did not sign the treaties, we would not improve the chances of reunification in any way. I knew that the men and women in the Soviet zone shared this view. I knew that they regarded the road taken by us as the only way that might one day lead them too out of their distress.

The question had further been raised whether the military strengthening of the West as a consequence of the treaties might not provoke Russia to change over to a hot war. Here too I thought that the opposite was the case, I was convinced that one cannot restrain a heavily armed totalitarian state by remaining as weak as possible. The history of the last twenty years gave two excellent examples of the point. When Hitler armed, nothing had at first been done by the other European countries or by the United States of America. Because Hitler knew that they were militarily weak, he lashed out the moment he thought he was strong enough to win a quick victory. If, when Hitler began to arm, other countries had increased their defence forces, Hitler would never have dared to go to war.

Events after 1945 were similar. Because Soviet Russia remained highly armed while the other countries disarmed, she made ruthless use of her military superiority by subjecting the countries that are now satellite states. I am convinced that Soviet Russia would not have done this if she had had to fear that the others would intervene to stop her. Every consolidation of the Western power of defence increased the probability that Soviet Russia would not proceed to a hot war.

The Federal Republic could not exist without the support of other countries. Germany's geographical situation is particularly unfavourable from the political point of view. She lies in the middle of Europe and has no protected frontiers. Ever since the 1870s Germany has looked for allies. At first it seemed as if the Three Emperors' League — Germany, Austria and Russia — in the year 1872 might provide allies and security. But Bismarck had soon seen that an alliance founded merely on the monarchist idea would have insufficient cohesion in the long run. Two alliance systems then developed: the Triple Alliance between Germany, Austria-Hungary and Italy in 1882 and the Triple Entente between England, France and Russia. Between 1900 and 1904 the Entente Cordiale was formed between France and Great Britain, and added to the existing Franco-Russian alliance. This development prepared the coming catastrophes.

We now needed allies more than ever to preserve our freedom. By joining the EDC which in its turn was connected with the North Atlantic Treaty, by the conclusion of the defensive agreement with Great Britain and by the security guarantee of the United States, we obtained for our country the greatest possible security. All these alliances and pacts had a purely defensive character which was not clearly expressed but also inherent in the structure of the whole system. The Western defence system could, it was my firm conviction, safeguard peace and freedom for Europe and ourselves. The tension between East and West existed. The powers of the countries of Europe, taken singly, were paralysed. They were now to be combined for the preservation of peace. The United States and Great Britain supported these endeavours with all their strength. I was convinced that these treaties would serve the cause of liberty, the creation of the new Europe, and the reunification of Germany in peace and freedom.

European Response
to Americanization

The attitude of Europeans toward "Americanization" has always been rather ambivalent. On the one hand, they have been suspicious of American mass society, mass production, and mass culture. Wherever Europeans stand on this question, however, they can hardly evade the relative decline of Europe's role in world affairs and the growing invasion of American capital and economic and cultural domination. Some, like De Gaulle, have viewed this as an American plot and have assumed a defensive posture. Others have insisted that the only way for Europe to maintain its independence and unique characteristics is to take the best that America has to offer. J.-J. Servan-Schreiber holds the latter viewpoint. He was born in 1924 and joined the French Resistance in 1943. He founded the highly successful and influential magazine L'Express *after the Second World War and further distinguished himself by exposing the brutality and terror of the French war effort in Algeria. His book* The American Challenge *appeared in 1967 and was a clarion call to Europe and France to scuttle the old politics and complacency and adopt the organizational techniques and methods needed to meet the challenge posed by the United States. Subsequently, he was elected deputy from Lorraine. Some have compared Servan-Schreiber to John F. Kennedy, arguing that his dynamism may present an important challenge to the regime of De Gaulle's successors.*

Servan-Schreiber's *American Challenge*

Fifteen years from now it is quite possible that the world's third greatest industrial power, just after the United States and Russia, may not be Europe, but *American industry in Europe.* Already, in the ninth year of the Common Market, this European market is basically American in organization.

The importance of U.S. penetration rests, first of all, on the sheer amount of capital invested — currently about $14 billion ($14,000,000,000). Add to this the massive size of the firms carrying out this conquest. Recent efforts by European firms to centralize and merge are inspired largely by the need to compete with the American giants like Interna-

From J.-J. Servan-Schreiber, The American Challenge, trans. Ronald Steel (New York: Atheneum, 1968), pp. 3–9, 26–30, 189–96, 203–07. Copyright © 1967 by Editions Denoel as Le Defi American; copyright © 1968, 1969 by Atheneum House, Inc., translation © 1960 by Atheneum House, Inc. Reprinted by permission of Atheneum Publishers and Hamish Hamilton Ltd.

tional Business Machines (IBM) and General Motors. This is the surface penetration. But there is another aspect of the problem which is considerably more subtle.

Every day an American banker working in Paris gets requests from French firms looking for Frenchmen "with experience in an American corporation." The manager of a German steel mill hires only staff personnel "having been trained with an American firm." The British Marketing Council sends 50 British executives to spend a year at the Harvard Business School — and the British government foots the bill. For European firms, so conservative and jealous of their independence, there is now one common denominator: American methods.

During the past ten years Americans in Europe have made more mistakes than their competitors — but they have tried to correct them. And an American firm can change its methods in almost no time, compared to a European firm. The Americans have been reorganizing their European operations. Everywhere they are setting up European-scale headquarters responsible for the firm's Continental business, with sweeping powers of decision and instructions not to pay any attention to national boundaries.

These U.S. subsidiaries have shown a flexibility and adaptability that have enabled them to adjust to local conditions and be prepared for political decisions taken, or even contemplated, by the Common Market.

Since 1958 American corporations have invested $10 billion in Western Europe — *more than a third* of their total investment abroad. Of the 6,000 new businesses started overseas by Americans during that period, *half* were in Europe.

One by one, American firms are setting up headquarters to coordinate their activities throughout Western Europe. This is true federalism — the only kind that exists in Europe on an industrial level. And it goes a good deal farther than anything Common Market experts ever imagined.

Union Carbide set up its European headquarters in Lausanne in 1965. The Corn Products Company, which now has ten European branches, moved its coordinating office from Zurich to Brussels and transformed it into a central headquarters. IBM now directs all its European activities from Paris. The Celanese Corporation of America has recently set up headquarters in Brussels; and American Express has established its European central offices in London.

Standard Oil of New Jersey has put its European oil (Esso Europe) headquarters in London, and its European chemical (Esso Chemical SA) command in Brussels. Both have been told to "ignore the present division between the Common Market and the free trade zone [Britain, Scandinavia]." For Esso, Europe now represents a market *larger than the United States,* and one growing *three times faster.*

Monsanto has moved its international department from St. Louis to

Brussels, where Mr. Throdahl, one of its vice-presidents, directs not only European operations but all business outside the United States. Monsanto is now building factories in France, Italy, Luxembourg, Britain, and Spain, and preparing plants for Scotland and Ireland. Half of its sales now come from Europe.

The greater wealth of American corporations allows them to conduct business in Europe faster and more flexibly than their European competitors. This *flexibility* of the Americans, even more than their wealth, is their major weapon. While Common Market officials are still looking for a law which will permit the creation of European-wide businesses, American firms, with their own headquarters, already form the framework of a real "Europeanization."

A leading Belgian banker recently stated: "The Common Market won't be able to work out a European corporate law in time, and during the next few years U.S. corporations will enjoy a decisive advantage over their European rivals." The American giants in Europe become bigger and stronger all the time, and are hiring "development" experts whose job is to seek new acquisitions.

While all this has been going on, Europeans have done little to take advantage of the new market. On the industrial level Europe has almost nothing to compare with the dynamic American corporations being set up on her soil. The one interesting exception is Imperial Chemical Industries (Britain), the only European firm to establish a Continental-scale headquarters to administer its 50 subsidiaries.

Efforts of other European corporations are timid by comparison. Among these the best known is the film company Agfa (part of the Bayer group), which two years ago decided to merge with its Belgian rival, Gevaert. But it was not a very romantic marriage. The two companies exchanged directors, put a hyphen between their names (Agfa-Gevaert), and combined their research departments. That's about all. Aside from that, they have announced their intention to form a truly unified firm the day the Common Market gives the go-ahead by passing a still non-existent statute permitting European-wide corporations. They are still waiting for legislation.

In the meantime, American firms continue to carve up Europe at their pleasure. In the words of a report by McGraw-Hill: "The founders of the Common Market, men like Robert Schuman, Jean Monnet, and Walter Hallstein, can be proud of helping break down the barriers dividing Europe. But it is American business that has understood their idea and is helping Europe understand its own potential by applying, with some variations, the same methods America used to build its own enormous market."

Europeans especially envy the ease with which American firms reorganize themselves to tap the full potential of the new market, and they are very much aware of the advantages this flexibility offers. The question they ask most often, says an American executive working in France, is simply: "How do you do it?"

Hand in hand with this industrial penetration another giant U.S. enterprise is taking shape in Europe — the creation of management consultant groups.

The three American consultant firms with European branches (Booz, Allen and Hamilton, Arthur D. Little, Inc., and McKinsey and Co.) have *doubled* their staffs *every year* for the past five years. The Americans are creating a "market consciousness" in their wake.

According to an American executive in Frankfurt: "If a German manager wants to increase his production, he studies all the factors that go into the manufacture of his product. But if I want to increase my production, I add to these same calculations our research and market predictions so that I will know not only how to produce, but how to produce the desired quantity at the lowest cost. What interests me is my profit margin. What interests my European competitor is a factory that produces. *It isn't the same thing.*" This science of marketing is new in Europe. Now there is hardly a major European executive today who does not put it at the top of his list of his concerns.

Thus, much beyond massive U.S. investments, it is American-style management that is, in its own special way, unifying Europe. As the American businessman from Frankfurt, quoted earlier, added: "The Treaty of Rome is the sweetest deal ever to come out of Europe. It's what brought us here. We're happy to be here. We're making money. And we're going to make a lot more. Whether the European negotiations in Brussels move ahead or not, prospects in commerce and industry are better for us here than they are in the United States."

It really is the sweetest deal anyone ever thought of. But why for the Americans and not for us? Why do they succeed better over here than we do ourselves? Simply by trying to find an answer to this question, we come across a whole new world.

. . . In short, Europeans are faced with a dilemma that might well be of historic significance.

If we allow American investments to enter freely under present conditions, we consign European industry — or at least the part that is most scientifically and technologically advanced and on which our future rests — to a subsidiary role, and Europe herself to the position of a satellite.

If, on the other hand, we adopt effective restrictive measures, we would be double losers — denying ourselves both the manufactured products we need and the capital funds that would then be invested in other countries. By trying to be self-sufficient we would only condemn ourselves to underdevelopment.

What can we do? The problem of American investments is only one special aspect of the problem of power, of the growing displacement of power from Europe to America.

Nothing would be more absurd than to treat the American investor as "guilty," and to respond by some form of repression. No matter how determined we are that Europe be mistress of her destiny, we ought not to forget what Alexander Hamilton said in 1791 about foreign investment in the United States: "Rather than treating the foreign investor as a rival, we should consider him a valuable helper, for he increases our production and the efficiency of our businesses."

If American investment is only part of the phenomenon of power, the problem for Europe is to become a power. What today seems like an enormous "rummage sale" of our industry to the Americans could, paradoxically, point to our salvation.

American power is no longer what it was after the end of the war. Its scale and even its nature have changed. We are learning about it because we are feeling its impact right here on our shores. This is all to the good. While it is a shock, shock is better than surprise because it forces us to pay attention.

During the *past ten years,* from the end of the cold war and the launching of the first Sputnik, American power has made an unprecedented leap forward. It has undergone a violent and productive internal revolution. Technological innovation has now become the basic objective of economic policy. In America today the government official, the industrial manager, the economics professor, the engineer, and the scientist have joined forces to develop coordinated techniques for integrating factors of production. These techniques have stimulated what amounts to a permanent industrial revolution.

The originality of this revolution consists precisely in the effect this fusion of talents has on decisions made by government agencies, corporations, and universities. This takes us a long way from the old image of the United States — a country where business was not only separate from government but constantly struggling with it, and where there was a chasm between professors and businessmen. Today, to the contrary, this combination of forces has produced the remarkable integrated entity that John Kenneth Galbraith calls a "technostructure."

If we continue to allow the major decisions about industrial innovation and technological creativity — decisions which directly affect our lives — to be made in Washington, New York, Cambridge, Detroit, Seattle, and Houston, there is a real danger that Europe may forever be confined to second place. We may not be able to build one of those great industrial-intellectual complexes on which a creative society depends. What kind of future do we want?

It is time for us to take stock and face the hard truth. Some of those who watched the decline of Rome or Byzantium also caught a glimpse of the future that was coming. But that was not enough to change the course of history. If we are to be master of our fate, we will need a rude awakening. If this doesn't come, then Europe, like so many other glorious civilizations, will gradually sink into decadence without ever understanding why or how it happened. In 1923 Spengler mused over "The Decline of the West." Today we have barely time enough to comprehend what is happening to us.

What threatens to crush us today is not a torrent of riches, but a more intelligent use of skills. While French, German, or Italian firms are still groping around in the new open spaces provided by the Treaty of Rome, afraid to emerge from the dilapidated shelter of their old habits, American industry has gauged the terrain and is now rolling from Naples to Amsterdam with the ease and the speed of Israeli tanks in the Sinai desert.

Confronted with this conquering force, European politicians and businessmen do not know how to react. Public opinion, confused by their contradictory statements and mysterious shifts of policy, has no way of judging whether American penetration is good or bad.

It is both. The stimulus of competition and the introduction of new techniques are clearly good for Europe. But the cumulative underdevelopment that could transform this assistance into a takeover is bad for us.

The danger is not in what the Americans can do, but what the Europeans cannot do, and in the vacuum between the two. This is why the various restrictions and prohibitions that we impose — or would like to impose — are either irrelevant to the problem or deal with it only peripherally. Putting an end to American influence will not fill the vacuum; it will only weaken us further.

While all this is taking place we show no signs of suffering. Our economy grows and our standard of living rises nicely. Why should we worry? Let's take a look over the horizon. . . .

The postwar generation was faced with the choice of seeing all Europe unified within the communist world or of trying to maintain an independent Western Europe. Today's generation faces a less dramatic, but equally clear choice of building an independent Europe or letting it become an annex of the United States. The sheer weight of American power is pushing our hesitant countries along the path of annexation, and the point of no return may be reached before today's ten-year-olds are able to vote.

It is still possible for us to catch up. But there is a great deal of dead weight to overcome. This does not mean we have to make real sacrifices, for by trying to become her own mistress, Europe will increase her power and wealth, and finally the well-being of her citizens. But perhaps it is asking too much of Europeans to adapt to global competition, shake themselves loose from entrenched national habits, pull together dispersed resources, adjust to severe new rules of management, and stop wasting precious men and capital. Is it reasonable to ask an old continent to show the vitality of a new nation — especially when the satellization of Europe is accompanied, at least initially, by a rising standard of living and by only a very gradual reduction of our freedom of thought? Our dependence will not stop Frenchmen from discussing politics or Germans from going to the opera. Why, then, try to oppose it?

Western Europeans look on self-determination as an acquired right; they cannot imagine it could really be threatened. Man's right to determine the shape of his society and his future seems entirely natural — and with good reason. The principle of self-determination was born in Europe, introduced during a time of slavery in ancient Greece, taken up by the more enlightened theology of the Middle Ages and the Renaissance, put into practice by England, the "mother of parliaments," proclaimed by the French Revolution, and extended to economics through the inspiration of the socialist movement.

It was first applied in the favored zones of the northern hemisphere, where less than a fifth of the world's population lives. Democracy might seem to be the result of chance, if history had not proved that it was an *idée fixe,* a central element of all the principles that have shaped European thought — and one strong enough, at least until now, to survive catastrophes and deception. This desire for self-determination, for freedom first from physical oppression, then from social restraints, is a hallmark of our civilization.

The day this drive weakens to the point that Europeans let "somebody bigger" do their work for them, the spirit of our civilization will have broken, as did that of the Arab and Indian civilizations centuries ago. We would be tainted by the knowledge of our own failure. Without suffering from poverty, we would nevertheless soon submit to a fatalism and depression that would end in impotence and abdication.

There is no way of leaving the "economic area" to the Americans so that we can get on with political, social, and cultural areas in our own way, as some people would like to believe. There is no such compartmentalization in the real world. Naturally there will not be any "American committee" to administer Europe, as Paul Valéry imagined. Citizens would continue to vote, trade unions to strike, and parliaments to deliberate. But it would all take place in a vacuum. With our growth rate, our investment priorities, and the distribution of our national income determined by the United States, it is not even necessary to imagine secret meetings between Wall Street bankers and European cabinet ministers to understand that the areas that really count would lie outside the democratic process.

The European elite would be trained at Harvard, Stanford, or Berkeley, continuing a precedent that has already begun. This elite would no doubt worm itself into a kind of Atlantic oligarchy, and even gain some influence over its decisions. But this would only raise another barrier between the governors and the governed: the aptitude for American *savoir-faire* and *savoir-vivre* would bestow privileges as great as those that now go with a degree from the École Polytechnique or Oxford.

A few leading firms, subsidiaries of American corporations, would decide how much European workers would earn and how they would live — work methods, human relations on the job, standards for wages and promotion, and job security. Employers, whether European or American, would be little more than clerks, enjoying some powers of initiative, but only within a framework worked out by the parent company and laid down to its subsidiaries around the world.

American capital and American management will not stop short at the gates of our society. No taboo of the sacred will keep these managers from crossing the threshold of the European sanctuary. They will take a majority interest in, and then control, the firms that dominate the market in publishing, the press, phonograph recordings, and television production. The formulas, if not all the details, of our cultural "messages" would be imported. Our system of education — in the large sense of channels of communication by which customers are transmitted and ways of life and thought formulated — would be controlled from the outside.

Cairo and Venice were able to keep their social and cultural identities during centuries of economic decline. But it was not such a small world then, and the pace of change was infinitely slower. A dying civilization could linger for a long time on the fragrance left in an empty vase. We will not have that consolation.

If France and Germany were really able to exercise the same rights as the state of New York or California, if Frenchmen and Germans could become "full-fledged citizens" of the American federation, our abdication would not be so great. We could then take part in the exercise of this world power, and while we sacrificed national identity, we would not also have to sacrifice self-government. But the American republic is a finished product. If Americans wanted to, they still could not change the federal system laid down in the Constitution. It is too late to contemplate such a solution. Even if a transatlantic union could maintain the essential principle of self-determination, Europeans would find the desire to preserve their own differences reason enough to remain separate.

Some of our characteristics stem, it is true, from a simple technological lag. Many signs of "Americanization" are really indications of a change that Europe would have gone through by herself if the United States were dragging up the rear instead of leading the way. The contempt and distrust of America felt by many Europeans is really their own fear of a future that was chosen by their fathers when they launched the first industrial revolution, and which they themselves reaffirmed by starting the second. But what makes Europe unique cannot be explained by a simple time lag.

Like many enlightened Americans today, Europeans have tried, in many cases successfully, to limit the power of money over the life of man. Despite prosperity, a man's income is not the same thing as his prestige; the most expensive medical care is available to the most impoverished; community needs and social services that cannot be bought on the market are better provided in Europe. Part of the Negro problem in the United States comes from a failure to recognize that this social fabric, while expensive, has a powerful ability to knit together individuals within a society.

It is often said that respect for intelligence and the protection of individuals from conformist pressures of society are historically linked to the feudal, or aristocractic, class structure of yesterday's Europe. But as Stanley Hoffmann has said, "There is no reason for giving up either. On the contrary, it is a reason for trying to adapt both to the age of democracy. All individuals, not just an elite, ought to be shown how to escape from the alienation of labor, from enslavement to technology, and from the shrill demands of the mass media, of the neighbors, or of all sorts of groups."

There is no excuse for Europeans to be passive or complacent, for they are free to examine the American experience critically, to make of tomorrow's Europe "an industrial society that will have its own profile, not simply because many of the old features will not have been erased by the plastic surgery of industrialization, but also because of a deliberate effort to preserve Europe's originality."

Will Europe, with infinitely greater means, resources, and power, be incapable of attempting as a world power what Sweden has done by specializing in a few areas? With the highest standard of living in the world (after the United States), this country of 8 million people has maintained its own identity — one sharply different from that of the United States. In Sweden they tear down old-age homes in perfectly good condition because advances in geriatrics allow society to offer something better to older people. This concern for non-commercial values has not prevented Sweden from producing highly competitive goods in certain carefully chosen areas.

The experience of Japan, while rather different, leads to a similar conclusion: economic growth can be adapted to social behavior and concepts of society far removed from the American model. Growth is compatible with a great variety of social institutions and individual behavior. "The power of Japan's example is not that it encourages us to imitate her society, but to accept a cultural relativism that allows each country to sink the roots of industrialization and economic progress into its own history." Varying balances can then be worked out between initiative and security, individual consumption and community development, private power and public power. A nation that is master of itself is free to stamp its own mark on society.

If Europe decides to do this, she would greatly improve the chances of building a decent world, one that could reconcile the unity of modern industrial society with the variety of national cultures that compose it. A polycentric world would ensure a growing exchange of goods and ideas, and the continuing competition between human societies that has always been the condition of human progress. Would an isolated Egypt, Greece, or Rome have done any better than the Mayas trapped in their jungle?

An independent Europe is essential for orderly world economic development. Is there any group of advanced nations — other than those of the Common Market, together with Britain — that could form a pole of attraction different from both America and Russia? A united Europe could bring about significant changes in the world power balance, and not only from the strength of her ideas. They would come, above all, from the very creation of a third great industrial power with no imperial pretensions — one whose only strategy is to help build a more unified international community. . . .

The success of other countries suggests that the *fundamental condition* for an industrial society to catch up is a high level of social integration — a kind of peaceful stability, or at least an absence of civil war, that will allow the society to concentrate on the mechanics of change. In particular this involves:

— the value placed on individual and social security in a time of technological development;
— the generally accepted importance of government leadership;
— a decision by the whole population to do what must be done to build a truly independent society.

We Europeans have to take all these factors into account if we hope to escape the alienation that gave birth to communism. We have to rely on the values and political forces that preserve Europe's special quality, and which are most likely to promote the adaptations necessary for growth. Otherwise there could be a legitimate revolt by those elements of the society most threatened by change.

This may be a debatable interpretation — especially since it underlines the continuing importance of traditional ideas that are linked with social democracy in Germany and Scandinavia, with the Labour party in Britain, or with the Left in Latin countries. We will limit ourselves to what is a personal interpretation, the interpretation of a man in the forty-year-old generation for whom the American challenge is the crucial question, one we cannot appeal. If the generation now assuming positions of power and determining the direction our societies will take is unable to meet this challenge, it will never have a second chance. The Europe we will pass on in 1980 to men who today are 20 years old will be a continent outside the mainstream of history, leading a life without vitality of purpose, under the shadow of its dependence on America.

This is the interpretation and commitment of a Frenchman persuaded, from a study of the objective material objectively presented here, that social integration and European recovery go hand-in-hand with a *new demand for justice* and with bringing up-to-date the old values of *confidence in man,* which are the natural heritage of what has been known historically as the Left. These are values, moreover, which have been applied in the development of the United States itself through the influence and action of the liberal wing of the Democratic Party.

The fate of Europe and the fate of the Left are linked together by the American challenge. If the Left, particularly in France, remains what it has been, the chances for social integration — the key to change — will be nil, and so will chances for Europe to raise her technological power up to the level of world competition.

Even if there is no real chance for social integration, change will be imposed upon us by technological evolution and international competition. But it will come painfully, provoking friction, jolts, and resistance.

If, however, the Left can overcome its instinctive reflexes of nervousness and fear when faced with the mounting tempo of progress, and can rediscover the traditional values for which it stands, it can liberate so much energy in France and throughout Europe that all the elements in the equation can be changed. Salvation can come only through such an awakening.

The word "Left," with all that it implies, is not being used in this book from ideology, nostalgia for the past, or a mania for classifications. It would be foolish to write off as profits and losses the intellectual, emotional, and historical capital of the Left at the very moment when it can help the cause of European development. The Left must put an end to the internecine conflicts and divisions which hold back French society, and whose resolution would make a real contribution to European recovery.

A country like France cannot achieve the degree of organization and efficiency it needs to play a key role in building the European community and replying to the American challenge so long as the various participants in the political, economic, and social game continue to contradict and ignore each other. So long as management persists in opposing labor, and labor refuses to cooperate with management, so long as the government denies the legitimacy of the opposition and the opposition that of the government, none of the necessary changes can take place. The rifts in French society will continue to cause terrible waste and to weaken Europe.

The Left is often accused of pursuing fantasies: general disarmament, abolition of class barriers, world government, etc. Here, for once, is a project which might achieve its goals. If it doesn't make the attempt, the Left will lose its *raison d'être,* which is to rally all men — not just the elite — to take the future into their hands. In a satellite Europe, plans for the democratization of education, knowledge, and business would become ludicrous, and debates on the meaning of democracy would be meaningless. We no longer have to ask whether Western Europe should choose the paths of Soviet bureaucratization. Our only choice is whether we want to be a poor imitation of the United States, or seek our goals by following our own special genius. Some of the things that are particularly European — efforts to go beyond the rationale of the market economy, the collectivization of risks, and limitations on the role of money — are in large part the contribution of the Left. The prospects for an independent Europe and for a revitalized Left are, as we shall see, intimately linked.

In 1936 the reformer who had been elected President of the United States, confronted with the gravest economic and social crisis his country had ever known, made his famous statement: "This generation of Americans has a rendezvous with destiny." These Americans assumed their responsibilities, and by a burst of support for the New Deal, launched the United States on the path of power at the very moment when she seemed to have lost all ambition.

This generation of Europeans, nearly half a century later, also has a rendezvous with destiny.

De-Stalinization

Although the death of Stalin in 1953 produced an almost immediate relaxation of the harshness of government practice in the Soviet Union, the great upsurge of de-Stalinization came in 1956 when Khrushchev delivered his secret report to the Twentieth Congress of the Communist party, denouncing Stalin's "cult of personality" and exposing Stalin's crimes and mistakes. The speech confirmed the transition from totalitarianism to authoritarianism and collective leadership. In order to understand its significance, however, one must bear in mind the monumental crimes committed by Stalin as well as the aura of infallibility and the godlike position associated with his name. To expose the crimes and to suggest that Stalin had made serious mistakes in his conduct of the war and foreign policy was to make certain implicit comments about the regime itself. Khrushchev, therefore, faced a delicate task. He had to defend the struggle against deviationists and the collectivization policy while attacking the methods by which they were implemented. At the same time, he had to explain why Stalin's successors had been unable to stop him, a matter of more than a little curiosity since Khrushchev, for example, had been boss of the Ukraine under Stalin's rule and was implicated in many of the crimes of the

*regime. Official history in the Soviet Union is seldom "definitive."
Khrushchev revised the Stalinist portrait of Stalin as a part of the
change in the style of Soviet leadership. When the regime finds it
necessary to assume a harder line, it upgrades Stalin. Nevertheless, the
1956 report was too devastating not to have lasting effects, and it is
doubtful whether the Soviet ruling class would be willing to return to
a Stalinist regime except in the most extreme emergency.*

Khrushchev's Secret Speech of February 25, 1956

Comrades! In the report of the Central Committee of the Party at the
XXth Congress, in a number of speeches by delegates to the Congress, as
also formerly during the plenary CC/CPSU sessions, quite a lot has
been said about the cult of the individual and about its harmful consequences.

After Stalin's death the Central Committee of the Party began to implement a policy of explaining concisely and consistently that it is im-
permissible and foreign to the spirit of Marxism-Leninism to elevate one
person, to transform him into a superman possessing supernatural characteristics akin to those of a god. Such a man supposedly knows everything, sees everything, thinks for everyone, can do anything, is infallible
in his behavior.

Such a belief about a man, and specifically about Stalin, was cultivated
among us for many years.

The objective of the present report is not a thorough evaluation of
Stalin's life and activity. Concerning Stalin's merits, an entirely sufficient
number of books, pamphlets and studies had already been written in his
lifetime. The role of Stalin in the preparation and execution of the
Socialist Revolution, in the Civil War, and in the fight for the construction of Socialism in our country is universally known. Everyone knows
this well. At the present we are concerned with a question which has
immense importance for the Party now and for the future — [we are
concerned] with how the cult of the person of Stalin has been gradually
growing, the cult which became at a certain specific stage the source of a
whole series of exceedingly serious and grave perversions of Party principles, of Party democracy, of revolutionary legality.

Because of the fact that not all as yet realize fully the practical consequences resulting from the cult of the individual, the great harm caused
by the violation of the principle of collective direction of the Party and
because of the accumulation of immense and limitless power in the hands
of one person — the Central Committee of the Party considers it absolutely necessary to make the material pertaining to this matter available

to the XXth Congress of the Communist Party of the Soviet Union. . . .

Marxism does not negate the role of the leaders of the workers' class in directing the revolutionary liberation movement.

While ascribing great importance to the role of the leaders and organizers of the masses, Lenin at the same time mercilessly stigmatized every manifestation of the cult of the individual, inexorably combated the foreign-to-Marxism views about a "hero" and a "crowd" and countered all efforts to oppose a "hero" to the masses and to the people.

Lenin taught that the Party's strength depends on its indissoluble unity with the masses, on the fact that behind the Party follow the people — workers, peasants and intelligentsia. "Only he will win and retain the power," said Lenin, "who believes in the people, who submerges himself in the mountain of the living creativeness of the people."

Lenin spoke with pride about the Bolshevik Communist Party as the leader and teacher of the people; he called for the presentation of all the most important questions before the opinion of knowledgeable workers, before the opinion of their Party; he said: "We believe in it, we see in it the wisdom, the honor, and the conscience of our epoch."

Lenin resolutely stood against every attempt aimed at belittling or weakening the directing role of the Party in the structure of the Soviet State. He worked out Bolshevik principles of Party direction and norms of Party life, stressing that the guiding principle of Party leadership is its collegiality. Already during the pre-revolutionary years Lenin called the Central Committee of the Party a collective of leaders and the guardian and interpreter of Party principles. "During the period between congresses," pointed out Lenin, "the Central Committee guards and interprets the principles of the Party."

Underlining the role of the Central Committee of the Party and its authority, Vladimir Ilyich pointed out: "Our Central Committee constituted itself as a closely centralized and highly authoritative group. . . ."

During Lenin's life the Central Committee of the Party was a real expression of collective leadership of the Party and of the nation. Being a militant Marxist-revolutionist, always unyielding its matters of principle, Lenin never imposed by force his views upon his co-workers. He tried to convince; he patiently explained his opinions to others. Lenin always diligently observed that the norms of Party life were realized, that the Party statute was enforced, that the Party congresses and the plenary sessions of the Central Committee took place at the proper intervals.

In addition to the great accomplishments of V. I. Lenin for the victory of the working class and of the working peasants, for the victory of our Party and for the application of the ideas of scientific Communism to life, his acute mind expressed itself also in this, that he detected in Stalin in time those negative characteristics which resulted later in grave consequences. Fearing for the future fate of the Party and of the Soviet nation, V. I. Lenin made a completely correct characterization of Stalin, pointing out that it was necessary to consider the question of transferring Stalin from the position of the Secretary General because of the fact that Stalin is excessively rude, that he does not have a proper attitude toward his comrades, that he is capricious and abuses his power.

In December 1922 in a letter to the Party Congress Vladimir Ilyich wrote: "After taking over the position of Secretary General Comrade Stalin accumulated in his hands immeasurable power and I am not certain whether he will always be able to use this power with the required care."

This letter – a political document of tremendous importance, known in the Party history as Lenin's "testament" – was distributed among the delegates to the XXth Party Congress. You have read it, and will undoubtedly read it again more than once. You might reflect on Lenin's plain words, in which expression is given to Vladimir Ilyich's anxiety concerning the Party, the people, the State, and the future direction of Party policy.

Vladimir Ilyich said: "Stalin is excessively rude, and this defect, which can be freely tolerated in our midst and in contacts among us Communists, becomes a defect which cannot be tolerated in one holding the position of the Secretary General. Because of this, I propose that the comrades consider the method by which Stalin would be removed from this position and by which another man would be selected for it, a man, who above all, would differ from Stalin in only one quality, namely greater tolerance, greater loyalty, greater kindness and more considerate attitude toward the comrades, a less capricious temper, etc."

This document of Lenin's was made known to the delegates at the XIIIth Party Congress, who discussed the question of transferring Stalin from the position of Secretary General. The delegates declared themselves in favor of retaining Stalin in this post, hoping that he would heed the critical remarks of Vladimir Ilyich and would be able to overcome the defects which caused Lenin serious anxiety. . . .

When we analyze the practice of Stalin in regard to the direction of the Party and of the country, when we pause to consider everything which Stalin perpetrated, we must be convinced that Lenin's fears were justified. The negative characteristics of Stalin, which, in Lenin's time, were only incipient, transformed themselves during the last years into a grave abuse of power by Stalin, which caused untold harm to our Party.

We have to consider seriously and analyze correctly this matter in order that we may preclude any possibility of a repetition in any form whatever of what took place during the life of Stalin, who absolutely did not tolerate collegiality in leadership and in work, and who practiced brutal violence, not only toward everything which opposed him, but also toward that which seemed to his capricious and despotic character, contrary to his concepts.

Stalin acted not through persuasion, explanation, and patient cooperation with people, but by imposing his concepts and demanding absolute submission to his opinion. Whoever opposed this concept or tried to prove his viewpoint, and the correctness of his position, was doomed to removal from the leading collective and to subsequent moral and physical annihilation. This was especially true during the period following the XVIIth Party Congress, when many prominent Party leaders and rank-and-file Party workers, honest and dedicated to the cause of Communism, fell victim to Stalin's despotism.

We must affirm that the Party had fought a serious fight against the Trotskyites, rightists and bourgeois nationalists, and that it disarmed ideologically all the enemies of Leninism. This ideological fight was carried on successfully, as a result of which the Party became strengthened and tempered. Here Stalin played a positive role. . . .

Worth noting is the fact that even during the progress of the furious ideological fight against the Trotskyites, the Zinovievites, the Bukharinites and others, extreme repressive measures were not used against them. The fight was on ideological grounds. But some years later when socialism in our country was fundamentally constructed, when the exploiting classes were generally liquidated, when the Soviet social structure had radically changed, when the social basis for political movements and groups hostile to the Party had violently contracted, when the ideological opponents of the Party were long since defeated politically — then the repression directed against them began.

It was precisely during this period (1935–1937–1938) that the practice of mass repression through the government apparatus was born, first against the enemies of Leninism — Trotskyites, Zinovievites, Bukharinites, long since politically defeated by the Party, and subsequently also against many honest Communists, against those Party cadres who had borne the heavy load of the Civil War and the first and most difficult years of industrialization and collectivization, who actively fought against the Trotskyites and the rightists for the Leninist Party line.

Stalin originated the concept "enemy of the people." This term automatically rendered it unnecessary that the ideological errors of a man or men engaged in a controversy be proven; this term made possible the usage of the most cruel repression, violating all norms of revolutionary legality, against anyone who in any way disagreed with Stalin, against those who were only suspected of hostile intent, against those who had bad reputations. This concept, "enemy of the people," actually eliminated the possibility of any kind of ideological fight or the making of one's views known on this or that issue, even those of a practical character. In the main, and in actuality, the only proof of guilt used, against all norms of current legal science, was the "confession" of the accused himself; and, as subsequent probing proved, "confessions" were acquired through physical pressures against the accused.

This led to glaring violations of revolutionary legality, and to the fact that many entirely innocent persons, who in the past had defended the Party line, became victims.

We must assert that in regard to those persons who in their time had opposed the Party line, there were often no sufficiently serious reasons for their physical annihilation. The formula, "enemy of the people," was specifically introduced for the purpose of physically annihilating such individuals. . . .

Facts prove that many abuses were made on Stalin's orders without reckoning with any norms of Party and Soviet legality. Stalin was a very distrustful man, sickly suspicious; we knew this from our work with him. He could look at a man and say: "Why are your eyes so shifty today," or "Why are you turning so much today and avoiding to look me directly in the eyes?" The sickly suspicion created in him a general distrust even toward eminent Party workers whom he had known for years. Everywhere and in everything he saw "enemies," "two-facers" and "spies."

Possessing unlimited power he indulged in great willfulness and choked a person morally and physically. A situation was created where one could not express one's own will.

When Stalin said that one or another should be arrested, it was necessary to accept on faith that he was an "enemy of the people." Meanwhile, Beria's gang, which ran the organs of state security, outdid itself in proving the guilt of the arrested and the truth of materials which it falsified. And what proofs were offered? The confessions of the arrested and the investigative judges accepted these "confessions." And how is it possible that a person confesses to crimes which he has not committed? Only in one way — because of application of physical methods of pressuring him, tortures, bringing him to a state of unconsciousness, deprivation of his judgment, taking away of his human dignity. In this manner were "confessions" acquired. . . .

The willfulness of Stalin showed itself not only in decisions concerning the internal life of the country but also in the international relations of the Soviet Union.

The July Plenum of the Central Committee studied in detail the reasons for the development of conflict with Yugoslavia. It was a shameful role which Stalin played here. The "Yugoslav Affair" contained no problems which could not have been solved through Party discussions among comrades. There was no significant basis for the development of this "affair"; it was completely possible to have prevented the rupture of relations with that country. This does not mean, however, that the Yugoslav leaders did not make mistakes or did not have shortcomings. But these mistakes and shortcomings were magnified in a monstrous manner by Stalin, which resulted in a break of relations with a friendly country. . . .

Comrades! If we sharply criticize today the cult of the individual which was so widespread during Stalin's life and if we speak about the many negative phenomena generated by this cult which is so alien to the spirit of Marxism-Leninism, various persons may ask: How could it be? Stalin headed the Party and the country for 30 years and many victories were gained during his lifetime. Can we deny this? In my opinion, the question can be asked in this manner only by those who are blinded and hopelessly hypnotized by the cult of the individual, only by those who do not understand the essence of the revolution and of the Soviet state, only by those who do not understand, in a Leninist manner, the role of the Party and of the nation in the development of the Soviet society.

The socialist revolution was attained by the working class and by the poor peasantry with the partial support of middle-class peasants. It was attained by the people under the leadership of the Bolshevik Party. Lenin's great service consisted of the fact that he created a militant Party of the working class, but he was armed with Marxist understanding of the laws of social development and with the science of proletarian victory in the fight with capitalism, and he steeled this Party in the crucible of revolutionary struggle of the masses of the people. During this fight the Party consistently defended the interests of the people, became its experienced leader, and led the working masses to power, to the creation of the first socialist state.

You remember well the wise words of Lenin that the Soviet state is strong because of the awareness of the masses that history is created by the millions and tens of millions of people.

Our historical victories were attained thanks to the organizational work of the Party, to the many provincial organizations, and to the self-sacrificing work of our great nation. These victories are the result of the great drive and activity of the nation and of the Party as a whole; they are not at all the fruit of the leadership of Stalin, as the situation was pictured during the period of the cult of the individual.

If we are to consider this matter as Marxists and as Leninists, then we have to state unequivocally that the leadership practice which came into being during the last years of Stalin's life became a serious obstacle in the path of Soviet social development.

Stalin often failed for months to take up some unusually important problems concerning the life of the Party and of the state whose solution could not be postponed. During Stalin's leadership our peaceful relations with other nations were often threatened, because one-man decisions could cause and often did cause great complications.

In the last years, when we managed to free ourselves of the harmful practice of the cult of the individual and took several proper steps in the sphere of internal and external policies, everyone saw how activity grew before their very eyes, how the creative activity of the broad working masses developed, how favorably all this acted upon the development of economy and of culture. (*Applause.*)

Some comrades may ask us: Where were the members of the Political Bureau of the Central Committee? Why did they not assert themselves against the cult of the individual in time? And why is this being done only now?

First of all we have to consider the fact that the members of the Political Bureau viewed these matters in a different way at different times. Initially, many of them backed Stalin actively because Stalin was one of the strongest Marxists and his logic, his strength and his will greatly influenced the cadres and Party work.

It is known that Stalin, after Lenin's death, especially during the first years, actively fought for Leninism against the enemies of Leninist theory and against those who deviated. Beginning with Leninist theory, the Party, with its Central Committee at the head, started on a great scale the work of socialist industrialization of the country, agricultural collectivization and the cultural revolution. At that time Stalin gained great popularity, sympathy and support. The Party had to fight those who attempted to lead the country away from the correct Leninist path; it had to fight Trotskyites, Zinovievites and rightists, and the bourgeois nationalists. This fight was indispensable. Later, however, Stalin, abusing his power more and more, began to fight eminent Party and government leaders and to use terroristic methods against honest Soviet people. As we have already shown, Stalin thus handled such eminent Party and government leaders as Kossior, Rudzutak, Eikhe, Postyshev and many others.

Attempts to oppose groundless suspicions and charges resulted in the opponent falling victim of the repression. This characterized the fall of Comrade Postyshev.

In one of his speeches Stalin expressed his dissatisfaction with Postyshev and asked him, "What are you actually?"

Postyshev answered clearly, "I am a Bolshevik, Comrade Stalin, a Bolshevik."

This assertion was at first considered to show a lack of respect for Stalin; later it was considered a harmful act and consequently resulted in Postyshev's annihilation and branding without any reason as a "people's enemy."

In the situation which then prevailed I have talked often with Nikolai Alexandrovich Bulganin; once when we two were traveling in a car, he said, "It has happened sometimes that a man goes to Stalin on his invitation as a friend. And when he sits with Stalin, he does not know where he will be sent next, home or to jail."

It is clear that such conditions put every member of the Political

Bureau in a very difficult situation. And when we also consider the fact that in the last years the Central Committee plenary sessions were not convened and that the sessions of the Political Bureau occurred only occasionally, from time to time, then we will understand how difficult it was for any member of the Political Bureau to take a stand against one or another injust or improper procedure, against serious errors and shortcomings in the practices of leadership.

As we have already shown, many decisions were taken either by one person or in a roundabout way, without collective discussions. . . .

Comrades! In order not to repeat errors of the past, the Central Committee has declared itself resolutely against the cult of the individual. We consider that Stalin was excessively extolled. However, in the past Stalin doubtlessly performed great services to the Party, to the working class, and to the international workers' movement.

This question is complicated by the fact that all this which we have just discussed was done during Stalin's life under his leadership and with his concurrence; here Stalin was convinced that this was necessary for the defense of the interests of the working classes against the plotting of the enemies and against the attack of the imperialist camp. He saw this from the position of the interest of the working class, of the interest of the laboring people, of the interest of the victory of socialism and Communism. We cannot say that these were the deeds of a giddy despot. He considered that this should be done in the interest of the Party; of the working masses, in the name of the defense of the revolution's gains. In this lies the whole tragedy!

Comrades! Lenin had often stressed that modesty is an absolutely integral part of a real Bolshevik. Lenin himself was the living personification of the greatest modesty. We cannot say that we have been following this Leninist example in all respects. It is enough to point out that many towns, factories and industrial enterprises, kolkhozes and sovkhozes, Soviet institutions and cultural institutions have been referred to by us with a title — if I may express it so — of private property of the names of these or those government or Party leaders who were still active and in good health. Many of us participated in the action of assigning our names to various towns, rayons, undertakings and kolkhozes. We must correct this. (*Applause.*)

But this should be done calmly and slowly. The Central Committee will discuss this matter and consider it carefully in order to prevent errors and excesses. I can remember how the Ukraine learned about Kossior's arrest. The Kiev radio used to start its programs thus: "This is radio [in the name of] Kossior." When one day the programs began without naming Kossior, everyone was quite certain that something had happened to Kossior, that he probably had been arrested.

Thus, if today we begin to remove the signs everywhere and to change names, people will think, that these comrades in whose honor the given enterprises, kolkhozes or cities are named, also met some bad fate and that they have also been arrested. (*Animation in the hall.*)

How is the authority and the importance of this or that leader judged? On the basis of how many towns, industrial enterprises and factories, kolkhozes and sovkhozes carry his name. It is not about time that we eliminate this "private property" and "nationalize" the factories, the industrial enterprises, the kolkhozes and the sovkhozes? (*Laughter, applause, voices: "That is right."*) This will benefit our cause. After all the cult of the individual is manifested also in this way.

We should in all seriousness consider the question of the cult of the individual. We cannot let this matter get out of the Party, especially not to the press. It is for this reason that we are considering it here at a closed Congress session. We should know the limits; we should not give ammunition to the enemy; we should not wash our dirty linen before their eyes. I think that the delegates to the Congress will understand and assess properly all these proposals. (*Tumultuous applause.*)

Comrades: We must abolish the cult of the individual decisively, once and for all; we must draw the proper conclusions concerning both ideological-theoretical and practical work.

It is necessary for this purpose:

First, in a Bolshevik manner to condemn and to eradicate the cult of the individual as alien to Marxism-Leninism and not consonant with the principles of Party leadership and the norms of Party life, and to fight inexorably all attempts at bringing back this practice in one form or another.

To return to and actually practice in all our ideological work the most important theses of Marxist-Leninist science about the people as the creator of history and as the creator of all material and spiritual good of humanity, about the decisive role of the Marxist Party in the revolutionary fight for the transformation of society, about the victory of Communism.

In this connection we will be forced to do much work in order to examine critically from the Marxist-Leninist viewpoint and to correct the widely spread erroneous views connected with the cult of the individual in the sphere of history, philosophy, economy and of other sciences, as well as in literature and the fine arts. It is especially necessary that in the immediate future we compile a serious textbook of the history of our Party which will be edited in accordance with scientific Marxist objectivism, a textbook of the history of Soviet society, a book pertaining to the events of the Civil War and the Great Patriotic War.

Secondly, to continue systematically and consistently the work done by the Party's Central Committee during the last years, a work characterized by minute observation in all Party organizations, from the bottom to the top, of the Leninist principles of Party leadership, characterized, above all, by the main principle of collective leadership, characterized by the observation of the norms of Party life described in the Statutes of our Party, and finally, characterized by the wide practice of criticism and self-criticism.

Thirdly, to restore completely the Leninist principles of Soviet socialist democracy, expressed in the Constitution of the Soviet Union, to fight willfulness of individuals abusing their power. The evil caused by acts violating revolutionary socialist legality which have accumulated during a long time as a result of the negative influence of the cult of the individual has to be completely corrected.

Comrades! The XXth Congress of the Communist Party of the Soviet Union has manifested with a new strength the unshakable unity of our Party, its cohesiveness around the Central Committee, its resolute will to accomplish the great task of building Communism. (*Tumultuous applause.*) And the fact that we present in all their ramifications the basic problems of overcoming the cult of the individual which is alien to Marxism-Leninism, as well as the problem of liquidating its burdensome consequences, is an evidence of the great moral and political strength of our Party. (*Prolonged applause.*)

We are absolutely certain that our Party, armed with the historical resolutions of the XXth Congress, will lead the Soviet people along the Leninist path to new successses, to new victories. (*Tumultuous, prolonged applause.*)

Long live the victorious banner of our Party — Leninism! (*Tumultuous, prolonged applause ending in ovation. All rise.*)

The Practice of Communism

Perhaps the most persuasive and important analysis of the tendencies of modern Communism has come from within the Socialist camp. Milovan Djilas is a leading Yugoslav Communist and the leading rival of Tito. In the latter capacity, he has suffered persecution and imprisonment. Although remaining committed to a Socialist system, Djilas has sought to reveal the realities of Communist practice, in contrast to its theory, as it "settles down." He rejects the notion that the Communists have created a classless society and urges them to face the reality that they have created a ruling class. He offers no solution, but he urges democratization within the Communist world and greater openness so that international peace and progress might be served by peaceful coexistence.

Djilas' New Class

Everything happened differently in the U.S.S.R. and other Communist countries from what the leaders — even such prominent ones as Lenin, Stalin, Trotsky, and Bukharin — anticipated. They expected that the state would rapidly wither away, that democracy would be strengthened. The reverse happened. They expected a rapid improvement in the standard of living — there has been scarcely any change in this respect and, in the subjugated East European countries, the standard has even declined. In every instance, the standard of living has failed to rise in proportion to the rate of industrialization, which was much more rapid. It was believed that the differences between cities and villages, between intellectual and physical labor, would slowly disappear; instead these differences have increased. Communist anticipations in other areas — including their expectations for developments in the non-Communist world — have also failed to materialize.

The greatest illusion was that industrialization and collectivization in the U.S.S.R., and destruction of capitalist ownership, would result in a classless society. In 1936, when the new Constitution was promulgated, Stalin announced that the "exploiting class" had ceased to exist. The capitalist and other classes of ancient origin had in fact been destroyed, but a new class, previously unknown to history, had been formed.

It is understandable that this class, like those before it, should believe that the establishment of its power would result in happiness and freedom for all men. The only difference between this and other classes was that it treated the delay in the realization of its illusions more crudely. It thus affirmed that its power was more complete than the power of any other class before in history, and its class illusions and prejudices were proportionally greater.

This new class, the bureaucracy, or more accurately the political bureaucracy, has all the characteristics of earlier ones as well as some new characteristics of its own. Its origin had its special characteristics also, even though in essence it was similar to the beginnings of other classes.

Other classes, too, obtained their strength and power by the revolutionary path, destroying the political, social, and other orders they met in their way. However, almost without exception, these classes attained power *after* new economic patterns had taken shape in the old society. The case was the reverse with new classes in the Communist systems. It did not come to power to *complete* a new economic order but to *establish* its own and, in so doing, to establish its power over society.

From Milovan Djilas, *The New Class: An Analysis of the Communist System* (New York: Praeger, 1957), pp. 37–41, 48–50, 52–54. Reprinted by permission of Praeger Publishers, Inc.

In earlier epochs the coming to power of some class, some part of a class, or of some party, was the final event resulting from its formation and its development. The reverse was true in the U.S.S.R. There the new class was definitely formed after it attained power. Its consciousness had to develop before its economic and physical powers, because the class had not taken root in the life of the nation. This class viewed its role in relation to the world from an idealistic point of view. Its practical possibilities were not diminished by this. In spite of its illusions, it represented an objective tendency toward industrialization. Its practical bent emanated from this tendency. The promise of an ideal world increased the faith in the ranks of the new class and sowed illusions among the masses. At the same time it inspired gigantic physical undertakings.

Because this new class had not been formed as a part of the economic and social life before it came to power, it could only be created in an organization of a special type, distinguished by a special discipline based on identical philosophic and ideological views of its members. A unity of belief and iron discipline was necessary to overcome its weaknesses.

The roots of the new class were implanted in a special party, of the Bolshevik type. Lenin was right in his view that his party was an exception in the history of human society, although he did not suspect that it would be the beginning of a new class.

To be more precise, the initiators of the new class are not found in the party of the Bolshevik type as a whole but in that stratum of professional revolutionaries who made up its core even before it attained power. It was not by accident that Lenin asserted after the failure of the 1905 revolution that only professional revolutionaries — men whose sole profession was revolutionary work — could build a new party of the Bolshevik type. It was still less accidental that even Stalin, the future creator of a new class, was the most outstanding example of such a professional revolutionary. The new ruling class has been gradually developing from this very narrow stratum of revolutionaries. These revolutionaries composed its core for a long period. Trotsky noted that in pre-revolutionary professional revolutionaries was the origin of the future Stalinist bureaucrat. What he did not detect was the beginning of a new class of owners and exploiters.

This is not to say that the new party and the new class are identical. The party, however, is the core of that class, and its base. It is very difficult, perhaps impossible, to define the limits of the new class and to identify its members. The new class may be said to be made up of those who have special privileges and economic preference because of the administrative monopoly they hold.

Since administration is unavoidable in society, necessary administrative functions may be coexistent with parasitic functions in the same person. Not every member of the party is a member of the new class, any more than every artisan or member of the city party was a bourgeois.

In loose terms, as the new class becomes stronger and attains a more perceptible physiognomy, the role of the party diminishes. The core and the basis of the new class is created in the party and at its top, as well as in the state political organs. The once live, compact party, full of initiative, is disappearing to become transformed into the traditional oligarchy of the new class, irresistibly drawing into its ranks those who aspire to join the new class and repressing those who have any ideals.

The party makes the class, but the class grows as a result and uses the party as a basis. The class grows stronger, while the party grows weaker; this is the inescapable fate of every Communist party in power.

If it were not materially interested in production or if it did not have within itself the potentialities for the creation of a new class, no party could act in so morally and ideologically foolhardy a fashion, let alone stay in power for long. Stalin declared, after the end of the First Five-Year Plan: "If we had not created the apparatus, we would have failed!" He should have substituted "new class" for the word "apparatus," and everything would have been clearer.

It seems unusual that a political party could be the beginning of a new class. Parties are generally the product of classes and strata which have become intellectually and economically strong. However, if one grasps the actual conditions in pre-revolutionary Russia and in other countries in which Communism prevailed over national forces, it will be clear that a party of this type is the product of specific opportunities and that there is nothing unusual or accidental in this being so. Although the roots of Bolshevism reach far back into Russian history, the party is partly the product of the unique pattern of international relationships in which Russia found itself at the end of the nineteenth and the beginning of the twentieth century. Russia was no longer able to live in the modern world as an absolute monarchy, and Russia's capitalism was too weak and too dependent on the interests of foreign powers to make it possible to have an industrial revolution. This revolution could only be implemented by a new class, or by a change in the social order. As yet, there was no such class.

In history, it is not important who implements a process, it is only important that the process be implemented. Such was the case in Russia and other countries in which Communist revolutions took place. The revolution created forces, leaders, organizations, and ideas which were necessary to it. The new class came into existence for objective reasons, and by the wish, wits, and action of its leaders. . . .

Although he did not realize it, Lenin started the organization of the new class. He established the party along Bolshevik lines and developed the theories of its unique and leading role in the building of a new society. This is but one aspect of his many-sided and gigantic work; it is the aspect which came about from his actions rather than his wishes. It is also the aspect which led the new class to revere him.

The real and direct originator of the new class, however, was Stalin. He was a man of quick reflexes and a tendency to coarse humor, not very educated nor a good speaker. But he was a relentless dogmatician and a great administrator, a Georgian who knew better than anyone else whither the new powers of Greater Russia were taking her. He created the new class by the use of the most barbaric means, not even sparing the class itself. It was inevitable that the new class which placed him at the top would later submit to his unbridled and brutal nature. He was the true leader of that class as long as the class was building itself up, and attaining power.

The new class was born in the revolutionary struggle in the Communist Party, but was developed in the industrial revolution. Without the revolution, without industry, the class's position would not have been secure and its power would have been limited.

While the country was being industrialized, Stalin began to introduce considerable variations in wages, at the same time allowing the development toward various privileges to proceed. He thought that industrialization would come to nothing if the new class were not made materially interested in the process, by acquisition of some property for itself. Without industrialization the new class would find it difficult to hold its position, for it would have neither historical justification nor the material resources for its continued existence.

The increase in the membership of the party, or of the bureaucracy, was closely connected with this. In 1927, on the eve of industrialization, the Soviet Communist Party had 887,233 members. In 1934, at the end of the First Five-Year Plan, the membership had increased to 1,874,488. This was a phenomenon obviously connected with industrialization: the prospects for the new class and privileges for its members were improving. What is more, the privileges and the class were expanding more rapidly than industrialization itself. It is difficult to cite any statistics on this point, but the conclusion is self-evident for anyone who bears in mind that the standard of living has not kept pace with industrial production, while the new class actually seized the lion's share of the economic and other progress earned by the sacrifices and efforts of the masses. . . .

Behind Lenin, who was all passion and thought, stands the dull, gray figure of Joseph Stalin, the symbol of the difficult, cruel, and unscrupulous ascent of the new class to its final power.

After Lenin and Stalin came what had to come; namely, mediocrity in the form of collective leadership. And also there came the apparently sincere, kind-hearted, non-intellectual "man of the people" — Nikita Khrushchev. The new class no longer needs the revolutionaries or dogmatists it once required; it is satisfied with simple personalities, such as Khrushchev, Malenkov, Bulganin, and Shepilov, whose every word reflects the average man. The new class itself is tired of dogmatic purges and training sessions. It would like to live quietly. It must protect itself even from its own authorized leader now that it has been adequately strengthened. Stalin remained the same as he was when the class was weak, when cruel measures were necessary against even those in its own ranks who threatened to deviate. Today this is all unnecessary. Without relinquishing anything it created under Stalin's leadership, the new class appears to be renouncing his authority for the past few years. But it is not really renouncing that authority — only Stalin's methods which, according to Khrushchev, hurt "good Communists."

Lenin's revolutionary epoch was replaced by Stalin's epoch, in which authority and ownership, and industrialization, were strengthened so that the much desired peaceful and good life of the new class could begin. Lenin's *revolutionary* Communism was replaced by Stalin's *dogmatic* communism, which in turn was replaced by *non-dogmatic* Communism, a so-called collective leadership or a group of oligarchs.

These are the three phases of development of the new class in the U.S.S.R. or of Russian Communism (or of every other type of Communism in one manner or another).

The fate of Yugoslav Communism was to unify these three phases in the single personality of Tito, along with national and personal characteristics. Tito is a great revolutionary, but without original ideas; he has attained personal power, but without Stalin's distrustfulness and dogmatism. Like Khrushchev, Tito is a representative of the people, that is, of the middle-party strata. The road which Yugoslav Communism has traveled — attaining a revolution, copying Stalinism, then renouncing Stalinism and seeking its own form — is seen most fully in the personality of Tito. Yugoslav Communism has been more consistent than other parties in preserving the substance of Communism, yet never renouncing any form which could be of value to it.

The three phases in the development of the new class — Lenin, Stalin, and "collective leadership" — are not completely divorced from each other, in substance or in ideas.

Lenin too was a dogmatist, and Stalin too was a revolutionary, just as collective leadership will resort to dogmatism and to revolutionary methods when necessary. What is more, the nondogmatism of the collective leadership is applied only to itself, to the heads of the new class. On the other hand, the people must be all the more persistently "educated" in the spirit of the dogma, or of Marxism-Leninism. By relaxing its dogmatic severity and exclusiveness, the new class, becoming strengthened economically, has prospects of attaining greater flexibility.

The heroic era of Communism is past. The epoch of its great leaders has ended. The epoch of practical men has set in. The new class has been created. It is at the height of its power and wealth, but it is without new ideas. It has nothing more to tell the people. The only thing that remains is for it to justify itself.

TENDENCIES
OF TWENTIETH-CENTURY
CIVILIZATION
Chapter 9

The civilization of the twentieth century is both confused and highly variegated, and the vast acceleration of the tempo of change makes it virtually impossible to pin down or predict with complete assurance the most significant and constant aspects and trends. It is reasonable to say and assume, however, that rapid scientific and technological advance provides the most critical foundation for the development of our civilization. It determines our possibilities and our problems. In the nineteenth century, scientific and technological advances were viewed with complete optimism by all but a few pessimistic intellectuals. Now, while there is a general recognition that it is impossible to set the clock back, the attitude toward the relation between science and "progress" is much more realistic. The development of the atomic bomb in 1945 marked a watershed in human possibilities. Mankind can now destroy itself quickly and efficiently, or it can harness atomic energy for constructive purposes. In any case, this century could with justification be called the age of anxiety. The technological revolution, however, has not been limited to atomic energy. The computer and the automation that accompanies it promise to revolutionize industrial processes and have made it possible for man to go to the moon. Yet the new techniques create technological unemployment and make possible the systematic invasion of privacy and the development of totalitarian techniques in ways that go beyond the frightening vision presented in George Orwell's famous novel *1984*. The problems created by modern technology have been brought home in a direct way by the increasing pollution of the environment throughout the industrialized areas of the world. The Volga River is as polluted as the Hudson, if not more so, and ecology has become an interest that crosses ideological barriers. It seems obvious that these problems can

248

be overcome only by a more sophisticated science and technology since the populations of the world can be supported only by the spread of industrialization, but it is no less obvious that new discoveries will create new problems just as they will solve old ones.

Scientific and technological developments present a challenge to education. They require expanded educational facilities and opportunities as well as new educational methods. The international crisis in higher education reflects many of these difficulties. Mass education and long periods of schooling have produced institutional and psychological problems that have been compounded by the loss of a sense of educational meaning and purpose. This loss has been created in part by the proliferation of knowledge and the increase of specialization. In Europe, the problems have been particularly severe because of the institutional backwardness of the university systems, the inordinate power of professors and their insufficient numbers, and the traditionalist rejection of both mass education and scientific-technological education. The dilemma of how to establish mass systems of higher education that will fruitfully and meaningfully combine the "two cultures" of science and humanities remains to be solved. In England, Germany, and France important innovations have been made as a result of the need for expanded higher education as well as because of student unrest, but the moral and intellectual problems of twentieth-century civilization continue to produce ferment in the schools.

Although the tendency of modern art to be abstract and meaningless in representational and ideational content has often been emphasized, it should also be recognized that the arts have pioneered in the effort to reestablish the sense of wholeness that seems to have been lost in modern society as well as in the effort to bridge the gap between the humanities and technology. Experimentation with various media, the combination of media, kinetic art, and the general interest in the machine shown by many artists today reflect these tendencies. Architecture has been particularly notable in the effort to combine esthetic, technological, and social concerns. Though the mass media have often produced and encouraged conformity and mediocrity, they have also spread culture to more people than ever before in history. Many have regretted the decline of the theater and the loss of direct contact between actors and audience, but the motion picture has often been employed with remarkable brilliance and originality and cannot be shunted aside as an art form.

The twentieth century has witnessed the rapid decline of religious faith and the loss of the absolute faith in science that had been so important in the Enlightenment and positivistic eras. Ideologies remain important, but the world's experience with Hitler and Stalin has produced a good deal of skepticism. The affirmation of life and its value thus seems to rest increasingly on an existential commitment, an affirmative acceptance of the human condition and its tasks despite manifold absurdities.

Science and the Humanities

C. P. Snow, a scientist and novelist, is one of few men who have comfortably bridged two cultures in their everyday activities. His discussions of the problem of the separation of the natural sciences and the humanities have attracted wide attention and respect in both intellectual disciplines. Snow has above all supported educational reform and a reduction of specialization as means of overcoming the intellectual crisis.

Snow's *Two Cultures*

. . . I believe the intellectual life of the whole of western society is increasingly split into two polar groups. When I say the intellectual life, I mean to include also a large part of our practical life, because I should be the last person to suggest the two can at the deepest level be distinguished. I shall come back to the practical life a little later. Two polar groups: at one pole we have the literary intellectuals, who incidentally while no one was looking took to referring to themselves as 'intellectuals' as though there were no others. . . .

Literary intellectuals at one pole — at the other scientists, and as the most representative, the physical scientists. Between the two a gulf of mutual incomprehension — sometimes (particularly among the young) hostility and dislike, but most of all lack of understanding. They have a curious distorted image of each other. Their attitudes are so different that, even on the level of emotion, they can't find much common ground. Non-scientists tend to think of scientists as brash and boastful. They hear Mr. T. S. Eliot, who just for these illustrations we can take as an archetypal figure, saying about his attempts to revive verse-drama that we can hope for very little, but that he would feel content if he and

From C. P. Snow, *The Two Cultures and a Second Look. An Expanded Version of The Two Cultures and the Scientific Revolution* (Cambridge: Cambridge University Press, 1965), pp. 3–9. Reprinted by permission of Cambridge University Press.

his co-workers could prepare the ground for a new Kyd or a new Greene. That is the tone, restricted and constrained, with which literary intellectuals are at home: it is the subdued voice of their culture. Then they hear a much louder voice, that of another archetypal figure, Rutherford, trumpeting: 'This is the heroic age of science! This is the Elizabethan age!' Many of us heard that, and a good many other statements beside which that was mild; and we weren't left in any doubt whom Rutherford was casting for the role of Shakespeare. What is hard for the literary intellectuals to understand, imaginatively or intellectually, is that he was absolutely right.

And compare 'this is the way the world ends, not with a bang but a whimper' — incidentally, one of the least likely scientific prophecies ever made — compare that with Rutherford's famous repartee, 'Lucky fellow, Rutherford, always on the crest of the wave.' 'Well, I made the wave, didn't I?'

The non-scientists have a rooted impression that the scientists are shallowly optimistic, unaware of man's condition. On the other hand, the scientists believe that the literary intellectuals are totally lacking in foresight, peculiarly unconcerned with their brother men, in a deep sense anti-intellectual, anxious to restrict both art and thought to the existential moment. And so on. Anyone with a mild talent for invective could produce plenty of this kind of subterranean back-chat. On each side there is some of it which is not entirely baseless. It is all destructive. Much of it rests on misinterpretations which are dangerous. I should like to deal with two of the most profound of these now, one on each side.

First, about the scientists' optimism. This is an accusation which has been made so often that it has become a platitude. It has been made by some of the acutest non-scientific minds of the day. But it depends upon a confusion between the individual experience and the social experience, between the individual condition of man and his social condition. Most of the scientists I have known well have felt — just as deeply as the non-scientists I have known well — that the individual condition of each of us is tragic. Each of us is alone: sometimes we escape from solitariness, through love or affection or perhaps creative moments, but those triumphs of life are pools of light we make for ourselves while the edge of the road is black: each of us dies alone. Some scientists I have known have had faith in revealed religion. Perhaps with them the sense of the tragic condition is not so strong. I don't know. With most people of deep feeling, however high-spirited and happy they are, sometimes most with those who are happiest and most high-spirited, it seems to be right in the fibres, part of the weight of life. That is as true of the scientists I have known best as of anyone at all.

But nearly all of them — and this is where the colour of hope genuinely comes in — would see no reason why, just because the individual condition is tragic, so must the social condition be. Each of us is solitary: each of us dies alone: all right, that's a fate against which we can't struggle — but there is plenty in our condition which is not fate, and against which we are less than human unless we do struggle.

Most of our fellow human beings, for instance, are underfed and die before their time. In the crudest terms, *that* is the social condition. There is a moral trap which comes through the insight into man's loneliness: it tempts one to sit back, complacent in one's unique tragedy, and let the others go without a meal.

As a group, the scientists fall into that trap less than others. They are inclined to be impatient to see if something can be done: and inclined to think that it can be done, until it's proved otherwise. That is their real optimism, and it's an optimism that the rest of us badly need.

In reverse, the same spirit, tough and good and determined to fight it out at the side of their brother men, has made scientists regard the other culture's social attitudes as contemptible. That is too facile: some of them are, but they are a temporary phase and not to be taken as representative. . . .

Those are two of the misunderstandings between the two cultures. I should say, since I began to talk about them — the two cultures, that is — I have had some criticism. Most of my scientific acquaintances think that there is something in it, and so do most of the practising artists I know. But I have been argued with by non-scientists of strong down-to-earth interests. Their view is that it is an oversimplification, and that if one is going to talk in these terms there ought to be at least three cultures. They argue that, though they are not scientists themselves, they would share a good deal of the scientific feeling. They would have as little use — perhaps, since they knew more about it, even less use — for the recent literary culture as the scientists themselves. J. H. Plumb, Alan Bullock and some of my American sociological friends have said that they vigorously refuse to be corralled in a cultural box with people they wouldn't be seen dead with, or to be regarded as helping to produce a climate which would not permit of social hope.

I respect those arguments. The number 2 is a very dangerous number: that is why the dialectic is a dangerous process. Attempts to divide anything into two ought to be regarded with much suspicion. I have thought a long time about going in for further refinements: but in the end I have decided against. I was searching for something a little more than a dashing metaphor, a good deal less than a cultural map: and for those purposes the two cultures is about right, and subtilising any more would bring more disadvantages than it's worth.

At one pole, the scientific culture really is a culture, not only in an intellectual but also in an anthropological sense. That is, its members need not, and of course often do not, always completely understand each other; biologists more often than not will have a pretty hazy idea of contemporary physics; but there are common attitudes, common standards and patterns of behaviour, common approaches and assumptions. This goes surprisingly wide and deep. It cuts across other mental patterns, such as those of religion or politics or class.

Statistically, I suppose slightly more scientists are in religious terms unbelievers, compared with the rest of the intellectual world — though there are plenty who are religious, and that seems to be increasingly so among the young. Statistically also, slightly more scientists are on the Left in open politics — though again, plenty always have called themselves conservatives, and that also seems to be more common among the young. Compared with the rest of the intellectual world, considerably more scientists in this country and probably in the U.S. come from poor families. Yet over a whole range of thought and behaviour, none of that matters very much. In their working, and in much of their emotional life, their attitudes are closer to other scientists than to non-scientists who in religion or politics or class have the same labels as themselves. If I were to risk a piece of shorthand, I should say that naturally they had the future in their bones.

They may or may not like it, but they have it. That was as true of the conservatives J. J. Thomson and Lindemann as of the radicals Einstein or Blackett: as true of the Christian A. H. Compton as of the materialist Bernal: of the aristocrats de Broglie or Russell as of the proletarian Faraday: of those born rich, like Thomas Merton or Victor Rothschild, as of Rutherford, who was the son of an odd-job handyman. Without thinking about it, they respond alike. That is what a culture means.

At the other pole, the spread of attitudes is wider. It is obvious that between the two, as one moves through intellectual society from the physicists to the literary intellectuals, there are all kinds of tones of feeling on the way. But I believe the pole of total incomprehension of science radiates its influence on all the rest. That total incomprehension gives, much more pervasively than we realise, living in it, an unscientific flavour to the whole 'traditional' culture, and that unscientific flavour is often, much more than we admit, on the point of turning anti-scientific. The feelings of one pole become the anti-feelings of the other. If the scientists have the future in their bones, then the traditional culture responds by wishing the future did not exist. It is the traditional culture, to an extent remarkably little diminished by the emergence of the scientific one, which manages the western world.

This polarisation is sheer loss to us all. To us as people, and to our society. It is at the same time practical and intellectual and creative loss, and I repeat that it is false to imagine that those considerations are clearly separable. But for a moment I want to concentrate on the intellectual loss.

The degree of incomprehension on both sides is the kind of joke which has gone sour. There are about fifty thousand working scientists in the country and about eighty thousand professional engineers or applied scientists. During the war and in the years since, my colleagues and I have had to interview somewhere between thirty to forty thousand of these — that is, about 25 per cent. The number is large enough to give us a fair sample, though of the men we talked to most would still be under forty. We were able to find out a certain amount of what they read and thought about. I confess that even I, who am fond of them and respect them, was a bit shaken. We hadn't quite expected that the links with the traditional culture should be so tenuous, nothing more than a formal touch of the cap.

As one would expect, some of the very best scientists had and have plenty of energy and interest to spare, and we came across several who had read everything that literary people talk about. But that's very rare. Most of the rest, when one tried to probe for what books they had read, would modestly confess, 'Well, I've *tried* a bit of Dickens,' rather as though Dickens were an extraordinarily esoteric, tangled and dubiously rewarding writer, something like Rainer Maria Rilke. In fact that is exactly how they do regard him: we thought that discovery, that Dickens had been transformed into the type-specimen of literary incomprehensibility, was one of the oddest results of the whole exercise.

But of course, in reading him, in reading almost any writer whom we should value, they are just touching their caps to the traditional culture. They have their own culture, intensive, rigorous, and constantly in action. This culture contains a great deal of argument, usually much more rigorous, and almost always at a higher conceptual level, than literary persons' arguments — even though the scientists do cheerfully use words in senses which literary persons don't recognise, the senses are exact ones, and when they talk about 'subjective,' 'objective,' 'philosophy' or 'progressive,' they know what they mean, even though it isn't what one is accustomed to expect.

Remember, these are very intelligent men. Their culture is in many ways an exacting and admirable one. It doesn't contain much art, with the exception, an important exception, of music. Verbal exchange, insistent argument. Long-playing records. Colour-photography. The ear, to some extent the eye. Books very little, though perhaps not many would go so far as one hero, who perhaps I should admit was further down the scientific ladder than the people I've been talking about — who, when asked what books he read, replied firmly and confidently: 'Books? I prefer to use my books as tools.' It was very hard not to let the mind wander — what sort of tool would a book make? Perhaps a hammer? A primitive digging instrument?

Of books, though, very little. And of the books which to most literary persons are bread and butter, novels, history, poetry, plays, almost nothing at all. It isn't that they're not interested in the psychological or moral or social life. In the social life, they certainly are, more than most of us. In the moral, they are by and large the soundest group of intellectuals we have; there is a moral competent right in the grain of science itself, and almost all scientists form their own judgments of the moral life. In the psychological they have as much interest as most of us, though occasionally I fancy they come to it rather late. It isn't that they lack the interests. It is much more that the whole literature of the traditional culture doesn't seem to them relevant to those interests. They are, of course, dead wrong. As a result, their imaginative understanding is less than it could be. They are self-impoverished.

But what about the other side? They are impoverished too — perhaps more seriously, because they are vainer about it. They still like to pretend that the traditional culture is the whole of 'culture,' as though the natural order didn't exist. As though the exploration of the natural order was of no interest either in its own value or its consequences. As though the scientific edifice of the physical world was not, in its intellectual depth, complexity and articulation, the most beautiful and wonderful collective work of the mind of man. Yet most non-scientists have no conception of that edifice at all. Even if they want to have it, they can't. It is rather as though, over an immense range of intellectual experience, a whole group was tone-deaf. Except that this tone-deafness doesn't come by nature, but by training, or rather the absence of training.

As with the tone-deaf, they don't know what they miss. They give a pitying chuckle at the news of scientists who have never read a major work of English literature. They dismiss them as ignorant specialists. Yet their own ignorance and their own specialisation is just as startling. A good many times I have been present at gatherings of people who, by the standards of the traditional culture, are thought highly educated and who have with considerable gusto been expressing their incredulity at the illiteracy of scientists. Once or twice I have been provoked and have asked the company how many of them could describe the Second Law of Thermodynamics. The response was cold: it was also negative. Yet I was asking something which is about the scientific equivalent of: *Have you read a work of Shakespeare's?*

I now believe that if I had asked an even simpler question — such as, What do you mean by mass, or acceleration, which is the scientific equivalent of saying, *Can you read?* — not more than one in ten of the highly educated would have felt that I was speaking the same language. So the great edifice of modern physics goes up, and the majority of the cleverest people in the western world have about as much insight into it as their neolithic ancestors would have had. . . .

There seems then to be no place where the cultures meet. I am not going to waste time saying that this is a pity. It is much worse than that.

Soon I shall come to some practical consequences. But at the heart of thought and creation we are letting some of our best chances go by default. The clashing point of two subjects, two disciplines, two cultures — of two galaxies, so far as that goes — ought to produce creative chances. In the history of mental activity that has been where some of the breakthroughs came. The chances are there now. But they are there, as it were, in a vacuum, because those in the two cultures can't talk to each other. It is bizarre how very little of twentieth-century science has been assimilated into twentieth-century art. Now and then one used to find poets conscientiously using scientific expressions, and getting them wrong — there was a time when "refraction" kept cropping up in verse in a mystifying fashion, and when "polarised light" was used as though writers were under the illusion that it was a specially admirable kind of light.

Of course, that isn t the way that science could be any good to art. It has got to be assimilated along with, and as part and parcel of, the whole of our mental experience, and used as naturally as the rest. . . .

There is only one way out of all this: it is, of course, by rethinking our education. In this country . . . that is more difficult than in any other. Nearly everyone will agree that our school education is too specialised. But nearly everyone feels that it is outside the will of man to alter it. Other countries are as dissatisfied with their education as we are, but are not so resigned.

The U.S. teach out of proportion more children up to eighteen than we do: they teach them far more widely, but nothing like so rigorously. They know that: they are hoping to take the problem in hand within ten years, though they may not have all that time to spare. The U.S.S.R. also teach out of proportion more children than we do: they also teach far more widely than we do (it is an absurd western myth that their school education is specialised) but much too rigorously. They know that — and they are beating about to get it right. The Scandinavians, in particular the Swedes, who would make a more sensible job of it than any of us, are handicapped by their practical need to devote an inordinate amount of time to foreign languages. But they too are seized of the problem.

Are we? Have we crystallised so far that we are no longer flexible at all? . . .

Somehow we have set ourselves the task of producing a tiny *élite* — far smaller proportionately than in any comparable country — educated in one academic skill. For a hundred and fifty years in Cambridge it was mathematics: then it was mathematics or classics: then natural science was allowed in. But still the choice had to be a single one.

It may well be that this process has gone too far to be reversible. I have given reasons why I think it is a disastrous process, for the purpose of a living culture. I am going on to give reasons why I think it is fatal, if we're to perform our practical tasks in the world. . . .

Student Unrest

The aims of European and American student protestors and revolutionaries have often mystified the government and the public. In contrast to the 1930's, very few of them are Communists, and they consider the Soviet Union as "repressive" as they do Western capitalist regimes. The dominant political strain seems to be anarchism, and the emphasis has been on direct democracy, worker control in the factories, and student control in the universities. Some student leaders have turned against the workers, who have been notoriously unfriendly toward the student radicals, as well as the bourgeoisie, on the grounds that they have become integrated into the bourgeois order. Most radical leaders, however, continue to hope for an alliance between the two groups in order to make the revolution. In Paris in May, 1968, this seemed for a moment to be possible. Student uprisings were combined with worker strikes in protest against the economic and social policies of the De Gaulle government. The trade unions (CGT) and Communist leaders, however, quickly abandoned the movement in return for concrete economic gains, and the student radicals had to settle for educational reforms. One of the most important and widely publicized leaders of the student revolt was Daniel Cohn-Bendit, who in an interview by the famous existentialist writer and philosopher Jean-Paul Sartre provides important clues to the causes and goals of student unrest as well as to the logic and ideology of contemporary student revolutionaries.

The French Student Revolt of May, 1968: Sartre's Interview with Daniel Cohn-Bendit

JEAN-PAUL SARTRE. Within a few days, although no one called for a general strike, France has been practically paralysed by work stoppages and factory occupations. And all because the students who took con-

From *The Student Revolt: The Activists Speak,* comp. Hervé Bourges, trans. Benjamin R. Brewster (London: Panther Books, 1968), pp. 97–107. Reprinted by permission of Hill & Wang, Inc., and Jonathan Cape Ltd. The interview appeared in *Le Nouvel Observateur.*

trol of the streets in the Latin Quarter. What is your analysis of the movement you have unleashed? How far can it go?

DANIEL COHN-BENDIT. It has grown much larger than we could have foreseen at the start. The aim is now the overthrow of the regime. But it is not up to us whether or no this is achieved. If the Communist Party, the CGT and the other union headquarters shared it there would be no problem; the regime would fall within a fortnight, as it has no counterthrust against a trial of strength supported by all working-class forces.

J.-P. S. For the moment there is an obvious disproportion between the massive nature of the strike movement, which does, indeed, make possible a direct confrontation with the regime, and the demands the trade unions have presented which are still limited ones: for wages, work organization, pensions, etc., etc.

D. C.-B. There has always been a disjunction in workers' struggles between the strength of the action and the initial demands. But it might be that the success of the action, the dynamism of the movement could alter the nature of the demands progressively. A strike launched for a partial victory may change into a movement for insurrection.

Even so, some of the demands put forward by the workers today are are very far-reaching: a real forty-hour week, for example, and at Renault's a minimum wage of a thousand francs per month. The Gaullist regime cannot accept them without a total loss of face and if it holds out, then there will be a confrontation. Suppose the workers hold out too and the regime falls. What will happen then? The left will come to power. Everything will then depend on what it does. If it really changes the system — I must admit I doubt if it will — it will have an audience, and all will be well. But if we have a Wilson-style government, with or without the Communists, which only proposes minor reforms and adjustments, then the extreme left will regain its strength and we shall have to go on posing the real problems of social control, workers' power, and so on.

But we have not reached that stage yet, and it is not at all certain even that the regime will fall.

J.-P. S. When the situation is a revolutionary one, a movement like your own may not be stopped, but it may be that its impetus will fade. In that case you will have to try to go as far as possible before you come to a halt. What irreversible results do you think the present movement will achieve, supposing that it soon stops?

D. C.-B. The workers will obtain the satisfaction of a number of material demands, and the moderates in the student movement and the teachers will put through important university reforms. These will not be the radical reforms we should like to see, but we shall still be able to bring some pressure to bear: we shall make particular proposals, and no doubt a few of them will be accepted because they won't dare refuse us everything. That will be some progress, of course, but nothing basic will have changed and we shall continue to challenge the system as a whole.

Besides, I don't believe the revolution is possible overnight like that. I believe that all we can get are successive adjustment, of more or less importance, but these adjustments can only be imposed by revolutionary action. That is how the student movement, which, even if it does temporarily lose its energy, will still have achieved an important university reform, can act as an example to many young workers. By using the traditional means of action of the workers' movement — strikes, occupations of the streets and work-places — we have destroyed the first barrier: the myth that 'nothing can be done about the regime.' We have proved that this is not true. And the workers rushed into the breach. Perhaps this time they won't go right to the end. But there will be other explosions later on. What matters is that the effectiveness of revolutionary methods has been proved.

The union of workers and students can only be achieved in the dynamic of action if the students' movement and the workers' movement each sustain their own impetus and converge on one aim. At the moment, naturally and understandably enough, the workers distrust the students.

J.-P. S. This distrust is not natural, it has been acquired. It did not exist at the beginning of the nineteenth century, and did not appear until after the massacres of June 1848. Before that, republicans — who were intellectuals and petty bourgeois — and workers marched together. This unity has been out of the question ever since, even in the Communist Party, which has always carefully separated workers and intellectuals.

D. C.-B. But something did happen during the crisis. At Billancourt the workers would not let the students into the factories. But even the fact that students went to Billancourt was new and important. In fact, there were three stages. First, open mistrust, not only in the working-class press, but among the workers themselves. They said, 'Who are all these daddies' boys who have come to annoy us?' Then, after the street battles, the students' struggle with the police, this feeling disappeared and solidarity was effectively achieved.

Now we are in a third stage: the workers and peasants have entered the struggle in their turn, but they tell us, "Wait a little, we want to fight our own battles for ourselves!" That is to be expected. Union can only take place later on if the two movements, the students' movement and the workers' movement, maintain their impetus. After fifty years of distrust, I don't think that what is called 'dialogue' is possible. It is not just a matter of talk. We should not expect the workers to welcome us with open arms. Contact will only be made when we are fighting side by side. We might for example set up common revolutionary action groups in which workers and students raise problems and act together. There are places where that will work, and others where it won't.

J.-P. S. The problem remains the same: adjustments or revolution. As you have said, everything you do by force is recovered positively by the reformists. Thanks to your action, the university will be readjusted, but only within the framework of a bourgeois society.

D. C.-B. Obviously, but I believe that that is the only way to advance. Take the examinations, for example. There can be no doubt that they will take place. But certainly not in the way they used to. A new formula will be found. And once they take place in an unusual way, an irreversible process of reforms will have been set moving. I don't know how far it will go, and I know it will be a slow process, but it is the only possible strategy.

I am not interested in metaphysics, in looking for ways to 'make the revolution.' As I have said, I think that we are moving towards a perpetually changing society, modified by revolutionary actions at each stage. A radical change in the structure of our society would only be possible, if, for example, a serious economic crisis, the action of a powerful workers' movement, and vigorous student activity suddenly converged. These conditions have not all been realized today. At best we can hope to bring down the government. We must not dream of destroying bourgeois society. That does not mean that there is nothing to be done; on the contrary, we must struggle step by step, on the basis of a global challenge.

I am not really interested in whether there can still be revolutions in advanced capitalist societies, and what we should do to induce them. Everyone has his own theory. Some say: the revolutions of the Third World will bring about a collapse of the capitalist world. Others: only thanks to revolution in the capitalist world can the Third World advance. All these analyses are more or less correct, but, to my mind, of little importance.

Look at what has just happened. Many people spent a long time searching for the best way to set off an explosion among the students. Finally — no one found it — an *objective situation* produced the explosion. There was the authorities' *coup de pouce,* of course — the police occupation of the Sorbonne — but it is clear that that absurd mistake was not the sole source of the movement. The police had already entered Nanterre several months earlier without setting off a chain reaction. This time there was a chain reaction that could not be stopped — which allows us to analyse the role an active minority can play.

What has happened in the last fortnight is to my mind a refutation of the famous theory of the 'revolutionary vanguard' as the force leading a popular movement. At Nanterre and Paris there was simply an objective situation, arising from what is vaguely called 'student unrest' and from a desire for action on the part of some young people disgusted by the inaction of the ruling classes. Because it was more conscious theoretically and better prepared, the active minority was able to light the fuse and make the breach. But that is all. The others could follow or not. They happened to have followed. But from then on no vanguard, neither the UEC, the JCR nor the Marxist-Leninists, has been able to seize control of the movement. Their militants can participate decisively in the actions, but they have been drowned in the movement. They are to be found on the co-ordination committees, where their role is important, but there has never been any question of one of these vanguards taking a leading position.

This is the essential point. It shows that we must abandon the theory of the 'leading vanguard' and replace it by a much simpler and more honest one of the active minority functioning as a permanent leaven, pushing for action without ever leading it. In fact, though no one will admit it, the Bolshevik Party did not 'lead' the Russian Revolution. It was borne along by the masses. It might have elaborated its theory en route, and pushed the movement in one direction or another, but it did not by itself launch the movement; that was largely spontaneous. In certain objective situations — with the help of an active minority — spontaneity can find its old place in the social movement. Spontaneity makes possible the forward drive, not the orders of a leading group.

J.-P. S. What many people cannot understand is the fact that you have not tried to work out a programme, or to give your movement a structure. They attack you for trying to 'smash everything' without knowing — or at any rate saying — what you would like to put in place of what you demolish.

D. C.-B. Naturally! Everyone would be reassured, particularly Pompidou, if we set up a party and announced, 'All these people here are ours now. Here are our aims and this is how we are going to attain them.' They would know who they were dealing with and how to counter them. They would no longer have to face 'anarchy,' 'disorder,' 'uncontrollable effervescence.'

Our movement's strength is precisely that it is based on an 'uncontrollable' spontaneity, that it gives an impetus without trying to canalize it or use the action it has unleashed to its own profit. There are clearly two solutions open to us today. The first would be to bring together half a dozen people with political experience, ask them to formulate some convincing immediate demands, and say, 'Here is the student movement's position, do what you like with it!' That is the bad solution. The second is to try to give an understanding of the situation not to the totality of the students nor even to the totality of demonstrators, but to a large number of them. To do so we must avoid building an organization immediately, or defining a programme; that would inevitably paralyse us. The movement's only chance is the disorder that lets men speak freely, and that can result in a form of self-organization. For example, we should now give up mass-spectacular meetings and turn to the formation of work and action groups. That is what we are trying to do at Nanterre.

But now that speech has been suddenly freed in Paris, it is essential first of all that people should express themselves. They say confused, vague things and they are often uninteresting things too, for they have been said a hundred times before, but when they have finished, this allows them to ask 'So what?' This is what matters, that the largest possible number of students say 'So what?' Only then can a programme and a structure be discussed. To ask us today, 'What are you going to do about the examinations?' is to wish to drown the fish, to sabotage the movement and to interrupt its dynamic. The examinations will take place and we shall make proposals, but give us time. First we must discuss, reflect, seek new formulae. We shall find them. But not today.

J.-P. S. You have said that the student movement is now on the crest of a wave. But the vacation is coming, and with it a deceleration, probably a retreat. The government will take the opportunity to put through reforms. It will invite students to participate and many will accept, saying either 'Reformism is all we want,' or 'It is only reformism, but it is better than nothing, and we have obtained it by force.' So you will have a transformed university, but the changes may be merely superficial ones, dealing particularly with the development of material facilities, lodgings, university restaurants. These things would make no basic changes in the system. They are demands that the authorities could satisfy without bringing the regime into question. Do you think that you could obtain any 'adjustments' that would really introduce revolutionary elements into the bourgeois university — for example, that would make the education given at the university contradictory to the basic function of the university in the present regime: the training of cadres who are well integrated into the system?

D. C.-B. First, purely material demands may have a revolutionary content. On university restaurants we have a demand which is basic. We demand their abolition as university restaurants. They must become youth restaurants in which all young people, whether students or not, can eat for one franc forty. No one can reject this demand: if young workers are working during the day, there seems no reason why they should not dine for one franc forty in the evening. Similarly with the *Cités Universitaires*. There are many young workers and apprentices who would rather live away from their parents but who cannot take a room because that would cost them 30,000 francs per month; let us welcome them to the *Cités,* where the rent is from 9,000 to 10,000 francs per month. And let the well-to-do students in law and *sciences-po* go elsewhere.

Basically, I don't think that any reforms the government might make would be enough to demobilize the students. There obviously will be a retreat during the vacation, but they will not 'break' the movement. Some will say, 'We have lost our chance,' without any attempt to explain what has happened. Others will say, 'The situation is not yet ripe.' But many militants will realize that we must capitalize on what has just taken place, analyse it theoretically and prepare to resume our action next term. For there will be an explosion then, whatever the government's reforms. And the experience of disorderly, unintentional, authority-provoked action we have just been through will enable us to make any action launched in the autumn more effective. The vacation will enable students to come to terms with the disarray they showed during the fortnight's crisis, and to think about what they want to do and can do.

As to the possibility of making the education given at the university a 'counter-education' manufacturing not well-integrated cadres but revolutionaries, I am afraid that that seems to me a somewhat idealistic hope. Even a reformed bourgeois education will still manufacture bourgeois cadres. People will be caught in the wheels of the system. At best they will become members of a *bien-pensant* left, but objectively they will remain cogs ensuring the functioning of society.

Our aim is to pursue successfully a 'parallel education' which will be technical and ideological. We must launch a university ourselves, on a completely new basis, even if it only lasts a few weeks. We shall call on left-wing and extreme left-wing teachers who are prepared to work with us in seminars and assist us with their knowledge — renouncing their 'professional' status — in the investigations which we shall undertake.

In all faculties we shall open seminars — not lecture courses, obviously — on the problems of the workers' movement, on the use of technology in the interests of man, on the possibilities opened up by automation. And all this not from a theoretical viewpoint (every sociological study today opens with the words 'Technology must be made to serve man's interests'), but by posing concrete problems. Obviously this education will go in the opposite direction to the education provided by the system and the experiment could not last long; the system would quickly react and the movement give way. But what matters is not working out a reform of capitalist society, but launching an experiment that completely breaks with that society, an experiment that will not last, but which allows a glimpse of a possibility: something which is revealed for a moment and then vanishes. But that is enough to prove that that something could exist.

We do not hope to make some kind of socialist university in our society, for we know that the function of the university will stay the same so long as the system is unchanged as a whole. But we believe that there can be moments of rupture in the system's cohesion and that it is possible to profit by them to open breaches in it.

J.-P. S. That presupposes the permanent existence of an 'anti-institutional' movement preventing the student forces from structuring themselves. In fact, you could attack UNEF for being a trade union, that is, a necessarily sclerosed institution.

D. C.-B. We attack it primarily for its inability to make any demands because of its forms of organization. Besides, the defence of the students' interests is something very problematic. What are their 'interests'? They do not constitute a class. Workers and peasants form social classes and have objective interests. Their demands are clear and they are addressed to the management and to the government of the bourgeoisie. But the students? Who are their 'oppressors,' if not the system as a whole?

J.-P. S. Indeed, students are not a class. They are defined by age and a relation to knowledge. By definition, a student is someone who must one day cease to be a student in any society, even the society of our dreams.

D. C.-B. That is precisely what we must change. In the present system, they say: there are those who work and those who study. And we are stuck with a social division of labour, however intelligent. But we can imagine another system where everyone will work at the tasks of production — reduced to a minimum thanks to technical progress — and everyone will still be able to pursue his studies at the same time: the system of simultaneous productive work and study.

Obviously, there would be special cases; very advanced mathematics or medicine cannot be taken up while exercising another activity at the same time. Uniform rules cannot be laid down. But the basic principle must be changed. To start with we must reject the distinction between student and worker.

Of course, all this is not immediately foreseeable, but something has begun and must necessarily keep going.

The New Architecture

Walter Gropius founded the Bauhaus school, the center of the new architecture and important artistic activity between 1919 and 1933. His fundamental concern was to develop an art that would combine esthetic quality with the technology of the machine age and the social needs of modern industrial society. There was no room in Germany for Gropius and his colleagues after Hitler came to power, and he left for the United States, where he became the head of the architecture department at Harvard University. His basic principles have had an enormous influence on contemporary architecture.

The Principles of Walter Gropius

Can the real nature and significance of the new Architecture be conveyed in words? If I am to attempt to answer this question it must needs be in the form of an analysis of my own work, my own thoughts and discoveries. I hope, therefore, that a short account of my personal evolution as an architect will enable the reader to discern its basic characteristics for himself.

A breach has been made with the past, which allows us to envisage new aspects of architecture corresponding to the technical civilization of the age we live in; the morphology of dead styles has been destroyed; and we are returning to honesty of thought and feeling. The general public, formerly profoundly indifferent to everything to do with building, has been shaken out of its torpor; personal interest in architecture as something that concerns every one of us in our daily lives has been very widely aroused; and the broad lines of its future development are already clearly discernible. It is now becoming widely recognized that although the outward forms of the new Architecture differ fundamentally in an organic sense from those of the old, they are not the personal whims of a handful of architects avid for innovation at all costs, but simply the inevitable logical product of the intellectual, social and technical conditions of our age. A quarter of a century's earnest pregnant struggle preceded their eventual emergence.

But the development of the new architecture encountered serious obstacles at a very early stage of its development. Conflicting theories and the dogmas enunciated in architects' personal manifestos all helped to confuse the main issue. Technical difficulties were accentuated by the general economic decline that followed the war. Worst of all, "modern"

From Walter Gropius, *The New Architecture and the Bauhaus*, trans. P. Morton Shand (Cambridge: M.I.T. Press, 1955), pp. 17–32. Reprinted by permission of Faber and Faber Ltd.

architecture became fashionable in several countries; with the result that formalistic imitation and snobbery distorted the fundamental truth and simplicity on which this renascence was based.

That is why the movement must be purged from within if its original aims are apt to be saved from the straight jacket of materialism and false slogans inspired by plagiarism or misconception. Catchphrases like "functionalism" and "fitness for purpose = beauty" have had the effect of deflecting appreciation of the New Architecture into external channels or making it purely one sided. This is reflected in a very general ignorance of the true motives of its founders: an ignorance that impels superficial minds, who do not perceive that the new architecture is a bridge uniting opposite poles of thought, to relegate it to a single circumscribed province of design.

For instance rationalization, which many people imagine to be its cardinal principle, is really only its purifying agency. The liberation of architecture from a welter of ornament, the emphasis on its structural function, and the concentration on concise and economical solutions, represent the purely material side of that formalizing process on which the *practical* value of the New Architecture depends. The other, the aesthetic satisfaction of the human soul, is just as important as the material. Both find their counterpart in that unity which is life itself. What is far more important than the structural economy and its functional emphasis is the intellectual achievement which has made possible a new spatial vision. For whereas building is merely a matter of methods and materials, architecture implies a mastery of space.

For the last century the transition from manual to machine production has so preoccupied humanity that, instead of pressing forward to tackle the new problem of design postulated by this unprecedented transformation, we have remained content to borrow our styles from antiquity and perpetuate historical prototypes in decoration.

That state of affairs is over at last. A new conception of building, based on reality, has emerged; and with it has come a new conception of space. These changes, and the superior technical resources we can now command as a direct result of them, are embodied in the very different appearance of the already-numerous examples of the New Architecture.

Just think of all that modern technique has contributed to this decisive phase in the renascence of architecture, and the rapidity of its development!

Our fresh technical resources have furthered the disintegration of solid masses of masonry into slender piers, with consequent far reaching economies in bulk, space, weight, and haulage. New synthetic substances — steel, concrete, glass — are actively superseding the traditional raw materials of construction. Their rigidity and molecular density have made it possible to erect wide-spanned and all but transparent structures, for which the skill of previous ages was manifestly inadequate. This enormous saving in structural volume was an architectural revolution in itself.

One of the outstanding achievements of the new constructional technique has been the abolition of the separating function of the wall. Instead of making the walls the element of support, as in a brick-built house, our new space-saving construction transfers the whole load of the structure to a steel or concrete framework. Thus the role of the walls becomes restricted to that of near screens stretched between the upright columns of this framework to keep out rain, cold, and noise. In order to save weight and bulk still further, these non-supporting and now merely partitioning walls are made of lightweight pumice-concrete, breeze, or other reliable synthetic materials, in the form of hollow blocks or thin slabs. Systematic technical improvement in steel and concrete, and nicer and nicer calculation of their tensile and compressive strengths, are steadily reducing the area occupied by supporting members. This, in turn, naturally leads to a progressively bolder (i.e. wider) opening up of the wall surfaces, which allows rooms to be much better lit. It is, therefore, only logical that the old type of window — a hole that had to be hollowed out of the full thickness of a supporting wall — should be giving place more and more to the continuous horizontal casement, subdivided by thin steel mullions, characteristic of the New Architecture. And as a direct result of the growing preponderance of voids over solids, glass is assuming an ever greater structural importance. Its sparkling insubstantiality, and the way it seems to float between wall and wall imponderably as the air, adds a note of gaiety to our modern homes.

In the same way the flat roof is superseding the old penthouse roof with its tiled or slated gables. For its advantages are obvious: (1) light, normally shaped top-floor rooms instead of poky attics, darkened by dormers and sloping ceilings, with their almost inutilisable corners; (2) the avoidance of timber rafters, so often the cause of fires; (3) the possibility of turning the top of the house to practical account as a sun-loggia, open-air gymnasium, or children's playground; (4) simpler structural provision for subsequent additions, whether as extra stories or new wings; (5) elimination of unnecessary surfaces presented to the action of wind and weather, and therefore less need for repairs; (6) suppression of hanging gutters, external rain-pipes, etc., that often erode rapidly. With the development of air transport the architect will have to pay as much attention to the bird's eye perspective of his houses as to their elevations. The utilisation of flat roofs as "grounds" offers us a means of reacclimatizing nature amidst the stony deserts of our great towns; for the plots from which she has been evicted to make room for buildings can be given back to her up aloft. Seen from the skies, the leafy housetops of the cities of the future will look like endless chains of hanging gardens. But the primary advantage of the flat roof is that it renders possible a much freer kind of interior planning.

STANDARDIZATION

The elementary impulse of all national economies proceeds from the desire to meet the needs of the community at less cost and effort by the improvement of its productive organizations. This has led progressively to mechanization, specialized division of labor, and rationalization: seemingly irrevocable steps in industrial evolution which have the same implications for building as for every other branch of organized production. Were mechanization an end in itself it would be an unmitigated calamity, robbing life of half of its fulness and variety by stunting men and women into subhuman, robot-like automations. (Here we touch the deeper causality of the dogged resistance of the old civilization of handicrafts to the new world-order of the machine.) But in the last resort mechanization can have only one object: to abolish the individual's physical toil of providing himself with the necessities of existence in order that hand and brain may be set free for some higher order of activity.

Our age has initiated a rationalization of industry based on the kind of working partnership between manual and mechanical production we call standardization, which is already having direct repercussions on building. There can be no doubt that the systematic application of standardization to housing would effect enormous economies — so enormous, indeed, that it is impossible to estimate their extent at present.

Standardization is not an impediment to the development of civilization, but, on the contrary, one of its immediate prerequisites. A standard may be defined as that simplified practical exemplar of anything in general use which embodies a fusion of the best of its anterior forms — a fusion preceded by the elimination of the personal content of their designers and all otherwise ungeneric or non-essential features. Such an impersonal standard is called a "norm," a word derived from a carpenter's square.

The fear that individuality will be crushed out by the growing "tyranny" of standardization is the sort of myth which cannot sustain the briefest examination. In all great epochs of history the existence of standards — that is the conscious adoption of type-forms — has been the criterion of a polite and well ordered society; for it is a commonplace that repetition of the same things for the same purposes exercises a settling and civilizing influence on men's minds.

As the basic cellular unit of that larger unit the street, the dwelling house represents a typical group-organism. The uniformity of the cells whose multiplication by streets forms the still larger unit of the city therefore calls for formal expression. Diversity in their sizes provides the necessary modicum in variation, which in turn promotes natural competition between dissimilar types developing side by side. The most admired cities of the past are conclusive proof that the reiteration of "typical" (i.e. typified) buildings notably enhances civic dignity and coherence. As a maturer and more final model than any of the individual prototypes merged in it, an accepted standard is always a formal common denominator of a whole period. The unification of architectural components would have the salutary effect of imparting that homogeneous character to our own towns which is the distinguishing mark of a superior urban culture. A prudent limitation of variety to a few standard types of buildings increases their quality and decreases their cost; thereby raising the social level of the population as a whole. Proper respect for tradition will find a truer echo in these than in the miscellaneous solutions of an often arbitrary and aloof individualism because the greater communal utility of the former embodies a deeper architectural significance. The concentration of essential qualities in standard types presupposes methods of unprecedented industrial potentiality, which entail capital outlay on a scale that can only be justified by mass production.

RATIONALIZATION

Building, hitherto an essentially manual trade, is already in course of transformation into an organised industry. More and more work that used to be done on the scaffolding is now carried out under factory conditions far away from the site. The dislocation which the seasonal character of building operations causes employers and employed alike — as, indeed, the community at large — is being gradually overcome. Continuous activity throughout the year will soon become the rule instead of the exception.

And just as fabricated materials have been evolved which are superior to natural ones in accuracy and uniformity, so modern practice in house construction is increasingly approximating to the successive stages of a manufacturing process. We are approaching a state of technical proficiency when it will become possible to rationalize buildings and mass-produce them in factories by resolving their structure into a number of component parts. Like boxes of toy bricks, these will be assembled in various formal compositions in a dry state: which means that building will definitely cease to be dependent on the weather. Ready-made houses of solid, fireproof construction, that can be delivered fully-equipped from stock, will ultimately become one of the principal products of industry. Before this is practicable, however, every part of the house — floor beams, wall slabs, windows, doors, staircases, and fittings — will have to be normed. The repetition of standardized parts, and the use of identical materials in different buildings, will have the same sort of coordinating and sobering effect on the aspect of our towns as uniformity of type in modern attire has in social life. But that will in no sense restrict the architect's freedom of design. For although every house and block of flats will bear the unmistakable impress of our age, there will always remain, as in the clothes we wear, sufficient scope for the individual to find expression for his own personality. The net result should be a happy architectonic combination of maximum standardization and maximum variety. Since 1910 I have consistently advocated prefabrication of houses in numerous articles and lectures; besides which I have undertaken a number of practical experiments in this field of research in conjunction with important industrial concerns.

Dry assembly offers the best prospects because (to take only one of its advantages) moisture in one form or another is the principal obstacle to economy in masonry or brick construction (mortar joints). Moisture is the direct cause of most of the weaknesses of the old methods of building. It leads to badly fitting joints, warping and staining, unforeseen piecework, and serious loss of time and money through delays in drying. By eliminating this factor, and so assuring the perfect interlocking of all component parts, the prefabricated house makes it possible to guarantee a fixed price and a definite period of construction. Moreover the use of reliable modern materials enables the stability and insulation of the building to be increased and its weight and bulk decreased. A prefabricated house can be loaded on to a couple of lorries at the factory — walls, floors, roofs, fittings and all — conveyed to the site, and put together in next to no time regardless of the season of the year.

The outstanding concomitant advantages of rationalized construction are superior economy and an enhanced standard of living. Many of the things that are regarded as luxuries today will be standard fitments in the homes of tomorrow.

So much for technique! — but what about beauty?

The New Architecture throws open its walls like curtains to admit a plenitude of fresh air, daylight and sunshine. Instead of anchoring buildings ponderously into the ground with massive foundations, it poises them lightly, yet firmly, upon the face of the earth; and bodies itself forth, not in stylistic imitation of ornamental frippery, but in those simple and sharply modelled designs in which every part merges naturally into the comprehensive volume of the whole. Thus its esthetic meets our material and psychological requirements alike.

For unless we choose to regard the satisfaction of those conditions which can alone animate, and so humanize, a room — spatial harmony, repose, proportion — as an ideal of some higher order, architecture cannot be limited to the fulfilment of its structural function.

We have had enough and to spare of the arbitrary reproduction of historic styles. In the progress of our advance from the vagaries of mere architectural caprice to the dictates of structural logic, we have learned to seek concrete expression of the life of our epoch in clear and crisply simplified forms.

Absurdity and Heroism

Albert Camus (1913–1960) received the Nobel Prize in 1957 for his contributions to literature. His existential novels and essays combine an emphasis on the absurdity and meaninglessness of life with a humanistic insistence on the need to affirm values and preserve one's existence by giving life meaning. At at a time when Western civilization in particular and humanity in general are being severely challenged, the affirmative side of Camus's thought appears particularly heartening. He finds in the ancient Greek myth of Sisyphus the key to the universal condition of man.

Camus: "The Myth of Sisyphus"

The gods had condemned Sisyphus to ceaselessly rolling a rock to the top of a mountain, whence the stone would fall back of its own weight. They had thought with some reason that there is no more dreadful punishment than futile and hopeless labor.

If one believes Homer, Sisyphus was the wisest and most prudent of mortals. According to another tradition, however, he was disposed to practice the profession of highwayman. I see no contradiction in this. Opinions differ as to the reasons why he became the futile laborer of the underworld. To begin with, he is accused of a certain levity in regard to the gods. He stole their secrets. Aegina, the daughter of Aesopus, was carried off by Jupiter. The father was shocked by that disappearance and complained to Sisyphus. He, who knew of the abduction, offered to tell about it on condition that Aesopus would give water to the citadel of Corinth. To the celestial thunderbolts he preferred the benediction of water. He was punished for this in the underworld. Homer tells us also that Sisyphus had put Death in chains. Pluto could not endure the sight of his deserted, silent empire. He dispatched the god of war, who liberated Death from the hands of her conqueror.

It is said also that Sisyphus, being near to death, rashly wanted to test his wife's love. He ordered her to cast his unburied body into the middle of the public square. Sisyphus woke up in the underworld. And there, annoyed by an obedience so contrary to human love, he obtained from Pluto permission to return to earth in order to chastise his wife. But when he had seen again the face of this world, enjoyed water and sun, warm stones and the sea, he no longer wanted to go back to the infernal darkness. Recalls, signs of anger, warnings were of no avail. Many years

From Albert Camus, *The Myth of Sisyphus and Other Essays*, trans. Justin O'Brien (New York: Knopf, 1961), pp. 119–23. Copyright © 1942 by Editions Gallimard; copyright © 1955 by Alfred A. Knopf, Inc. Reprinted by permission of Alfred A. Knopf, Inc., and Hamish Hamilton Ltd.

more he lived facing the curve of the gulf, the sparkling sea, and the smiles of earth. A decree of the gods was necessary. Mercury came and seized the impudent man by the collar and, snatching him from his joys, led him forcibly back to the underworld, where his rock was ready for him.

You have already grasped that Sisyphus is the absurd hero. He *is*, as much through his passions as through his torture. His scorn of the gods, his hatred of death, and his passion for life won him that unspeakable penalty in which the whole being is exerted toward accomplishing nothing. This is the price that must be paid for the passions of this earth. Nothing is told us about Sisyphus in the underworld. Myths are made for the imagination to breathe life into them. As for this myth, one sees merely the whole effort of a body straining to raise the huge stone, to roll it and push it up a slope a hundred times over; one sees the face screwed up, the cheek right against the stone, the shoulder bracing the clay-covered mass, the foot wedging it, the fresh start with arms outstretched, the wholly human security of two earth-clotted hands. At the very end of his long effort measured by skyless space and time without depth, the purpose is achieved. Then Sisyphus watches the stone rush down in a few moments toward that lower world whence he will have to push it up again toward the summit. He goes back down to the plain.

It is during that return, that pause, that Sisyphus interests me. A face that toils so close to stones is already stone itself! I see that man going back down with a heavy yet measured step toward the torment of which he will never know the end. That hour like a breathing-space which returns as surely as his suffering, that is the hour of consciousness. At each of those moments when he leaves the heights and gradually sinks toward the lairs of the gods, he is superior to his fate. He is stronger than his rock.

If this myth is tragic, that is because its hero is conscious. Where would his torture be, indeed, if at every step the hope of succeeding upheld him? The workman of today works every day in his life at the same tasks, and this fate is no less absurd. But it is tragic only at the rare moments when it becomes conscious. Sisyphus, proletarian of the gods, powerless and rebellious, knows the whole extent of wretched condition: it is what he thinks of during his descent. The lucidity that was to constitute his torture at the same time crowns his victory. There is no fate that cannot be surmounted by scorn.

If the descent is thus sometimes performed in sorrow, it can also take place in joy. This word is not too much. Again I fancy Sisyphus returning toward his rock, and the sorrow was in the beginning. When the images of earth cling too tightly to memory, when the call of happiness becomes too insistent, it happens that melancholy rises in man's heart: this is the rock's victory, this is the rock itself. The boundless grief is too heavy to bear. These are our nights of Gethsemane. But crushing truths perish from being acknowledged. Thus, Oedipus at the outset obeys fate without knowing it. But from the moment he knows, his tragedy begins. Yet at the same moment, blind and desperate, he realizes that the only bond linking him to the world is the cool hand of a girl. Then a tremendous remark rings out: "Despite so many ordeals, my advanced age and the nobility of my soul make me conclude that all is well." Sophocles' Oedipus, like Dostoevsky's Kirilov, thus gives the recipe for the absurd victory. Ancient wisdom confirms modern heroism.

One does not discover the absurd without being tempted to write a manual of happiness. "What! by such narrow ways — ?" There is but one world, however. Happiness and the absurd are two sons of the same earth. They are inseparable. It would be a mistake to say that happiness necessarily springs from the absurd discovery. It happens as well that the feeling of the absurd springs from happiness. "I conclude that all is well," says Oedipus, and that remark is sacred. It echoes in the wild and limited universe of man. It teaches that all is not, has not been, exhausted. It drives out of this world a god who had come into it with dissatisfaction and a preference *for* futile sufferings. It makes of fate a human matter, which must be settled among men.

All Sisyphus' silent joy is contained therein. His fate belongs to him. His rock is his thing. Likewise, the absurd man, when he contemplates his torment, silences all the idols. In the universe suddenly restored to its silence, the myriad wondering little voices of the earth rise up. Unconscious, secret calls, invitations from all the faces, they are the necessary reverse and price of victory. There is no sun without shadow, and it is essential to know the night. The absurd man says yes and his effort will henceforth be unceasing. If there is a personal fate, there is no higher destiny, or at least there is but one which he concludes is inevitable and despicable. For the rest, he knows himself to be the master of his days. At that subtle moment when man glances backward over his life, Sisyphus returning toward his rock, in that slight pivoting he contemplates that series of unrelated actions which becomes his fate, created by him, combined under his memory's eye and soon sealed by his death. Thus, convinced of the wholly human origin of all that is human, a blind man eager to see who knows that the night has no end, he is still on the go. The rock is still rolling.

I leave Sisyphus at the foot of the mountain! One always finds one's burden again. But Sisyphus teaches the higher fidelity that negates the gods and raises rocks. He too concludes that all is well. This universe henceforth without a master seems to him neither sterile nor futile. Each atom of that stone, each mineral flake of that night-filled mountain, in itself forms a world. The struggle itself toward the heights is enough to fill a man's heart. One must imagine Sisyphus happy.